CONTROVERSIES IN THE ADDICTION'S FIELD: Volume One

Edited by:

Ruth C. Engs, R.N., Ed.D.
Professor, Applied Health Science
Indiana University, Bloomington, IN

D1526755

American Council
on Alcoholism, Inc.
The Health
Education Center
White Marsh
Business Center
5024 Campbell Blvd.
Suite H
Baltimore, MD 21236
1-800-527-5344

KENDALL/HUNT PUBLISHING COMPANY
2460 Kerper Boulevard   P.O. Box 539   Dubuque, Iowa 52004-0539

ORGANIZATION OF BOOK AND ACKNOWLEDGEMENTS

This book has been organized in the following manner. The first section encompasses various theories related to the nature of alcoholism and other drug dependencies. The next five sections discuss general public policy issues followed by specific prevention and intervention issues intrinsic to policy. Finally the last three sections focus on education and treatment issues.

The editor was fully responsible for organizing the material and selecting the writers for this publication. Since the authors were not able to review their page proofs due to time contraints, any textual errors are the full responsibility of the editor.

Any publication such as this needs to acknowledge individuals who have been most helpful in the process of its production. Therefore, I would like to thank David Hanson for his encouragement and help, Bud Pidgeon and Jerry Hart for their continued moral support during discouraging times, Jamee Wissink for eagle eyed copy editing, my husband Jeffrey Franz for just being there, and all the authors for their donated time and talent in making this book possible.

Ruth C. Engs (Editor) February 1990

Copyright © 1990 by the American Council on Alcoholism, Inc.

ISBN 0–8403–6057–6

Printed in the United States of America
10 9 8 7 6 5 4 3 2 1

CONTENTS

iii

FOREWORD

The American Council on Alcoholism, Inc. is delighted to be the host association for the book entitled *Controversies in the Addiction Field*.

The American Council on Alcoholism, since its inception, has promoted the process of open discussion concerning the alcoholism issue. It is our membership's belief that open dialogue provides intellectual growth and ultimately achieves the basic mission of our organization. Namely, to help provide a leadership role in identifying ways to reduce the incidence of abuse.

Controversies in the Addiction Field provides a genuine opportunity to review the major issues that are currently affecting our field and to measure the varying debates on each of those issues.

Our Council has, and will continue, to provide avenues to express the opinions of its members concerning these issues. The Council, for the purpose of intellectual thought, has not influenced this publication in any matter and will remain neutral in all ways concerning this publication.

Controversies in the Addiction Field provides you, the reader, with a rare opportunity to review the opinions and research of scholars who present varied or opposite points of views. This is made possible through the diligent work of Dr. Ruth Engs, the book's editor, and the voluntary effort of each contributing scholar.

We thank each and everyone of them for their vital contribution.

Walter P. Pidgeon, Jr., CAE
National President, American
Council on Alcoholism, Inc.

INTRODUCTION

As a researcher and educator who has investigated drinking patterns for almost twenty years, I have become deeply concerned over increased polarization between different factions in the field during the past decade in the United States and to a minor extent in Canada. I am concerned that this hostility has not only led to disharmony and discord but has, even more importantly, profoundly prevented workable solutions towards alcohol and other drug abuse problems in North America. As part of this accelerating conflict, conferences and publications have been forthcoming with only ONE side of a particular issue being presented, usually as the sole way to solve a problem. Individuals with dissenting viewpoints have not been encouraged or even invited to partake of these forums. Consequently the previous publications and conferences have all been one sided.

Therefore, as a scholar I felt that the airing of conflicting ideas, in one book, could be a step towards mutual understanding and acceptance and a vehicle to help bridge the divide between differing points of views and philosophies. Thus the purpose of this publication was to get under one cover differing opinions concerning various controversial issues and to discuss these differences in a scholarly manner based upon the research.

The mark of a scholar and of a scholary publication is to be tolerant of differing viewpoints and to assure that all sides have an open forum for presentation. As neutral editor for this book, I have strived for completely fair and scholarly representation of all sides of each issue presented. In this light I would like to mention that in two of the sections I have either previously co-authored, or have been closely involved professionally, with the authors writing on all sides of the issue. Also I should mention that as editor, in the process of putting this book together, I have discovered that this work itself is considered controversial by some.

This first volume addresses only a few of the controversial issues found in the addiction field. There are other issues of interest and an additional publication is being planned where additional controversies such as: should drugs be legalized, should there be mandatory treatment for pregnant alcohol/drug using women, etc. can be discussed.

In soliciting authors for the volume, noted researchers and scholars, known for a particular viewpoint, were contacted. Because of time commitments some were not able to contribute but readily offered names of colleagues. A few for political reasons and personal philosophies, which will be further discussed below, declined the invitation. In a few sections, where researchers could not be found, nationally know advocates for a particular issue were asked to participate. Also, some emerging scholars and academicians were asked to contribute so that there would be a mixture of seasoned authors and new emerging talent in the field.

Authors were not directed as to the style or manner of writing their manuscript. They were only asked to limit their manuscripts to approximately ten pages plus the bibliography and tables. Therefore, there are a variety of styles ranging from very light to very serious presentations. In some cases authors on each side of the issue used the same research data and related literature. Depending upon their interpretations they often came to different conclusions.

Any manuscript changes, other than minor spelling and punctuation by the copy-editor, were made with the approval of the authors(s). Though the authors did not see each other's works, in the case of the school based education issue, the authors on their own volition decided to share papers. Also, it needs to be mentioned that neither the editor nor the writers have been renumerated in any way for this publication as it is considered service to the field.

In two sections, namely the "nature of alcoholism and drug addictions" and the "effectiveness of school based education", because of the multifaceted nature of the area, more than two authors were obtained to gather a spectrum of viewpoints. In other subject areas, ideally it would have been more interesting to have multi-authors but this was not feasible because of page constraints or non-availability of potential writers at this time.

Is such a publication concerning controversies in the addictions field even needed ? After talking with a variety of potential authors throughout North America, I found that most encouraged the concept and welcomed an opportunity to discuss their point of view and research in an open forum. However, some were hostile towards its whole idea.

Sadly I talked with some potential authors who did not agree with or believe in the concept of open forum and debate. Some had punitive attitudes towards individuals or groups who had opinions or values different from their own. Some were even hostile to the concept of the book. I am distressed by the attitudes of these individuals, all of whom are very well known in their area of specialities. I regret that they declined to participate in this publication and would like to list some of their reasons as they appear to be symptomatic of the deep fissions characteristic of the alcohol/drug field today, particularly in the United States. The reasons as follows are:

1) There is only one correct point of view or only one right way to solve the problem and the individual was appalled that anyone could have a different viewpoint; 2) ACA as an organization receives funding from individuals associated with the beverage industry; or 3) ACA receives funding from the treatment industry and they would not want to be

associated with anything even remotely connected with the alcohol beverage or treatment industry; 4) When given the name of certain authors who had agreed to write chapters, some of the potential writers felt that these authors should not be given a forum because of their "dangerous", "non-academic", or "out of date" viewpoints and did not wish to be presented in the same book with them.

I was amazed by these attitudes. Certainly in academia all attitudes and ideas are welcome to be discussed in open forum. Individuals with different research results, values, agendas, or monetary affiliations are encouraged to discuss their point of view. I was amazed that some of these individuals apparently did not believe in the concept of open forum where a variety of individuals with various opinions could freely entertain their professional opinion concerning a controversial issues. I am deeply disturbed by these values as, in my opinion, they contribute to increased division and hostility rather than efforts to look for compromise and workable solutions to solve the problems in our field.

I would like briefly to inform the reader as to the process of how this publication came to be. After I had finished editing the book *Women: Alcohol and Other Drugs* for the Alcohol Drug Problems Association, I discussed with Kendall-Hunt, the publisher, the possibility of undertaking a book focused upon various controversies in the addiction field. This was because, as I have previously mentioned, I was concerned with increased polarization of factions within the field. I felt that a book discussing current controversial issues could serve as an open forum for differing viewpoints under one cover thereby helping to bridge the gap between the differences. Since this philosophy was compatible with the American Council on Alcoholism(ACA), I approached them with the idea for the book and they agreed to become the host sponsoring organization, as is required by the publisher for this type of service oriented text.

In summary, as a society we cannot afford to think uni-dimensionally or dichotomize the field because all the issues discussed in this book are extremely complex. In all probability there is no simplistic solution or one answer to any of the problems or issues discussed. As it may have become apparent to the reader there are various shades of gray for each of the items discussed. No issue is really black or white. Perhaps after enough time and effort we may find that there are numerous etiologies for alcohol and other addictions and a variety of potentially successful prevention, education, treatment and public policy solutions. However, we must begin to start listening to each other. We must start to work together by openly discussing our differences if we are to successfully solve the alcohol and other drug abuse problems in our culture today.

Ruth C. Engs, RN, Ed.D. (Editor)

LIST OF AUTHORS *

Ruth C. Engs, RN, Ed.D. (Editor)
  Professor, Department Applied Health Science
  HPER Room 116
  Indiana University, Bloomington, IN 47405

Ernest Abel, Ph.D.
  Professor, Department of Obstetrics and Gynecology
Robert Sokol, M.D.
  Dean, School of Medicine
  Wayne State University
  C. S. Mott Center for Human Growth and Development
  275 E. Hancock Detroit, MI 48201

Howard T. Blane, Ph.D.
  Director/Research Institute on Alcoholism/Research Professor
  of Psychology, SUNY at Buffalo
  1021 Main St. University of Buffalo, Buffalo, NY 14203

Sterling K. Clarren, M.D.
  Aldrich Professor of Pediatrics/Head, Division Embryology,
  Teratology, and Congenital Defects
  University of Washington, School of Medicine
  Childrens Hospital and Medical Center
  P.O. Box C-5371. Seattle, WA 98195

Thomas J. Delaney, Jr. M.S.W. M.P.A.
  Executive Director
  Employee Assistance Professionals Association
  4601 N. Fairfax Dr. Suite 1001 Arlington, VA 22203

Robert L. DuPont, M.D.
  President, Institute for Behavior and Health, Inc.
  Clinical Professor of Psychiatry, Georgetown Medical School
  6191 Executive Blvd.
  Rockville, MD 20852

* Title and affiliation of principle author

ix

Herbert Fingarette, Ph.D.
Professor, Department of Philosophy
University of California Santa Barbara, CA 93106

Stuart W. Fors, Ed.D.
Associate Professor, Department of Health Promotion and Behavior
Stegeman Hall, University of Georgia
Athens, GA 30602

Louis Gliksman, Ph.D.
Scientist
Cynthia Smythe, M.Ed.
Addiction Research Foundation
The University of Western Ontario
London, Ontario Canada N6A5B9

Richard J. Goeman, B.S.
Research Associate, Department Applied Health Science
Indiana University Bloomington, IN 47405

Donald W. Goodwin, M.D.
Professor and Chair, Department of Psychiatry
University of Kansas Medical Center, College of Health Science
39 Rainbow Blvd. at 39th.
Kansas City, Kansas 66103

David M. Hanson, Ph.D.
Professor, Sociology
State University of New York at Potsdam
Potsdam, NY 13676

Dwight B. Heath, Ph.D.
Professor, Department of Anthropology
Box 1921
Brown University Providence, RI 02912

Reid K. Hester, Ph.D.
Research Associate Professor/Clinical Psychologist
Center for Research on Addictive Behaviors and BehaviorTherapy
Associates

Nancy Sheehy, M.A.
    Department of Psychology, University of New Mexico
    Albuquerque, NM 87131-1161

Karol L. Kumpfer, Ph.D.
    Associate Professor, Health Education
Eric P. Trunnell, Ph.D
Henry O. Whiteside, Ph.D.
    Department of Health Education
    HPERN - 215 University of Utah
    Salt Lake City, Utah 84112

Ting-Kai Li, M.D.
    Distinguished Professor,
    Indiana University School of Medicine and
    V.A. Medical Center
    545 Barnhill Dr. Indianapolis, IN 46204

Gail G. Milgram, Ed.D.
    Professor/Director of Education and Training Division
    Center of Alcohol Studies
    Rutgers University
    New Brunswick, NJ 08903

Robert D. Myers, Ph.D.
    Professor, Pharmacology and Psychiatric Medicine,
    School of Medicine/Editor-in-Chief, *Alcohol,*
    International Biomedical Journal
    East Carolina University
    Greenville, NC 27858-4354

Kimberly A. Neuendorf, Ph.D.
    Associate Professor, Department of Communication
    Cleveland State University
    Cleveland, OH 44115

David Pittman, Ph.D.
    Professor, Department of Sociology
    Box 1113 Washington University
    St. Louis, MO 63130

Donna L. Polowchena, M.A.
    Executive Director, Alcohol Substance Abuse Council of St.
    Lawrence County
    7 Main St. Canton, N.Y. 13617

Robin Room, Ph.D.
    Scientific Director, Alcohol Research Group/
    Adjunct Professor, School of Public Health
    Medical Research Institute of San Francisco
    1816 Scenic Ave. Berkeley, CA 94709

Martha Sanchez-Craig, Ph.D.
    Senior Research Scientist
    Addiction Research Foundation 33 Russell St.
    Toronto, Ontario Canada M5S 2S1

Harold A. Shoup, B.A.
    Executive Vice President, American Association of
    Advertising Agencies
Christine Dobday, M.B.A.
    American Association of Advertising Agencies
    1899 L. Street N.W. 700 Washington, DC 20036

John Wallace, Ph.D.
    Director of Treatment, Edgehill Newport/Clinical Associate
    Professor of Community Health, Brown University
    200 Harrison Ave. Newport, RI 02840

WHAT IS THE NATURE OF ALCOHOLISM AND/OR DRUG ADDICTION?

CHAPTER 1

The Grand Unification Theory of Alcohol Abuse: It's Time to Stop Fighting Each Other and Start Working Together

Reid K. Hester, Ph.D.
Nancy Sheehy, M.A.

Introduction

The number of other chapters in this section demonstrate the wide diversity of current theories of alcohol abuse. While these chapters are representative of the current crop of perspectives, space limitation precludes an exhaustive discussion of all of the current and historical theories of alcohol abuse. Indeed, by 1960 Jellinek presented a summary of over 200 definitions, theories of etiology, and conceptualizations of the phenomena of alcoholism.

The purpose of this chapter is to review current and historical theories of alcoholism within a framework which allows us to examine each theory's causal factors, appropriate agents and mechanisms for change, and implied interventions. By presenting the theories in this fashion we will show how each theory can account for some aspect of what we know about alcohol abuse. With one exception, however, each theory is short-sighted and limited in its ability to *comprehensively* explain all that we know about alcohol abuse on a macro level. After discussing current and historical theories of alcohol abuse, we will present a model which is integrative and comprehensive.

Model Descriptions

Moral Models. Moral models have historically emphasized deficits in personal responsibility or spiritual strength as the cause of excessive drinking or drunkenness. While many might consider that the moral model is something of a historical artifact, it is still alive and well. Consider that driving under the influence of alcohol is a crime regardless of whether the individual is diagnosed as alcoholic or not. Indeed, while the vast majority of criminal acts are committed under the influence of alcohol or drugs, intoxication has rarely been a justifiable defense in the United States. Clearly, the judicial system holds individuals *personally* accountable for their actions. The implied agents of change include the clergy, to act as spiritual motivators, and law enforcement to punish acts of "willful misconduct."

The Temperance Model. In the late 1800s the temperance model was developed and emphasized the moderate use of alcohol. While sometimes confused with the moral models, the temperance model viewed alcohol itself as a dangerous drug which was to be consumed cautiously. As the temperance movement became more popular and increased its political influence, its perspective of alcohol became more extreme. Alcohol came to be viewed as an extraordinarily dangerous drug which no one could use, even in moderation, without progressing down the road to ruination and death. Sustained moderate consumption in any form was not considered possible. This movement eventually resulted in Congress passing the 18th amendment to the Constitution which began the era of Prohibition. While the law proved to be unpopular and encouraged the expansion of organized crime, it did significantly reduce alcohol consumption and alcohol-related problems in the U.S. during this time. The repeal of Prohibition in 1933 by the 21st amendment rang the death knoll for the temperance movement.

Key assumptions of the temperance model have survived, however, and influence our thinking about alcohol and drugs to this day. The model emphasized the hazardous aspects of the drug alcohol. This, in turn, has influenced our investigation of many of the physically debilitating consequences of excessive drinking. Viewing alcohol as dangerous is also similar to how cocaine, marijuana, and heroin are viewed today.

The temperance model implies that prevention and intervention should be conducted by abstainers who can act as role models in exhorting others to abstain. Legislation to restrict the availability and promotion of alcohol is another appropriate intervention with this model.

The American Disease Model. Two years after the repeal of prohibition, Alcoholics Anonymous came into being and with it the American disease model. The central assumption of this model is that alcoholism is a progressive, irreversible condition characterized primarily by loss of control over drinking. It cannot be cured, only arrested by complete abstinence. Alcoholics are somehow different constitutionally form non-alcoholics and this individual difference makes it impossible for them to drink moderately or without problems for anything but short periods of time. Denial of alcoholism is another cardinal symptom of the disease. Until strongly confronted, alcoholics will deny their disease.

The disease model had an immediate advantage for alcoholics: Humane treatment rather than derision or prison. It also enabled society to accept moderate drinking for most but not all people. Eventually the disease model was accepted by the medical community. As a disease it

3

required medical treatment. Finally, it was embraced by the liquor industry because of its implication that most people can drink with impunity without risk of becoming alcoholic.

The American disease model implies that the most appropriate agents for intervention are recovering alcoholics. Because of the unique aspect of denial, recovering alcoholics are best able to spot it and intervene with confrontation. Prevention is best accomplished by early identification of those at highest risk from a constitutional standpoint for becoming alcoholic.

Educational Models. A central assumption in educational models is that alcohol abuse stems from a deficit in knowledge about the harmful effects of alcohol and heavy drinking. Once armed with this knowledge, individuals will understand that alcohol abuse or alcoholism causes significant harm to themselves as well as to their families and society. Abstention from drinking is then a logical conclusion. The implied intervention then is educational lectures about the harmful effects of alcohol by educators.

Characterological Models. These models focus on psychopathology or deficits in personality functioning as the cause of alcohol abuse. Rooted initially in psychoanalysis and evolving after World War II, alcoholics were thought to be fixated at some stage in their personality development, usually the oral stage. Other psychoanalytic theories have considered alcoholism to be a manifestation of sex-role conflicts, latent homosexuality, or low self-esteem. Given these causes, the natural agent for intervention is the psychoanalytically-oriented psychotherapist.

Conditioning Models. The premise of conditioning models, as they are applied to alcoholism, is that excessive drinking is a pattern of learned behavior which has been reinforced. As a learned behavior it is subject to the same laws of reinforcement as other behaviors. It is also subject to change through relearning and different patterns of reinforcement. Treatment then, is a matter of counterconditioning (e.g., aversion therapies), altering contingencies for drinking and sobriety (e.g., community reinforcement approach or "disenabling"), and/or relearning new ways to reduce tension or deal with conflicts which have precipitated heavy drinking. Prevention efforts might focus on factors which create positive expectations about drinking (e.g., advertising) and incentives which encourage heavy drinking (e.g., 2 for 1 happy hours). The implied agents of intervention are behavior therapists.

Biological Models. Biological models have emphasized genetic and physiological factors resulting in alcoholism. The genetic models are supported by evidence of higher levels of alcoholism among the offspring of alcoholics, even if not raised by their biological parents. The implied intervention here is risk identification by diagnosticians and the urging of

4

caution about the use of alcohol in individuals at high risk. The concept of pharmacological addiction represents another biological model. The assumed causal factor here is alcohol itself. The implied agents of intervention are physicians and the intervention is medically-oriented treatment.

Social Learning Models. These models go beyond the conditioning models by emphasizing the social context in which heavy drinking occurs. Causal factors include deficits in coping skills, peer pressures and modeling of heavy drinking, positive expectancies about drinking, and psychological dependence. In the latter, heavy drinking is seen as a strategy for altering psychological states or coping with problems. In these models the appropriate agents of intervention include cognitive-behavior therapists and role models.

General Systems Models. These models focus on the larger social system in which the alcohol abuser is but one part of a whole. Most often the social system is the family. The implied causal factor is a dysfunctional family an individual is a part of while he or she grows up. Because the family system is seen as having an inherent drive to maintain the status quo, changing the individual with treatment without addressing the family dynamics has a low chance of succeeding. Consequently the agents of intervention are family therapists and the intervention is systems-oriented family therapy.

Sociocultural Models. These models emphasize the roles of societal norms about drinking, the cost and availability of alcohol, and the nature of the drinking environment itself. For example, per capita consumption of alcohol is strongly influenced by its cost and availability. An important assumption here is that the more alcohol consumed in a society, the more alcohol-related problems it has. Recent moves to increase the liability of those who serve alcoholic beverages is another recognition that the environment in which a person drinks is, in itself, an important influence on how much a person consumes. In the view of the sociocultural models, the agents of intervention include legislators and makers of social policy. The implied interventions include legislation to restrict access and to increase the price of alcohol and training of servers of alcohol.

Summary. Table 1.1 summarizes the models we have described thus far. Until recently proponents of each of these models have squared off against each other in futile attempts to defend their model as the most important. This is unfortunate, as it has led to more conflict and strife than there needs to be. It is beyond the scope and space limitations of this chapter to even summarize the evidence supporting each model. Suffice it to say that each has evidence to support its validity. At the same time, each model is limited in its ability to account for *all* that we know about alcohol abuse.

5

Table 1.1 A Developmental History of Models of
Addictive Behaviors and Their Implications for Intervention

MODEL	EXAMPLES	EMPHASIZED CASUAL FACTORS	IMPLIED INTERVENTIONS	APPROPRIATE INTERVENTION AGENT
MORAL	Abuse as sin Abuse as crime	Spirituality Personal responsibility	Spiritual direction, Moral suasion, Social sanctions	Clergy Law enforcement agents
TEMPERANCE	Prohibition WCTU	Alcohol	Exhortation Abstinence/prohibition	Abstainers Legislators
AMERICAN DISEASE	A.A. N.A.	Irreversible constitutional Abnormality of individual	Identification/confrontation Lifelong abstinence	Recovering alcoholics Peer support
EDUCATIONAL	Lectures Affective educ.	Lack of knowledge Lack of motivation	Education	Educators
CHARACTERO-LOGICAL	Psychoanalysis	Personality Traits/dispositions Defense mechanisms	Psychotherapy Risk identification Self-image modification	Psychotherapists
CONDITIONING	Classical cond. Operant cond.	Conditioned response Reinforcement	Counterconditioning Altered contingencies Relearning "Disenabling"	Behavior therapists
BIOMEDICAL	Heredity Brain (THIQ)	Genetic Physiological	Risk identification Medical treatment	Diagnosticians Physicians
SOCIAL LEARNING	Cognitive therapy Relapse prevention	Modeling Expectancies Skill deficits	Appropriate models/goals Cognitive restructuring, Skill training, Self-control training	Cognitive-behavior therapists Appropriate models
GENERAL SYSTEMS	Transactional analysis "Adult children of alcholics"	Family dysfunction	Family therapy Recognition, peer support	Family Therapist Support groups
SOCIOCULTURAL	Control of consumption	Environmental Cultural norms	Supply-side intervention Social policy Server intervention	Lobbyists/legislators Social policy makers Retailers/servers
PUBLIC HEALTH	World Health Organization National Academy of Sciences	Interactions of host, agent, and environment	Comprehensive, multifaceted	Interdisciplinary

Fortunately, in recent years the Public Health model has been promoted by public health professionals as an approach which integrates all of the models we have described thus far.

Public Health Model

Public health professionals conceptualize health problems in terms of an interaction among three factors: the agent, the host, and the environment. Most often the agent is an organism (e.g., a virus) but, in this case, it is ethanol. This involves such issues as the chemical action of alcohol at a celluar level, its impact on organ functions, and its interaction with disease processes. The second factor in the model is the host. As a causal factor, the host involves intraindividual consideration of the many biological, sociological, and psychological variables which influence drinking behavior and mediate its effects. Subjects for investigation within this category include genetic predispositions to the effects of alcohol, personality disorders, and an individual's positive expectancies about drinking. The environment includes the social, cultural, political, and economic variables which affect alcohol use and its consequences. Issues of concern here include sociocultural norm for drinking and availability of alcohol. The public health approach to the etiology, course, and outcome of a health problem, therefore, involves the examination of the complex interaction of the multitude of variables affecting the agent, the host, and the environment.

While each of the models discussed earlier contributes to our understanding of the nature of alcohol-related problems, the public health model is more comprehensive (Miller and Hester, 1989). Other models emphasize one aspect, either the host, the agent, or the environment, to the exclusion of the others. For example, the temperance model emphasizes the agent—alcohol—as the cause of alcohol problems and excludes the role of the environment and the host. Moral, disease, educational, characterological, and biological models emphasize aspects of the host that lead to the susceptibility for alcohol abuse while excluding effects of the environment and the agent. Conditioning, general systems, and sociocultural models consider the environment as the crucial element in the etiology of alcoholism and minimize or exclude its interaction with the agent and the host and their separate contributions.

Although the public health perspective acknowledges the interactive effects of the host and the environment, the agent—ethanol—is recognized as a hazardous drug and its use at any level of consumption, low or high, can lead to problems. Consequently, one form of primary prevention efforts focuses on decreasing access to, and the availability of alcohol. Legitimate criticisms have been directed at these control-of-supply recommendations (Peele, 1987). Proponents of the public health perspective recognize that the acceptance of this form of prevention depends upon the public's understanding of the rationale, need, and benefits to be received from such controls (Ashley and Rankin, 1988). This model also recognizes that the social context of drinking is important and that some individuals may be at greater risk for developing alcohol-related problems. Consequently, the primary prevention efforts implied by this model are multidimensional and broad spectrum.

In addition to primary prevention, the public health model emphasizes secondary prevention; the early detection of heavy drinking and reduction of alcohol consumption before chronic use leads to extensive and irreversible health problems. Its emphasis on public health makes primary health care (PHC) settings (e.g., emergency rooms, ambulatory care clinics, obstetrics units) appropriate sites for screening and prevention efforts. Evidence of the effectiveness of brief interventions in these settings is increasing (Chafetz, Blane, Abram, Clark, Golner, Hastie, and McCourt, 1964; Kristenson, Ohlin, Hulten-Nosslin, Trell, and Hood, 1983; Chick, Lloyd, and Crombie, 1985).

Unlike the other models previously mentioned, the public health model does not support one mode of intervention over others. Through its inclusion of the agent, the host, and the environment as causal factors, the public health model implies that different treatments are appropriate for different individuals. This approach to treatment is consistent with the evidence of the effectiveness of different treatment approaches (Miller and Hester, 1986). There is no single treatment approach which is most effective for everyone. Rather, the evidence suggests that there are a number of alternatives which are effective. The public health model, then, holds the promise of bringing together many professionals who have fought each other for so long. This field could benefit substantially from more cooperation and less confrontation.

REFERENCES

Ashley, M.J., and Rankin, J.G. (1988). A public health approach to the prevention of alcohol-related health problems. *Annual Review of Public Health*, 9 233-271.

Babor, T.E., Ritson, E.B., and Hodgson, R.J. (1986). Alcohol-related problems in the primary health care setting: A review of early intervention strategies. *British Journal of Addiction*, 81 23-46.

Chafetz, M.E., Blane, H.T., Abram, H.S., Clark, E., Golner, J.H., Hastie, E.L, and McCourt, W.F. (1964). Establishing treatment relations with alcoholics: A supplementary report. *Journal of Nervous and Mental Disease*, **138** 390-393.

Chick, J., Lloyd, G., and Crombie, E. (1985). Counselling problem drinkers in medical wards: A controlled study. *British Medical Journal*, **290** 965-967.

Jellinek, E.M. (1960) *The Disease Concept of Alcoholism*. Hillhouse Press: New Haven.

Kristenson, H., Ohlin, H., Hulten-Nosslin, M., Trell, E., and Hood, B. (1983). Identification and intervention of heavy drinkers in middle-aged men: Results and follow-up of 24-60 months of long-term study with randomized controls. *Journal of Alcoholism, Clinical and Experimental Research*, **7** 203-209.

Miller, W.R., and Hester, R.K. (1986). The effectiveness of alcoholism treatment: What research reveals. In W. R. Miller, , and N. Heather (Eds.), *Treating addictive behaviors: Processes of change* (pp. 121-174). Plenum: New York, NY.

Miller, W.R., and Hester, R.K. (1989). Treating alcohol problems: Toward an informed eclecticism. In W.R. Miller, and R.K. Hester (Eds.), *Handbook of Alcoholism Treatment Approaches: Effective Alternatives*. Pergammon Press: New York.

Peele, S. (1987). The limitations of control-of-supply models for explaining and preventing alcoholism and drug addictions. *Journal of Studies on Alcohol*, **48** 61-89.

Skinner, H.A., and Holt, S. (1983). Early intervention for alcohol problems. *Journal of the Royal College of General Practitioners*, **33** 787-791.

CHAPTER 2

Evidence for a Genetic Factor in Alcoholism

Donald W. Goodwin, M.D.

Three types of evidence support the possibility that heredity may contribute to alcoholism: family studies, adoption studies, and twins studies. Each will be reviewed briefly, followed by some comments about etiology.

Family Studies. Alcoholism runs in families. An estimated 20-25% of sons of alcoholics become alcoholic and about 5% of the daughters (Cotton, 1979). Estimates of the rate of alcoholism in the general population vary widely, but the rates for first degree relatives of alcoholics are several fold higher than most population estimates. A family history of alcoholism represents the strongest known risk factor for alcoholism.

Similarly, about 20-25% of male siblings of alcoholics become alcoholic and about 5% of female siblings. The observation that alcoholism runs in families dates to classical times and is one of the most documented facts in the field of substance abuse.

Not everything that runs in families is inherited. Languages, for example, run in families. For many years it was believed that alcoholism was "learned" in the way that languages were learned: largely emulation. Twin and adoption studies tend to challenge this belief.

Adoption Studies. Studying adoptees is one way to separate nature from nurture. If there is alcoholism in the biological parents and the disorder has a partial genetic basis, one would predict that children of alcoholics adopted in infancy to nonalcoholics would still have a relatively high rate of alcoholism. Four such studies have been conducted.

The first by Roe (1944) found no difference between children of alcoholics and children of nonalcoholics when both groups had been raised by adoptive parents who presumably were not alcoholic. There were no alcoholics in either group. The sample size was small and it was not clear that the biological parents would be classified as alcoholic today. Many had a history suggestive of antisocial personality. Also, the adoptees were young at the time they were studied and may had not entered the age of risk for alcoholism.

The 1970s saw a renewed interest in biological factors in alcoholism. Three adoption studies were conducted in three countries: Denmark (Goodwin et al., 1973), Sweden (Bohman, 1978) and the United States (Cadoret, Cain, and Grove, 1979) Although methologically dissimilar, the three studies came to similar conclusions:

1. Grownup children of alcoholics raised by nonalcoholic adoptive parents continued to have a high rate of alcoholism—about as high as that found in children of alcoholics raised by alcoholic parents.
2. Having an alcoholic biological parent apparently did not increase the risk of the adoptees having other psychiatric disorders.

In the Danish study, four groups of individuals were interviewed: sons and daughters of alcoholic parents who were adopted out and raised by nonalcoholic, unrelated, adoptive parents, and their brothers and sisters raised by the alcoholic parent. No difference in alcoholism rates in same-sex siblings were found. Nor did the adopted-out children of alcoholics have elevated rates of other psychiatric pathology compared to controls (adopted-out children of nonalcoholics). Alcoholism ran true to type. Having an alcoholic parent did not even increase the chance of the adopted-out offspring being classified as heavy drinkers.

The Swedish and Iowa studies initially reported similar findings. In the Swedish study, criminality in the biological parents did not predict criminality in the offspring, nor did alcoholism predict criminality. The data were later reanalyzed by Cloninger (Cloninger, Bohman, and Sigvardsson, 1981) who identified environmental factors (e.g., income) as important in one group of adoptees but not in the other. In the first group (called Type I alcoholism) both sexes were susceptible to what seemed a rather mild form of alcoholism and heredity seemed relatively unimportant. In Type II alcoholism, men were mainly susceptible and there was a strong history of alcoholism in the biological parents. Also, Cloninger reported that Type II alcoholism was associated with antisocial personality.

Originally, the Iowa study also found that alcoholism ran true to type; that is, a family history of alcoholism in the biological parents did not increase the likelihood of other psychiatric illnesses occurring in the adopted-out offspring. Further study found a tendency for the adopted-out children to misuse drugs and also found that alcoholism in the adoptive parents somewhat raised the chance of alcoholism occurring in their adopted children (Cadoret et al., 1984). At present, the issue remains unclear about whether alcoholism in parents increased the chance of other psychiatric disorders occurring in their adopted-out offspring.

Twin Studies. Single egg monozygotic twins share the same DNA and presumably have identical susceptibility to genetic illnesses. Twin egg dizygotic twins share a familial susceptibility to genetic illnesses to the extent to which they share the same genes.

Four twin studies have examined drinking patterns and alcohol dependence. A Swedish study (Kaij, 1960) found that identical twins were more concordant for alcoholism than fraternal twins. A large Finnish study (Partanen, Bruun, and Markkanen, 1977) found similarities of drinking patterns, but no difference between identical and fraternal twins regarding "loss of control" (believed by some to be the sine qua non of alcoholism). However, there was a discrepancy in concordance rates for younger twins, with young identical twins more likely to be concordant for alcoholism than young fraternal twins. A review of Veterans Administration records in the United States lent support to a genetic factor (Hrubec and Omenn, 1981), finding that identical twins were more often concordant for alcoholism than fraternal twins. Finally, an ongoing study in England has failed so far to find differences between identical and fraternal twins with respect to alcoholism (Murray and Gurlin, 1983).

Like the adoption studies, most of the twin data are consistent with the presence of genetic factors in alcoholism, but there are exceptions, and the relative importance of environmental and genetic factors remains to be ascertained.

What is Inherited?

To the extent that alcoholism is influenced by heredity, what is inherited? The answer is that nobody knows. The cause of alcoholism is unknown.

Nevertheless, there is much speculation. Often the word multifactorial is used. What is meant by this?

Multifactorial is a mathematical-sounding word usually uttered in tones which suggest that our ignorance about alcoholism may be total, but that we at least agree that it is "multifactorial." When we do not know the cause of alcoholism (which means that it could just as easily be unifactorial as multifactorial), I believe we should admit it and not disguise our ignorance with big words.

One reason why alcoholism is called multifactorial may be that it seems a nice thing to say—politic, diplomatic. Meetings on alcoholism are attended by people from a variety of specialties: medicine, psychiatry, psychology, social work, etc. When alcoholism is attributed to multiple factors—biologic, sociologic, psychologic—everyone feels useful. There is a kind of unspoken agreement that, because experts form diverse backgrounds study alcoholism, alcoholism must have diverse origins.

In one sense this is obviously true. Genes give us the enzymes to metabolize alcohol; society gives us the alcohol to metabolize; and our psyches respond in wondrous ways to these combined gifts. Nevertheless, beyond this obvious level, the evidence for multiple causes of alcoholism is no better or worse than the evidence for a single cause.

The etiology of alcoholism may *actually* involve a single cause—a single chemical "switch." If someone ever finds the switch, the next step will be to learn how to turn it off. This is relatively easy once a switch is found (as has been done in other illnesses). Lewis Thomas says the same thing about cancer (Thomas, 1979). When people interested in cancer get together at meetings, they also use terms like multifactorial. But Thomas believes cancer may also involve a single switch:

"The record of the past half century has established, I think, two general principles about human disease. First, it is necessary to know a great deal about underlying mechanisms before one can really act effectively..."

"Second, for every disease there is a single key mechanism that dominates all others...This generalization is harder to prove... but I believe that the record thus far tends to support it. The most complicated, multicellular, multitissue, and multiorgan disease I know of are tertiary syphilis, chronic tuberculosis, and pernicious aniema... Before they came under scientific appraisal each was thought to be what we now call a "multifactorial" disease, far too complex to allow for any single causative mechanism. And yet, when all the necessary facts were in, it was clear that by simply switching off one thing—the spirochete, the tubercle bacillus, or a single vitamin deficiency—the whole array of disordered and seemingly unrelated pathologic mechanisms could be switched off, at once..."

"I believe that a prospect something like this is the likelihood for the future of medicine. I have no doubt that there will turn out to be dozens of separate influences that can launch cancer...but I think there will turn out to be a single switch at the center of things...I think that schizophrenia will turn out to be a neurochemical disorder, with some central, single chemical event gone wrong. I think there is a single causative agent responsible for rheumatoid arthritis...I think that the central vascular abnormalities that launch coronary occlusion and stroke have not yet been glimpsed, but they are there, waiting to be switched on or off."

Thomas did not include alcoholism in his list of potential single-switch disorders, but I suspect he would have, had he attended a few multidisciplinary conferences on alcoholism. (In the case of cancer, single switches *were* found, called oncogenes, long after Thomas wrote the above words.)

Two possible switches might turn on alcoholism. One involves producing too little of something. The second involves producing too much of something.

To illustrate the former: Let's assume that some alcoholics lack the gene(s) for optimal production of Substance H (H for happiness). They are born, so to speak, unhappy. Sometime in their teens they discover that having two or three beers or drinks makes them happy. Someone once said that you never feel better than when you feel good after feeling bad, and, for some alcoholics—those who start life feeling bad—drinking alcohol feels so good it becomes habit-forming. But all is not bliss. Ten minutes or so after the H-deficient person has a drink, he wants another. He is feeling unhappy again—unhappier than before he had the drink. The unhappiness now has a special quality sometimes called craving. A drink relieves this new special unhappiness and even restores the original happiness, but just briefly. Another drink, and another, is needed to overcome the unhappy feeling produceed by the same drug that produced the happy feeling— alcohol. "It lifts you up and puts you down," as the saying goes, and some people are lifted up and put down more than others, possibly because of genes.

Substance H (if it exists) has not been identified. Let's assume, for the sake of speculation, that it is serotonin. Perhaps the pre-alcoholic has too little serotonin. Alcohol brings his serotonin level to normal and even above normal, making the act of drinking highly reinforcing. Alcohol does this by releasing serotonin from brain cells. Brain cells contain limited amounts of serotonin and, after a short time, they run out of serotonin. Now the pre-alcoholic who had low levels of serotonin to begin with has even lower levels, and because drinking, for him, is so strongly reinforced and habit-forming, he wages a desperate battle to overcome his serotonin deficiency by drinking more and more alcohol. It is a battle he will inevitable lose; his cells cannot keep up with the demand for serotonin. As a result, there is considerable stress and strain on the organism. Stimulant chemicals like epinephrine pitch in to help, but ultimately make matters worse by leaving the drinker in a hyperstimulated state when he stops drinking (as he eventually must).

A second chemical possibility involves overproduction. Alcohol produces substances in the brain that resemble morphine. Conceivably, alcohol produces more morphine-like substances in some brains than in others—again because of genes. The pre-alcoholic is the person whose brain overproduces morphine when he drinks alcohol—or overproduces *something* that makes drinking unusually rewarding, habit-forming, ad-

14

dictive. Chemical mediators of addiction (if they exist) may not be like morphine at all, but the overproduction model is a good one to pursue.

Conclusion

In summary, alcoholism runs in families. It runs in families even when the children are raised by nonalcoholic adoptive parents. Thus the transmission of alcoholism cannot be attributed entirely to conditions of upbringing. This is as far as our knowledge goes. Terms like multifactorial merely disguise our ignorance. But knowing that alcoholism involves a biological susceptibility—possibly genetic—is new and important information. It has led to some biochemical theories that deserve pursuing.

REFERENCES

Bohman, M. (1978). Some genetic aspects of alcoholism and criminality: A population of adoptees. *Archives of General Psychiatry*, **35** 269-276.

Cadoret, R.J., Cain, C.A., and Grove, W.M. (1979). Development of alcoholism in adoptees raised apart from alcoholic biologic relatives. *Archives of General Psychiatry*, **37** 561-563.

Cadoret, R.J., O'Gorman, T.W., Troughton, E., and Heywood, E. (1984). Alcoholism and antisocial personality: Interrelationships, genetic and environmental factors. *Archives of General Psychiatry*, **42** 161-167.

Cloninger, C.R., Bohman, M., and Sigvardsson, S. (1981). Inheritance of alcohol abuse: Cross-fostering analysis of adopted men. *Archives of General Psychiatry*, **36** 861-868.

Cotton, N.S. (1979). The familial incidence of alcoholism: A review. *Journal of Studies on Alcoholism*, **40** 89-116.

Goodwin, D.W., Schulsinger, F., Hermansen, L., Guze, S.B., and Winokur, G. (1973). Alcohol problems in adoptees raised apart form alcoholic biological parents. *Archives of General Psychiatry*, **28** 238-242.

Hrubec, A. and Omenn, G. (1981). Evidence of genetic predisposition to alcoholic cirrhosis and psychosis: Twin concordances for alcoholism and its biological end points by zygosity among male veterans. *Alcoholism Clinical and Experimental Research*, **5** 207-215.

Kaij, L. (1960). *Studies on the Etiology and Sequels of Abuse of Alcohol*. University of Lund: Lund, Sweden.

Murray, R.M. and Gurlin, C.C. (1983). Twin and alcoholism studies. *Recent developments in Alcoholism*, edited by M. Galanter, Volume 1, Chapter 5, Gardner Press: New York.

Partanen, J., Bruun, K. and Markkanen, T. (1977). Inheritance of drinking behavior: A study on intelligence, personality, and use of alcohol of adult twins. *Emerging Concepts of Alcohol Dependence*, edited by E.M. Pattison, M.B. Sobell, L.C. Sobell, Chapter 10. Springer Publishing Co., Inc.: New York.

Roe, A. (1944). The adult adjustment of children of alcoholic parents raised in foster homes. *Quarterly Journal of Studies on Alcohol*, **5** 378-393.

Thomas, L. (1979). *The Medusa and the Snail*. Viking Press: New York.

CHAPTER 3

Neurobiological and Genetic Basis for Alcoholism Based Upon Research in Animal Models

Ting-Kai Li, M.D.

Alcoholism is a disorder of alcohol (drug)-seeking behavior. This abnormal "appetite" for alcohol results in loss of control over drinking and tolerance to the pharmacological actions of the drug. Both psychological and physical dependence develop over time. Alcoholism, also known as the alcohol dependence syndrome (Edwards and Gross, 1976), is expressed as intense reinforced-responding for alcohol.

Alcohol-drinking or alcohol self-administration behavior is a quantitative trait. As with most quantitative traits (e.g., height, blood pressure or serum cholesterol), expression is influenced by both genetic and environmental factors. It is now known that there are significant genetic contributions to the normal ranges of variation in human behavior, including various dimensions of personality, cognitive abilities, and intelligence. There is also a genetic component to the variance in alcohol-drinking behavior (Jardine and Martin, 1984). Genetic influence is also seen in a number of behavioral disorders, including alcoholism (Goodwin et al., 1973). Subtypes of familial alcoholism have been identified, in which genetic and environmental factors appear to have different degrees of influence (Cloninger, 1986). Because ethanol is a weak drug which is effective only at concentrations thousands of times higher than that of other drugs of abuse, such as opiates, cocaine or amphetamine, genetic susceptibility becomes an important etiological consideration in our quest to understand the pathogenesis of alcoholism. The identification of genetic vulnerability in subgroups of alcoholics does not diminish the importance of environmental influences, as is evident from the large number of "sporadic" (nonfamilial) cases in the affected population.

There is at this time still very little understanding about the biological mechanisms that promote abnormal alcohol-seeking behavior; however, studies in genetically-developed animal models are beginning to provide interesting leads that appear to be relevant to the human disorder. This

17

chapter will review some of the advances in this area. The animal models were developed with the notion that the neuropsychopharmacological actions of ethanol and how different individuals react to them can be important biological determinants. Ethanol's action is biphasic, i.e., it can be reinforcing (rewarding) in the low concentration range, but aversive at high concentrations (Pohorecky, 1977). Perception by the individual of the reinforcing actions of ethanol might be expected to maintain alcohol-seeking behavior, whereas aversive effects would be expected to extinguish this behavior. Continued exposure can evoke neuroadaptive and metabolic changes of different degree that attenuate the effects of ethanol.

Genetic Variability in Response to Alcohol in Humans

In looking at various biological responses to ethanol that can serve as feedback loops to influence alcohol drinking behavior in humans, it is noteworthy that a number of them, as well as drinking behavior itself, have shown a large degree of between-individual variability which are, in part, genetically determined (McClearn and Erwin, 1982; Li, 1985). These include: alcohol elimination rate, the sensitivity of the brain to the actions of alcohol (as exemplified by patterns of ethanol-induced change in the electroencephalogram), and systemic reactivity to ethanol's metabolism, as evidenced by the alcohol-flush reaction.

The alcohol-flush reaction is aversive and occurs in approximately 50% of Asian populations. It is caused by a genetic variation in the mitochondrial form of aldehyde dehydrogenase ($ALDH_2$) that renders it inactive. The $ALDH_2$ deficiency, acetaldehyde, which is quite toxic, accumulates in the body and provokes the flush reaction (Harada et al., 1981). The $ALDH_2$ deficiency trait is protective against heavy drinking and individuals with this genetic trait represent a very small proportion (less than 10%) of Asian alcoholics as compared with the approximately 50% prevalence rate in the general population (Harada et al., 1983) The mutation on the $ALDH_2$ gene that causes this trait has been identified, and it has been shown that $ALDH_2$-deficiency is inherited as an autosomal dominant trait (Crabb et al., 1989). In other words, the dominant gene allele that codes for the inactive or low activity $ALDH_2$ is protective against heavy drinking and alcoholism, whereas the recessive gene allele that codes for the active $ALDH_2$ enzyme is permissive of heavy drinking. This is the first gene identified to have an important impact on drinking behavior and alcoholism.

It can be expected that other responses to alcohol's actions, such as individual differences in sensitivity to the reinforcing effects of ethanol, in capacity for developing tolerance to the aversive effects of ethanol, and in severity of withdrawal reactions owing to physical dependence might

18

also be attributable, in part, to genetic factors. Experiments on the heritability of the high dose aversive effects of alcohol and of the chronic effects of ethanol administration (tolerance and physical dependence) are difficult to justify in humans for ethical reasons. Clearly, such studies and the study of the relation to alcohol-seeking behavior of these responses to ethanol are more appropriately carried out in experimental laboratory animals. For similar reasons, exploration of the neuroanatomical, neurophysiological, and neurochemical substrates of alcohol-seeking behavior can only be pursued with use of laboratory animals that exhibit differences in degree of alcohol preference or alcohol-seeking behavior.

Genetic Variability in Responses to Alcohol in Experimental Animals

In experimental animals, genetic influence has been documented for a variety of responses to ethanol including alcohol preference, alcohol metabolic rate, neuronal sensitivity to the acute effects of ethanol, the capacity to develop tolerance, and severity of withdrawal reactions (Li, 1985; McClearn and Erwin, 1982). A recent review (Crabbe, 1989) summarizes the various inbred mouse strains and selectively bred mouse and rat lines that differ in the above traits. The process of selective breeding systematically mates chosen individuals that exhibit the most extreme levels of a given phenotype (e.g., high or low measures of alcohol drinking preference) through successive generations. Over time, the selected lines would have a high or low frequency of the genes influencing that trait, while the frequencies for genes not affecting that trait should be randomly distributed. Apart from demonstrating experimentally that the phenotype in question is genetically influenced, these pharmacogenetically different animals provide useful tools for investigating mechanisms, since associated traits are likely to share common mechanisms through common gene action.

Genetic Animal Models for the Study of Alcohol-Seeking Behavior and Alcoholism

To elucidate the neurobiological mechanisms that underlie abnormal alcohol-seeking behavior, it is necessary to have experimental animals that would orally self-administer alcoholic solutions, (for the drug properties of ethanol) in amounts comparable to that in the human alcoholic. A major roadblock to studies of this nature in the past has been that most species of laboratory animals do not like to drink unflavored aqueous solutions containing moderate (10%) to high concentrations of ethanol. However, through selective breeding, rat lines that exhibit high and low alcohol-drinking preference have been raised. Two pairs of these, the alcohol-preferring P and HAD lines and the alcohol nonpreferring NP and LAD lines were raised in our laboratory from Wistar and N/Nih foundation stocks, respectively.

Studies in the past 12 years have shown that the P rats satisfy the major criteria for an animal model of alcoholism (Lester and Freed, 1973; Cicero, 1979). Specifically, the P rats:

1. Voluntarily drink ethanol solutions (10-30%, v/v, in water in quantities that elevate blood alcohol concentrations (BACs) into pharmacologically meaningful ranges (Li et al., 1979, Lumeng and Li, 1986). Blood ethanol concentrations as high as 200 mg% have been observed.

2. Develop, with chronic drinking, metabolic and neuronal tolerance (Lumeng and Li, 1986; Gatto et al., 1987a), and physical dependence as evidenced by withdrawal signs (Waller et al., 1982).

3. Work by operant responding (bar-pressing) to obtain ethanol in concentrations as high as 30%, but not because of the caloric value, taste or smell of the ethanol solutions (Penn et al., 1978; Murphy et al., 1989). The NP rats will not bar-press for ethanol in concentrations higher than 5%. Importantly, the P, but not the NP rats would self-administer ethanol even by direct intragastric infusion (Waller et al., 1984). Blood alcohol concentrations as high as 400 mg% were observed.

Associated Traits of Alcohol-Seeking Behavior

Comparison of the P rats with the selectively bred, alcohol-nonpreferring NP line of rats has revealed differences that suggest new avenues for exploration of the neurobiological basis of alcohol-seeking behavior. Compared with the NP rats:

1. The P rats are behaviorally stimulated by low doses of ethanol and are less affected by sedative-hypnotic doses of ethanol (Waller et al., 1986). The NP rats are more sensitive to the aversive properties of ethanol than the P rats (Froehlich et al., 1988a).

2. The P rats develop tolerance more quickly within a single session of exposure to a sedative-hypnotic dose of ethanol (acute tolerance), and this tolerance persists (as tested by a second dose of ethanol) for a much longer period of time (Waller et al., 1983; Gatto et al., 1987b). With chronic free-choice drinking, P rats develop tolerance to the aversive properties of ethanol. Concomitantly, the free-choice drinking of ethanol increases (unpublished data).

3. Ethanol-naive P rats exhibit lower levels of serotonin (5-HT) and

20

dopamine (DA) in certain brain regions (Murphy et al., 1982), most notably the nucleus accumbens (Murphy et al., 1987). Higher densities of 5-HT receptors in some of these regions (cerebral cortex and hippocampus) have been found in the P rats as compared with NP rats (Wong et al., 1988). Preliminary immunocytochemical studies suggest that the P rats may have fewer 5-HT fibers in the affected regions as compared with NP rats (unpublished observations). The administration of 5-HT uptake inhibitors attenuates the alcohol-seeking behavior of the P rats (McBride et al., 1988).

The difference between lines in response to ethanol suggests that both the enhanced responsiveness to the low-dose reinforcing effects of ethanol, and the rapid development and persistence of tolerance to the high-dose, aversive effects of ethanol are important in promoting high alcohol-seeking behavior. Recent comparison studies in HAD and LAD rats have shown that, as with the P rats, selection for ethanol drinking preference (10%, v/v, vs. H^2O) produced lines (HAD) that exhibit operant responding for ethanol as reward in concentrations as high as 30%. As with NP rats, LAD rats responded very little for ethanol when alcohol concentration exceeded 5% (Levy et al., 1988). Furthermore, as was found in the P and NP rats, HAD animals exhibit longer persistence of tolerance after a single, sedative-hypnotic dose of ethanol than do the LAD animals (Froehlich et al., 1987). Therefore, the salient features of the hypothesis formulated from the studies of the P and NP rats appear generalizable.

More recently, the contents of dopamine (DA), serotonin (5-HT), and their primary acid metabolites were assayed in 10 brain regions of the HAD and LAD lines of rats (Gongwer et al., 1989). Compared with the LAD line, the contents of 5-HT and/or 5-hydroxyindoleacetic acid were lower in several brain regions (cerebral cortex, striatum, nucleus accumbens, septal nuclei, hippocampus and hypothalamus) of the HAD line. The levels of DA, 3,4-dihydroxyphenylacetic acid, and homovanillic acid were also lower in the nucleus accumbens and anterior striatum of the HAD rats. These data agree generally with the neurochemical findings in P and NP rats and implicate the involvement of 5-HT and DA pathways in mediating alcohol-drinking behavior. Other neurotransmitter systems that may have an important role in ethanol preference are gamma-aminobutyric acid (GABA) and the opioid peptides (Froehlich et al., 1988b). Immunocytochemical and morphometric studies have revealed more GABAergic terminals in the nucleus accumbens of the P and HAD rats than in that of the NP and LAD rats (Hwang et al., 1988). How these neurotransmitter systems interface in producing alcohol-seeking behavior is currently under active investigation. It is our hope that understanding gained through such studies can lead to better treatment modalities for alcoholism.

REFERENCES

Cicero, T.J. (1979). A critique of animal analogues of alcoholism. In: *Biochemistry and Pharmacology of Ethanol, Vol. 2*. Majchrowicz, E. and Noble, E.P., eds. Plenum Press: New York, pp. 533-560.

Cloninger, C.R. (1986). Genetics of alcoholism. *Alcoholism: Clinical and Experimental Research,* **9** 479-482.

Crabb, D.W., Edenberg, H.J., Bosron, W.F., and Li, T.-K. (1989). Genotypes for aldehyde dehydrogenase deficiency and alcohol sensitivity: The inactive $ALDH^2$ allele is dominant. *Journal of Clinical Investigation,* **83** 314-316.

Crabbe, J.C. (1989). Genetic animal models in the study of alcoholism. *Alcoholism: Clinical and Experimental Research,* **13** 120-127.

Edwards, G. and Gross, M.M. (1976). Alcohol dependence: Provisional description of a syndrome. *British Medical Journal,* **1** 1058-1051.

Froehlich, J.C., Harts, J., Lemeng, L., and Li, T.-K. (1988a). Differences in response to the aversive properties of ethanol in rats selectively bred for oral ethanal preference. *Pharmacology, Biochemistry, and Behavior,* **31** 215-222.

Froehlich, J.C., Harts, J., Lumeng, L., and Li, T.-K. (1988b). Enkephalinergic involvement in voluntary ethanol consumption. *Excerpta Medica International Congress Series,* **805** 235-238.

Froehlich, J.C., Hostetler, J., Lumeng, L., and Li, T.-K. (1987). Association between alcohol preference and acute tolerance. *Alcoholism: Clinical and Experimental Research,* **11** 199 (Abstract).

Gatto, G.J., Murphy, J.M., Waller, M.B., McBride, W.J., Lumeng, L., and Li, T.-K. (1987a). Chronic ethanol tolerance through free-choice drinking in the P line of alcohol-preferring rats. *Pharmacology Biochemistry and Behavior,* **28** 111-115.

Gatto, G.J., Murphy, J.M., Waller, M.B., McBride, W.J., Lumeng, L., and Li, T.-K. (1987b). Persistence of tolerance to a single dose of ethanol in the selectively bred alcohol-preferring P rats. *Pharmacology Biochemistry and Behavior,* **28** 105-110.

Goodwin, D.W., Schulsinger, F., Hermansen, L., Guze, S.B, and Winokur, G. (1973). Alcohol problems in adoptees raised apart from alcoholic biological parents. *Archives of General Psychiatry,* **28** 238-243.

Gongwer, M.A., Lumeng, L., Murphy, J.M., McBride, W.J., Li, T.-K. (1989). Regional brain contents of serotonin, dopamine and their metabolites in the selectively bred high- and low-alcohol-drinking lines of rats. *Alcohol,* 6 317-320.

Harada, S., Agarwal, D.P. and Goedde, H.W. (1981). Aldehyde dehydrogenase deficiency as cause of facial flushing reaction to alcohol in Japanese. *Lancet,* ii 982.

Harada, S., Agarwal, D.P., Goedde, H.W., and Ishikawa, B. (1983). Aldehyde dehydrogenase isoenzyme variation and alcoholism in Japan. *Pharmacology Biochemistry and Behavior,* 18 (Suppl. 1) 151-153.

Hwang, B.H., Lumeng, L., Wu, J.-Y., Li, T.-K. (1988). GABAergic neurons in nucleus accumbens: a possible role in alcohol preference. *Alcoholism: Clinical and Experimental Research,* 12 306 (abstract).

Jardine, R. and Martin, N.G. (1984). Causes of variation in drinking habits in a large twin sample. *Acta Geneticae Medicae et Gemellogiae,* 33 435-450.

Lester, D. and Freed, E.X. (1773). Criteria for an animal model of alcoholism. *Pharmacology Biochemistry and Behavior,* 1 103-107.

Levy, A.D., McBride, W.J., Murphy, J.M., Lumeng, L., and Li, T.-K. (1988). Genetically selected lines of high and low alcohol-drinking rats: operant studies. *Abstracts from the Society for Neuroscience,* 14 41.

Li, T.-K., (1985). Genetic variability in response to ethanol in humans and experimental animals. *Proceedings: NIAAA-WHO Collaborating Center Designation Meeting and Alcohol Research Seminar.* L.H. Towle, ed. U.S. Government Printing Office: Washington, DC, pp. 50-62.

Li, T.-K., Lumeng, L., McBride, W.J., Waller, M.B., and Hawking, D.T. (1979). Progress toward a voluntary oral-consumption model of alcoholism. *Drug and Alcohol Dependence,* 4 45-60.

Loehlin, J.C., Willerman, L., and Horn, J.M. (1988). Human behavior genetics. *Annual Review of Psychology,* 39 101-133.

Lumeng, L. and Li, T.-K. (1986). The development of metabolic tolerance in the alcohol-preferring P rats: Comparison of forced and free-choice drinking of ethanol. *Pharmacology Biochemistry and Behavior,* 25 1013-1020.

McBride, W.J., Murphy, J.M., Lumeng, L., and Li, T.-K. (1988). Effects of Ro 15-4513, fluoxetine and desipramine on the intake of ethanol, water and food by the alcohol-preferring (P) and -nonpreferring (NP) lines of rats. *Pharmacology Biochemistry and Behavior,* 30 1045-1050.

McClearn, G.E. and Erwin, V.G. (1982). Mechanisms of genetic influence on alcohol-related behaviors. *Alcohol and Health Monograph I. Alcohol Consumption and Related Problems.* U.S. Government Printing Office: Washington, DC, pp. 263-289.

Murphy, J.M., Gatto, G.J., McBride, W.J., Lumeng, L., and Li, T.-K. (1989). Operant responding for oral ethanol in the alcohol-preferring P and alcohol-nonpreferring (NP) lines of rats. *Alcohol*, **6** 127-131.

Murphy, J.M., McBride, W.J., Lumeng, L., and Li, T.-K. (1982). Regional brain levels of monoamines in alcohol-preferring and -nonpreferring lines of rats. *Pharmacology Biochemistry and Behavior*, **16** 145-149.

Murphy, J.M., McBride, W.J., Lumeng, L., and Li, T.-K. (1987). Contents of monoamines in forebrain regions of alcohol-preferring (P) and -nonpreferring (NP) lines of rats. *Pharmacology Biochemistry and Behavior*, **26** 389-392.

Penn, P.E., McBride, W.J., Lumeng, L., Gaff, T.M., and Li, T.-K. (1978). Neurochemical and operant behavioral studies of a strain of alcohol-preferring rats. *Pharmacology Biochemistry and Behavior*, **8** 475-481.

Pohorecky, L.A., (1977). Biphasic action of ethanol. *Biobehavioral Reviews*, **1** 231-240.

Waller, M.B., McBride, W.J., Gatto, G.J., Lumeng, L., and Li, T.-K. (1984). Intragastric self-infusion of ethanol by the P and the NP (alcohol-preferring and -nonpreferring) lines of rats. *Science*, **225** 78-80.

Waller, M.B., McBride, W.J., Lumeng, L., and Li, T.-K. (1982). Induction of dependence on ethanol by free-choice drinking in alcohol-preferring rats. *Pharmacology Biochemistry and Behavior*, **16** 501-507.

Waller, M.B., McBride, W.J., Lumeng, L., and Li, T.-K. (1983). Initial sensitivity and acute tolerance to ethanol in the P and NP lines of rats. *Pharmacology Biochemistry and Behavior*, **19** 683-686.

Waller, M.B., Murphy, J.M., McBride, W.J., Lumeng, L. and Li, T.-K. (1986). Effect of low dose ethanol on spontaneous motor activity in alcohol-preferring and -nonpreferring lines of rats. *Pharmacology Biochemistry and Behavior*, **24** 617-625.

Wong, D.T., Lumeng, L., Threlkeld, P.G., Reid, L.R., and Li, T.-K. (1988). Serotonergic and adrenergic receptors of alcohol preferring and non-preferring rats. *Journal of Neural Transmission*, **71** 207-218.

CHAPTER 4

Neurobiological Basis of Alcohol Reinforcement and Drinking

R.D. Myers, Ph.D.

"Absence of proof is not proof of absence...of anything."
C. Pert (1989).

Introduction

Controversy is in the mind of the beholder. Unlike the eye required for perceiving beauty, controversy feeds solely on thought, be it logical or illogical. In the domain of science, the processes of scientific thought and of experimental research should not, by definition, necessarily generate controversy. When the scientific method is precisely followed with all documented rules and internal controls in place, an observation is obtained which is factual. It is immutable; it does not lie. How then can a relatively specialized area of scientific inquiry evolve into an outright controversy? Several reasons are readily identified.

First, a moral, religious, or other belief system can hinder the acceptance of a new scientific or theoretical viewpoint. When such a belief system is instilled strongly enough in one's childhood, for example, a subsequent interpretation of a scientific finding can be unbending in an individual, depending largely on the intensity and circumstances of early indoctrination. To illustrate, an activity as commonplace as transportation has been a vehicle for controversy over the generations with people divided into two camps: those who will travel in a conveyance and those who will not. My great-grandfather would never ride on a trolly car—too dangerous; my grandmother would not drive an automobile—too dangerous; my own father would not fly in an airplane—too dangerous. Of course, I would never consider a trip in a space shuttle—obviously, too dangerous!

Second, because of private conviction held in a specific area of scientific study, the revelation of a new observation may be dismissed regardless of the evidence presented. Consequently, a preconceived viewpoint about the operation of a biological or other process simply blots out the data. As a consequence, new experimental results may be transformed to suit one's own subjective view. This is not uncommon in individuals trained competently in a given scientific discipline. Installed over the entrance to a coffee lounge at a Northeastern University was a placard which simply stated ... "Don't confuse me with facts: my mind is made up!"

Third, even though bench-top data acquired by different scientists under diverse circumstances may collectively verify a new experimental result and substantiate a new theory, the experimental procedures of one study may vary to such a degree that a "negative" result is obtained. A scientist then may choose to ignore the set of positive findings, perhaps unintentionally, cite only the negative, and reject the theory. Consequently, the interpretation of the data can be misconstrued and the conclusion drawn erroneous.

These circumstances apply to both physical and biological sciences. In atomic research, the stakes encompassing an issue such as cold-fusion are high and of world-wide impact. Disciplines which focus on fundamental clinical-social research, such as addiction to neuroactive drugs are equally affected. In the field of alcohol research, for example, virtually every facet of experimental endeavor has been plagued by persistent debate or disbelief.

Basis of Discrepancy. Typically, the basis of an experimental discrepancy and contradictory interpretation rests usually in the design and actual conduct of the experiment. When a laboratory scientist attempts conscientiously to repeat another's observation, subtle deviations from the path of replication ordinarily arise. Why? Often one seeks to do the experiment "better," with more subjects or more "precise" measurement. Alternatively, the specific question is attacked from a different perspective using, for example, a different drug or schedule of testing. Other variables such as strain or age of animal may be introduced with the intention of ascertaining whether the original finding is applicable to a related theory or hypothesis.

Moreover, because the natural phenomenon of biological variation is so pervasive, a replication experiment is unlikely to generate an identical result. Thus, the degree to which instrumentation, methods, test subjects, and procedures match the original study will determine the magnitude of concordance of the data obtained. Since the replicating scientist rarely duplicates in detail the study of the first experimenter, the findings of the original observation may be eschewed or rejected.

Controversy in a given discipline of science can be very healthy for the field. It can lead to a serious re-evaluation of a question, stimulate new thinking, instigate the collection of new data, and kindle fresh ideas. On the other hand, controversy may be harmful to an issue and potentially

26

destructive to a discipline; it can prevent any further experimental study. This happens particularly when a negative result either is misinterpreted and blown out of proportion, or if zealousness develops on either or both sides of the issue. Alternatively, a controversy may not really matter sufficiently to have any substantial impact on the thinking extent in the field.

Controversy in Alcohol Research

A plethora of controversy exists in many areas of basic research into the biological phenomena associated with alcohol drinking and the disease concept of alcoholism: the role of liver factors in tolerance; membrane fluidity and alcohol's action; role of membrane and cytosolic calcium; effects of aldehyde dehydrogenase, isoenzymes and aldehyde metabolites on alcohol drinking; the chloride channel and benzodiazepine receptors in intoxication; role of brain endorphins and enkephalins in alcoholism; and biological markers such as serum transferrin. This chapter will deal with one of these controversies: the role of aldehyde metabolites in the reinforcing properties of alcohol and abnormal drinking.

Nature of Reinforcement. One can conceive of at least three internal levels of perceived experiences which are reinforcing. First, many persons frequent the theater, art museums and concerts, or play cards with friends. Others may play a musical instrument or engage actively in golf or tennis. Still others experience great pleasure by eating gourmet food at a sophisticated restaurant and sampling a Premier Crux from Bordeaux. Each sequence of behavior becomes part of a reinforced pattern and is fulfilling to an individual in a unique way. One may become so habituated to a specific activity that life without it is unfulfilling.

A second level of behavioral response may be more intensely reinforcing for certain individuals but somewhat less acceptable by one's peers or society. Such activity typically involves physiological events which provide the signal for the pleasurable sensation. The involvement may extend to such a point that personal obligations to one's family and occupation are relinquished: persistent sexual promiscuity, compulsive overeating to the point of obesity, incessant jogging, or other exercise. Some individuals report a transient or prolonged "high" from repetition of the activity, which is extremely gratifying. although exogenous chemical substances are not involved, humoral factors in the brain may underlie the intensity of the reinforcement. Enhanced levels of trophic hormones released from the pituitary, or endorphins and other opiate substances synthesized in the brain's limbic system (Gianoulakis, 1989) may promote further entrainment of the activity.

A third type of behavior is the self-administration of an addictive compound taken repeatedly for its reinforcing quality. Upon entry into the brain, certain drugs can become incorporated in the cellular machinery responsible for the function of nerve cells in structures of the limbic system. They can act to: release neurotransmitters which enable nerve impulses to traverse the synaptic cleft from one neuron to another; perturb receptor binding characteristics for these neurothransmitters; interfere pre- or postsynaptically with the transport of cellular constituents including Cl^- or Ca^{2+} ions; and promote new synthesis of substances which are themselves addictive. Because limbicforebrain pathways ostensibly underlie rewarding sensations, the stage is set whereby one or more of these interneuronal events can trigger an all-consuming demand to continue self-administration of the compound at all costs.

The nature of this chemical reinforcement contrasts sharply against the first two types. This is not to imply that the intense pleasure derived from an activity involving art, music, eating, or sport is not represented in the brain by an intricate network of neuronal systems comprising the substrate for reward. Rather, the addictive compound introduced into this same neuronal system may simply engulf and override the activity which is normally gratifying and pleasurable.

Brain Metabolites, Opiate Receptors, and Alcoholism

Since the 1960s, neurotransmitter systems in the brain have been implicated in the processes leading to the addictive drinking of alcohol. Serotonin (5-HT), which is involved in functional control mechanisms for body temperature and sleep (Myers, 1974) is one candidate possibly responsible for several aspects of the alcohol drinking mechanism. A pharmacologically induced disturbance to 5-HT in the brain can markedly alter alcohol drinking in the rat (Myers and Veale, 1968; Myers et al., 1972; Myers, 1978a). Studies in which dopamine pathways are ablated by a neurotoxin also implicated catecholamine neurotransmitters in alcohol drinking, in that alcohol intake post-lesion increases sharply and persists for several weeks (Kiianmaa et al., 1975). Thus, a basis for a direct link between neurochemical systems in the brain for reward and the magnitude of alcohol drinking is being established gradually (Myers, 1979a; 1989; Blum et al., 1989).

In 1970, a new theory emerged which traced the etiology of alcoholism to the formation of unique metabolites following alcohol's degradation (Davis and Walsh, 1970; Cohen and Collins, 1970). The theory is summarized as follows (See Myers, 1989). When alcohol is consumed, the enzyme, aldehyde dehydrogenase, degrades acetaldehyde, the toxic metabolite of alcohol. An insufficiency of this crucial enzyme or its preferential diversion to the breakdown of acetaldehyde can lead to an accumulation of other biogenic aldehydes. These aldehydes can react instantaneously with a neurotransmitter or precursor to form a new compound either in brain or periphery or both. One product arising from a dopamine-dopaldehyde reaction is the biological precursor to morphine in the opium poppy, tetrahydropapaveroline (THP). Another class of derivatives, tetrahydro-B-carbolines (THBC), arise from an indoleamine-aldehyde reaction and act to evoke intense anxiety.

Following alcohol drinking, two of the classes of compound detected peripherally and in brain (e.g., Sjöquist et al, 1981; Rommelspacher et al., 1984) are found to exert a myriad of neurobiological actions: they bind to opiate and other receptors in the brain (Gianoulakis, 1989), act as false transmitters, and alter vital functions including blood pressure (Myers, 1980; Melchior and Collins, 1982; Myers, 1985a; b). Drinking to excess, therefore, is hypothesized to lead to even more drinking because of the addictive/anxiogenic nature of the metabolites.

THP–Induced Alcohol Drinking. To test a part of this theory, THP or salsolinol (SAL), a dopamine-acetaldehyde metabolite, was infused directly into the brain of the rat. Water and ethanol were always available to the animal in increasing concentrations ranging from a palatable 3% to a highly aversive 30%. Almost immediately after the THP infusions began, alcohol intake increased sharply even in the aversive concentrations offered (Myers and Melchior, 1977a). THBC infused similarly evoked an identically intense shift in alcohol drinking (Myers and Melchior, 1977b). Thus, the "Multiple Metabolite" theory of alcoholism was born which states that prolonged alcohol drinking promotes synthesis of aldehyde-catechol- or indole-amine metabolites which sequester in specific structures in the brain. Their presence in critical anatomical sites mediate not only the rewarding or pleasurable property of alcohol but serve to sustain alcohol consumption. They even intensify drinking irreversibly to the point of clinical permanency (Myers, 1989).

Evidence for the "Multiple Metabolite" theory is summarized as follows: (1) increasing amounts of alcohol are consumed by a test animal at higher concentrations of alcohol following chronic infusions of either THP or THBC into the cerebral ventricles (ICV) (Myers and Melchior, 1977a; b; Myers and Oblinger, 1977); (2) elevated preference for alcohol is pharmacologically specific since alcohol is preferred over both palatable solutions (Melchior and Myers, 1977) and other drugs (Rommelspacher et al., 1987); (3) re-tests of drinking 1-6 months after exposure to metabolites reveals a permanent shift in alcohol selection (Duncan and Deitrich, 1980; Huttunen and Myers, 1987; Myers and Melchior, 1977b; Myers and Oblinger, 1977; Myers and Privette, 1989) reminiscent of the alcoholic patient; (4) THP-induced drinking is attenuated transiently by

29

opiate receptor antagonists (Critcher et al., 1983; Myers and Critcher, 1982; Myers et al., 1986); (5) blood alcohol levels reach pharmacologically significant amounts during drinking induced by THP (Critcher et al., 1983; Melchior and Myers, 1977); (6) patterns of alcohol intake vary diurnally with bouts of drinking occurring during the active part of the day-night cycle (Melchior and Myers, 1977; Myers, 1978b); (7) withdrawal symptoms are comparable to those described after the rat is withdrawn from morphine (Myers and Oblinger, 1977; Sinclair and Myers, 1982); (8) THP-induced alcohol intake is dose-dependent, a high dose generally suppressing intake and a low dose enhancing it (Myers, 1989; Myers and Oblinger, 1977); (9) lesions of metabolite-sensitive sites in the brain do not augment alcohol preference (Myers et al., 1983; 1982b; Swartzwelder and Myers, 1983); (10) intake of calories derived from solid food remains unchanged by metabolite injections; (11) gustatory discrimination is not impaired by the metabolites (Myers and Oblinger, 1977); (12) anatomical sites mapped in the brain of the rat which are reactive to THP and mediate alcohol drinking correspond to dopamine-enkephalin pathways (Duncan and Fernando, 1990; Myers, 1990; Myers and Privette, 1989); (13) salsolinol is detected in CSF of the alcoholic patient (Sjöquist et al., 1981; 1982a) and increases in concentration postmortem in dopaminergic-rich regions of the brain of alcoholics (Sjöquist et al., 1982b); (14) alcohol-dependent synthesis of B-carbolines arises endogenously (Collins, 1985) in volunteers who drink alcohol (Peura et al., 1981) as well as in alcoholic patients, whose urinary levels remain elevated after two weeks (Rommelspacher and Schmidt, 1985); (15) after the rat consumes alcohol chronically for a period of up to 10 months, postmortem levels of salsolinol rise sharply in the limbic-system (Matsubara et al., 1987; Myers et al., 1985a; b; Sjöquist et al., 1982b); (16) alcohol-dependent synthesis of THP in the brain occurs after alcohol is administered to the L-dopa treated rat (Cashaw et al., 1987); and (17) a similar time-dependent rise in an indole-aldehyde adduct in the brain of the rat arises after alcohol is ingested (Rommelspacher et al., 1984).

Table 4.1 presents an annotated survey of reports in which an amine-aldehyde metabolite significantly alters alcohol drinking.

A Unique Controversy

Shortly after the initial announcement of the new theory, two articles came forth to activate and then sustain a controversy on this new concept on the etiology of alcoholism (Haluska and Hoffman, 1970; Seevers, 1970). Although alcoholics and heroin addicts are indeed differentiated clinically, the sentiments of the critiques were neurochemically premature. Concerning the abyss of ignorance at that time on receptor mecha-

TABLE 4.1 Changes in National Ethanol Intake Following TIQ or B-Carboline Administration*

COMPOUND	ROUTE	REGIMEN	ANIMAL STRAIN	ETOH DRINKING	COMMENT	REFERENCE
THBC	IP	ACUTE	S.D.	↑d		GELLER & PURDY, 1975
THP	ICV	CHRONIC	S.D.	↑	WDL	MYERS & MELCHIOR, 1977a
THP	ICV	CHRONIC	S.D.	↑d	WDL	MELCHIOR & MYERS, 1977
THP	ICV	ACUTE	S.D	↑	WDL	MYERS & OBLINGER, 1977
SAL	ICV	CHRONIC	S.D.	↑d	WDL	MYERS & MELCHIOR, 1977b
SAL'	ICV	ACUTE	S.D.	↑	WDL	MYERS & OBLINGER, 1977
THBC	ICV	CHRONIC	S.D.	↑	WDL	MYERS & MELCHIOR, 1977b
THBC	ICV	ACUTE	S.D.	↑	WDL	MYERS & OBLINGER, 1977
THP	ICV	CHRONIC	S.D. & L.E.	↑d		DUNCAN & DIETRICH, 1980
THP	ICV	CHRONIC	WISTAR	→	ETOH	SMITH ET AL., 1980
SAL	ICV	ACUTE	WISTAR	↑	ETOH	SMITH ET AL., 1980
SAL	SC	ACUTE	S.D.	↑		PURVIS ET AL., 1980
SAL	ICV	CHRONIC	S.D. & L.E.	↑d		DUNCAN & DIETRICH, 1980
THP	ICV	ACUTE	L.E.	↑v	WDL	SINCLAIR & MYERS, 1982
THP	ICV	ACUTE	MACAQUE MONKEY	↑d		MYERS ET AL., 1982a
THP	ICV	ACUTE	S.D.	↑	WDL	CRITCHER, 1982
THP	ICV	ACUTE	S.D.	↑		MYERS & CRITCHER, 1982
SAL	ORAL	CHRONIC	CF1 MOUSE	↑		COLLINS & KAHN, 1982
THBC	ICV	CHRONIC	WISTAR	↑d		TUOMISTO ET AL., 1982
THP	ICV	ACUTE	S.D.	↑d		CLOW ET AL., 1983
THP	ICV	ACUTE	S.D.	↑		CRITCHER ET AL., 1983
PBR	ICV	ACUTE	S.D.	↑		CRITCHER ET AL., 1983
THBC	ICV	CHRONIC	WISTAR	↑d		AIRAKSININ ET AL., 1983
THBC	ICV	ACUTE	WISTAR	↑		ROMMELSPACHER ET AL., 1987
THP	HIPPOCAMPUS	ACUTE	S.D.	↑		HUTTUNEN & MYERS, 1987
THP	LIMBIC SITES	ACUTE	S.D.	↑		PRIVETTE ET AL., 1988
THP	LIMBIC SITES	ACUTE	S.D.	↑		MYERS & PRIVETTE, 1989
THP	THALAMUS; C.N.	ACUTE	S.D.	→		PRIVETTE & MYERS, 1989
THP	LIMBIC SITES	ACUTE	S.D.	↑d		PRIVETTE & MYERS, 1989
THP	ICV	ACUTE	S.D.	↓↑d		MINANO ET AL., 1989
THP	LIMBIC SITES	ACUTE	S.D.	↑		DUNCAN & FERNANDO, 1990

Abbreviations and Notes: d= Dose Dependent/High Dose Suppresses Intake, ↑=Infused with THBC, ICV=Intracerebroventricular, SC= Subcutaneous, PBR=Protoberberine, IP=Intraperitoneal, S.D.=Sprague-Dawley, L.E.=Long-Evans, C.N.=Caudate Nucleus, WDL=Withdrawal Signs Seen, ETOH=Alcohol Drinkers Used
* From Myers, 1990

31

nisms in the brain controlling vegetative functions such as drinking, craving for a drug, tolerance and withdrawal, it was remarkable how rapidly minds were made up.

Then a decade later, a paper appeared which reported that neither THP nor salsolinol infused ICV had an effect on alcohol drinking in the rat (Smith et al., 1980). In retrospect, however, the differences between procedures of the original experiments (Myers and Melchior, 1977 a; b) and the latter report were so substantial that the study hardly constituted a replication. These differences are enumerated as follows: (1) aseptic surgical procedures were not described; (2) stereotaxic coordinates for intracranial implantation of the THP/salsolinol infusion cannula were dissimilar; (3) the test rats were much smaller thereby affecting the anatomical site of implantation; (4) the purity of the compounds was not ascertained; (5) two drinking tubes instead of three were used for testing alcohol preference; (6) in a part of the study, those rats not consuming 8 ml of 15% alcohol were eliminated from the study, thus biasing the population sample in favor of genetic drinkers; (7) hydrochloric acid was used to adjust the infused solution to an acid pH; (8) ascorbic acid was not used as an anti-oxidant; (9) in a part of the study, some rats inexplicable doubled their alcohol intake during the baseline period prior to metabolite infusion; (10) the inbred sub-strain of rat was different; (11) baseline alcohol intakes of the metabolite-infused and control groups differed substantially; and (12) Ringers solution rather than an artificial CSF was used as the control vehicle.

In spite of these conspicuous differences in the experimental protocol, the data show that salsolinol infusions seemingly enhanced alcohol intake two-fold, from 2.0 to 4.0 gm/kg/day (Smith et al., 1980). Nevertheless, the "replication" was interpreted as unsuccessful.

Perpetuation of the Controversy

Without conscientious scrutiny of this report in light of the evidence from experiments presented in Table 4.1, some individuals have "thrown out the baby with the bath water." Skeptics from the 1970s astonishingly pounced on this report to dismiss outright any involvement of an aldehyde metabolite in alcohol or in the etiology of alcoholism. How frightening if the sample of THP had been contaminated! Or if it had been degraded in the brain because of the absence of an anti-oxidant!

At a recent symposium the view was expressed that "...Unfortunately, there is little in the way of solid, consistent data to support this "Multi-Metabolite" theory (Smith and Amit, 1987). These authors conclude that " ... further research in this area may be more fruitfully directed to other avenues of investigation." Recently, other individuals have espoused the

32

same viewpoint. In reviewing neurotransmitter systems implicated in the reinforcing effects of alcohol, for example, Kranzler and Orrok (1989) have deduced from the Smith-Amit paper that "...Despite the high face validity of this mechanism for the reinforcing effects of ethanol, the bulk of available evidence argues against a role for condensation products such as tetrahydroisoquinolines." Clearly, the only conclusion is that the bulk of the vast amount of data readily available, superficially condensed in Table 4.1, has neither been considered nor contemplated in balanced fashion.

Conclusion

To comprehend the reasoning behind a resolute stance of negativity which may promulgate a controversy is indeed challenging. Several explanations are forthcoming. First, the apparent evaluation of the pertinent literature has not been a critical one. Second, the "bulk of evidence" simply has not been analyzed, weighed, and then judged. Third, academic, institutional or other professional pressures conceivably may lead to error or oversight in the review and resultant pondering over the relevant literature. Fourth, it is much simpler intellectually to repudiate a viewpoint out-of-hand than to probe scientifically in-depth into each of the experiments pertaining to the controversy; thus any attempt to reach a reconciliation is nullified.

When the pendulum of controversy swings too far to the point of ultimate negativity, an experimental issue ordinarily is taken out of the realm of science. The consequences can be disastrous. Younger scientists are afraid to venture into a field when a discouraging pronouncement by a well-known scientist is made on a topic. The attitude of rejection of a proposition can even creep into the halls of a governmental granting agency or other institution supporting creative research. Today, this is critical since decisions are made to fund or not to fund projects which are now touched by the controversy. Finally, this sort of swing in a sense represents an obstacle to the fundamental principles of science. The outcome is a tragic loss in the goal of every rational individual involved in the quest for the truth about any complex mechanism in the nature— including the neurobiological mechanisms of alcohol reinforcement.

Summary

Clear-cut evidence now exists for alcohol-contingent synthesis *in vivo* of aminealdehyde metabolites in the brain which are active pharmacologically in altering alcohol drinking. Under the conditions of acute and chronic exposure to alcohol, aldehyde metabolites are readily detectable when appropriate and sensitive analytical techniques are employed. Except for one report from one laboratory, numerous investigators have demonstrated unequivocally in several species, the significant changes in volitional drinking of alcohol produced by THP, THBC, and other amine-aldehyde metabolites. Alterations in alcohol consumption depend on the metabolite selected, genetic background of the individual, the specific dose of the metabolite injected intracerebrally, regimen of administration, and the specific anatomical sites in the brain into which the compound is injected. Although the controversy surrounding the role of these metabolites in the etiological mechanisms of alcoholism may be "in the mind of the beholder," history alone will prove the validity of their involvement. The truth will triumph ultimately, but only if well-designed scientific experiments continue.

REFERENCES

Airaksinen, M.M., Mahonen, M., Tuomisto, L., Peura, P. and Eriksson, C.J.P. (1983). Tetrahydro-B-carbolines: effect of alcohol intake in rats. *Pharmac. Biochem. Behav.*, **18** 525-529.

Blum, K., Briggs, A.H., and Trachtenberg, M.C. (1989). Ethanol ingestive behavior as a function of central neurotransmission. *Experientia*, **45** 444-451.

Cashaw, J.L., Geraghty, C.A., McLaughlin, B.R., and Davis, V.E. (1987). Effect of acute ethanol administration on brain levels of tetrahydropapaveroline in L-dopa-treated rats. *J. Neurosci. Res.*, **18** 497-503.

Clow, A., Stolerman, I.P., Murray, R.M., and Sandler, M. (1983). Ethanol preference in rats: Increased consumption after intraventricular administration of tetrahydropapaveroline. *Neuropharmacology*, **22** 563-565.

Cohen, G. and Collins, M. (1970). Alkaloids from catecholamines in adrenal tissue: Possible role of alcoholism. *Science*, **167** 1749-1751.

Collins, M.A. (1985). ed., *Aldehyde Adducts in Alcoholism*. Alan Liss: New York.

Collins, M.A. and Kahn, A.J. (1982). Attraction to ethanol solutions in mice: induction by a tetrahydroisoquinoline derivative of L-Dopa. *Subs. Alc. Actions/Misuse*, **3** 299-302.

Critcher, E.C., (1982). Indications of an Opioid Mechanism in TIQ-induced alcohol drinking: Studies in the food-restricted and food-satiated rat. Unpublished Ph.D. thesis, University of Tennessee, Knoxville.

Critcher, E.C. and Myers, R.D. (1987). Cyanamide given ICV or systematically to the rat alters subsequent alcohol drinking. *Alcohol*, **4** 347-

353.

Critcher, E.C., Lin, C.I., Patel, J., and Myers, R.D. (1983). Attenuation of alcohol drinking in tetrahydroisoquinoline-treated rats by morphine and naltrexone. *Pharmac. Biochem. Behav.*, **18** 225-229.

Davis, V.E. and Walsh, M.J. (1970). Alcohol, amines and alkaloids: a possible biochemical basis for alcohol addiction. *Science*, **167** 1005-1007.

Duncan, C. and Deitrich, R.A. (1980). A critical evaluation of tetrahydroisoquinoline induced ethanol preference in rats. *Pharmac. Biochem. Behav.*, **13** 265-281.

Duncan, C. and Fernando, D.P. (1990). Effects of tetrahydropapaveroline in the nucleus accumbens and the ventral tegmental area on the rat's ethanol preference. In press.

Geller, I. and Purdy, R. (1975). Alteration of ethanol preference in rats; effects of B-carbolines. In: *Alcohol Intoxication and withdrawal II*, ed., M.M. Gross. Plenum Press: New York, pp. 295-302.

Gianoulakis, C. (1989). The effect of ethanol on the biosynthesis and regulation of opioid peptides. *Experientia*, **45** 428-435.

Haluska, P.V. and Hoffmann, P.C. (1970). Alcohol Addiction and tetrahydropapaveroline. *Science*, **169** 1104-1105.

Huttunen, P. and Myers, R.D. (1987). Anatomical localization in hippocampus of tetrahydro-B-carboline-induced alcohol drinking in the rat. *Alcohol*, **4** 181-187.

Kiianmaa, K., Fuxe, K., Jonsson, G. and Ahtee, L. (1975). Evidence for involvement of central NA neurones in alcohol intake. Increased alcohol consumption after degeneration of the NA pathway to the cortex cerebri. *Neurosci. Lett.*, **1** 41-45.

Kranzler, H.R., and Orrok, B. (1989). The pharmacotherapy of alcoholism. In: *Review of Psychiatry*; American Psychiatric Press: Washington, pp. 359-379.

Matsubara, K., Fukushima, S. and Fukui, Y. (1987). A systematic regional study of brain salsolinol levels during and immediately following chronic ethanol ingestion in rats. *Brain Res.*, **413** 336-343.

Melchior, C. and Collins, M.A. (1982). The route and significance of endogenous sythesis of alkaloids in animals. In: *CRC Critical Reviews in Toxicology*, pp 313-356.

Melchior, C.L. and Myers, R.D. (1977). Preference for alcohol evoked by tetrahydropapaveroline (THP) chronically infused in the cerebral ventricle of the rat. *Pharmac. Biochem. Behav.*, **7** 19-35.

Minano, F.J., McMillen, B.A., and Myers, R.D. (1989). Interaction of tetrahydropapaveroline with inhibition of dopa-decarboxylase by R04-4602 in brain: Effects on alcohol drinking in the rat. *Alcohol*, **6** (2) 133-

137.

Myers, R.D. (1974). Handbook of Drug and Chemical Stimulation of the Brain. Van Nostrand Reinhold Company: New York.

Myers, R.D. (1978a). Psychopharmacology of alcohol. *Ann. Rev. Pharmacol. Toxicol.*, **18** 125-144.

Myers, R.D. (1978b). Tetrahydroisoquinolines in the brain: The basis of an animal model of alcoholism. *Alcohol Clin. Exp. Res.*, **2** 145-154.

Myers, R.D. (1980). Pharmacological effects of amine-aldehyde condensation products. In: *Alcohol Tolerance and Dependence*, eds., H. Rigter and J. Crabbe, pp. 339-370. Elsevier: The Netherlands.

Myers, R.D. (1985a). Multiple metabolite theory, alcohol drinking and the alcogene. In: *Aldehyde Adducts in Alcoholism*, ed., M.A. Collins, pp. 201-220. Alan Liss: New York.

Myers, R.D. (1985b). Alkaloid Metabolites and addictive drinking of alcohol. *NIAAA Research Monograph* 17, Eds. N.C. Change and H.M. Chao, pp. 268-284.

Myers, R.D. (1989). Isoquinolines, beta-carbolines and alcohol drinking: Involvement of opioid and dopaminergic mechanisms. *Experientia*, **45** 436-443.

Myers, R.D. (1990). Anatomical "circuitry" in the brain mediating alcohol drinking: Analysis of THP-reactive sites in the rat's limbic system. *Alcohol*, **7** (In press).

Myers, R.D. and Critcher, E.C. (1982). Naloxone alters alcohol drinking induced in the rat by tetrahydropapaveroline (THP) infused ICV. *Pharmac. Biochem. Behav.*, **16** 827-836.

Myers, R.D. and Melchior, C.L. (1977a). Alcohol drinking: Abnormal intake caused by tetrahydropapaveroline in brain. *Science*, **196** 554-556.

Myers, R.D. and Melchior, C.L. (1977b). Differential actions on voluntary alcohol intake of tetrahydroisoquinolines or a B-carboline infused chronically in the ventricle of the rat. *Pharmac. Biochem. Behav.*, **7** 381-392.

Myers, R.D. and Oblinger, M. (1977). Alcohol drinking in the rat induced by acute intracerebral infusion of two tetrahydroisoquinolines and a B-carboline. *Drug and Alcohol Dependence*, **2** 469-483.

Myers, R.D. and Privette, T.H. (1989). Alcohol drinking in the rat: Mapping of anatomical sites in the brain reactive to tetrahydropapaveroline. *Brain Res. Bull.*, **22** 899-911.

Myers, R.D. and Veale, W.L. (1968). Alcohol preference in the rat: Reduction following depletion of brain serotonin. *Science*, **160** 1469-1471.

Myers, R.D., Borg, S., and Mossberg, R. (1986). Antagonism by naltrexone of voluntary alcohol selection in the chronically drinking macaque monkey. *Alcohol*, **3** 383-388.

Myers, R.D., Evans, J.E. and Yaksh, T.L. (1972). Ethanol preference in the rat: Interactions between brain serotonin and ethanol, actaldehyde, paraldehyde, 5-HT and 5-HTOL. *Neuropharmacol*, **11** 539-549.

Myers, R.D., McCaleb, M.L., and Ruwe, W.D. (1982a). Alcohol drinking induced in the monkey by tetrahydropapaveroline (THP) infused into the cerebral ventricle. *Pharmac. Biochem. Behav.*, **16** 995-1000.

Myers, R.D., Swarzwelder, H.S., and Dyer, R.S. (1982b). Acute treatment with trimethyltin alters alcohol self-selection. *Psychopharmac.*, **78** 19-22.

Myers, R.D. Swartzwelder, H.S., and Holahan, W. (1983). Effect of hippocampal lesions produced by intracerebroventricular kainic acid on alcohol drinking in the rat. *Brain Res. Bull.*, **10** 333-338.

Myers, W.D., Ng, K.T., Singer, G., Smythe, G.A., and Duncan, M.W. (1985a). Dopamine and salsolinol levels in rat hypothalami and striatum after schedule-induced self-injection (SISI) of ethanol and acetaldehyde. *Brain res.*, **358** 122-128.

Myers, W.D., Mackenzie, L., Ng, K.T., Singer, G., Smythe, G.A., and Duncan, M.W. (1985b). Salsolinol and dopamine in rat medial basal hypothalamus after chronic ethanol exposure. *Life Sci.*, **36** 309-314.

Pert, C.B. (1989). The naloxone methodology and the discovery of opiate receptors. *Current Contents*, **40** 16-17.

Peura, P., Airaksinen, M., Tuomisto, L., Saano, V., and Eriksson, P. (1981). L-methyl-tetrahydro-B-carboline in human blood after alcohol intake. *Proc. Finn. Symp. Biol. Med. Eff. Alc.*, 1135.

Privette, T.H., Hornsby, R.L., and Myers, R.D. (1988). Buspirone alters alcohol drinking induced in rats by tetrahydropapaveroline injected into brain monoaminergic pathways. *Alcohol*, **5** 147-152.

Privette, T.H., and Myers, R.D. (1989). Anatomical mapping of tetrahydropapaveroline reactive sites in brain mediating suppression of alcohol drinking in the rat. *Brain Res. Bull.*, **22** (6) 1039-1048.

Purvis, P.L., Hirst, M. and Baskerville, J.C. (1980). Voluntary ethanol consumption in the rat following peripheral administrations of 3-carboxysalsolinol. *Sub. Alc. Act./Misuse*, **1** 439-445.

Rommelspacher, H., and Schmidt, L. (1985). Increased formation of B-carbolines in alcoholic patients following ingestion of ethanol. *Pharmacopsychiat.*, **18** 153-154.

Rommelspacher, H., Buchau, C., and Weiss, J. (1987). Harman induces preference for ethanol in rats: Is the effect specific for ethanol. *Pharmac. Biochem. Behav.*, **26** 749-755.

Rommelspacher, H., Damm, H., Strauss, S., and Schmidt, G. (1984).

Ethanol induces an increase of harmane in the brain and urine of rats. *Naunyn Schmiedeberg's Arch. Pharmacol.*, **327** 107-113.

Seevers, M.H. (1970). Morphine and ethanol physical dependence: a critique of a hypothesis. *Science*, **170** 1113-1114.

Sinclair, J.D. and Myers, R.D. (1982). Cerbroventricular tetrahydropapaveroline infusions and ethanol consumption in the rat. *Sub. Alc. actions/ Misuse*, **3** 5-24.

Sjöquist, B., Borg, S., and Kvande, H. (1981). Catecholamine derived compounds in urine and cerebrospinal fluid from alcoholics during and after long-standing intoxication. *Sub. Alc. Act./Misuse*, **2** 63-72.

Sjöquist, B., Liljequist, S., and Engel, J., (1982a). Increased salsolinol levels in rat striatum and limbic forebrain following chronic ethanol treatment. *J. Neurochem.*, **39** 259-262.

Sjöquist, B., Eriksson, A., and Winblad, B. (1982b). Salsolinol and catecholamines in human brain and their relation to alcoholism. In: *B-carbolines and Tetrahydroisoquinolines*, eds. F. Bloom, J. Barchas, M. Sandler and E. Usdin, pp. 57-67, Alan Liss: New York.

Smith, B.R. and Amit, Z. (1987). False neurotransmitters and the effects of ethanol on the brain. *Ann. NY Acad. Sci.*, **492** 384-389.

Smith, B.R., Brown, Z.W. and Amit, Z. (1980). Chronic intraventricular administration of tetrahydroisoquinoline alkaloids: Lack of effect on voluntary ethanol consumption in the rat. *Sub. Alc. Act./Misuse*, **1** 209-221.

Swartzwelder, H.S. and Myers, R.D. (1983). Kainic acid lesioning of alkaloid-sensitive brain-sites and ethanol ingestion in the rat. *Neurosci. Lett.*, **36** 99-104.

Tuomisto, L., Airaksinen, M.M., Peura, P., and Eriksson, C.J.P. (1982). Alcohol Drinking in the rat: increases following intracerebroventricular treatment with tetrahydro-B-carbolines. *Pharmac. Biochem Behav.*, **17** 831-836.

CHAPTER 5

Environmental Basis for Alcoholic Disorders: Future Prospects*

Howard T. Blane, Ph. D.

After making a broad case for the historical importance of studying environment in the etiology of alcoholism and related problems, this chapter describes developments in alcohol research during the 1980s as a prelude to focusing upon the environmental aspects of family history of alcoholism as a risk factor for alcoholic disorders. Environmental bases for alcoholic disorders may be sought in sociocultural, social interactional, and psychological factors and models. An emphasis on environment hardly precludes the contribution of biological factors, including genetic and congenital aspects. Indeed, modern alcohol research (that is, since the 1940s) is perhaps unique in that it traditionally viewed alcohol problems as multiply-determined, the product of the interactions between biological, psychological, social, and cultural factors, though it was rare that this paradigm guided research. More typically scientists pursued topics within the scientific conventions and agendas of their own disciplines, with little consideration of contributions, corroborations, contradictions, or interactions from or with other levels of inquiry. In the past decade, however, there is considerable evidence that this situation is changing and an increasing amount of research involves interdisciplinary protocols. Nonetheless, the case for the influence of environmental factors in and of themselves is strong and compelling, founded on research findings accumulated over the years and derived from differing methods, approaches, and social-behavioral disciplines. This vast body of research and theory is touched upon briefly in order to treat more fully recent developments in family history research that are now energizing etiological research.

Sociocultural factors may be seen as establishing the conditions that shape the incidence and prevalence of alcoholic disorders as well as the social boundaries or definitions within which such disorders are expressed. The production, distribution, and cost of alcoholic beverages and

*Preparation of this chapter was supported in part by a grant (AA 06114) from the National Institute on Alcohol Abuse and Alcoholism.

the sanction structure which accompanies them — in a word, availability — comprise some of these conditions. They are the product of complex and incompletely understood processes involving cultural and social values and beliefs and the interplay of political, economic, and religious institutions. A commonly cited example is the near complete absence of drinking and alcoholism in Muslim societies. The total or almost total nonavailability of alcohol in these societies derives from religious proscriptions against alcohol permeating all political, legal, and social structures, thereby creating the extreme of a true abstinence society. Deviations from the near-universal norm are treated harshly without extenuation, but with popular approval. This example illustrates the power sociocultural forces can exert in the determination of behavior regarding the use, or nonuse, of alcoholic beverages.

The forms that drinking and alcoholic disorders assume among individuals are highly varied across and within societies; these variations can be reliably traced to cultural beliefs and values. The classic treatment of such variations and their nonbiological explanation is MacAndrew's and Edgerton's *Drunken Comportment* (1969). The wide differences in alcoholism rates among societies where alcohol is readily available are most parsimoniously explained within a socialization of cultural values framework. For instance, the oft-quoted and repeatedly substantiated resistance of Jews to alcoholism, despite the fact that drinking is not prohibited and most of them drink, has been variously attributed to sanctions against drunkenness and excess, the need to maintain vigilance against external incursions, and the value placed upon experiences that enhance and expand rather than dull and narrow mental function. In the case of the Jews, the strength of the forces involved are apparently so great that they have withstood prolonged contact with and extensive assimilation into cultural and societal contexts that include heavy drinking and proneness to alcoholic disorders. This is not always the case: Italian-Americans and Irish-Americans, for example, each show different ways of accommodating to the shift from Europe to the United States (Blane, 1977). The former appear to have adopted a unique pattern that blends both traditional Italian and American drinking norms with a consequent reduction of the high cirrhosis rates characteristic in Italy. Irish-Americans, on the other hand, perhaps as the consequence of fewer socioeconomic constraints in the States, show much higher rates of cirrhosis and other indicators of severe alcoholism than in Ireland. Culture-based arguments and research have been advanced to explain alcohol problem rates in other societies such as the wine-drinking cultures of the Mediterranean, Scandinavia, and other European countries.

At psychological and social levels of analysis, the independent contribution of nonbiological variables to almost every aspect of the human response to alcohol has been demonstrated; the findings are robust and many have been replicated. Areas relevant to alcoholic disorders include the importance of socialization influences on problem drinking in adolescence and early adulthood (e.g., Barnes, 1990; Huba and Bentler, 1982; Donovan, R. Jessor, and L. Jessor, 1983); early dispositional and social influences on subsequent development of alcoholism (e.g., Fillmore,1975; Jones, 1968; 1971; Kammeier, Hoffmann, and Loper, 1973; W. McCord and J. McCord, 1960); and learning influences on the phenomena of tolerance and withdrawal (e.g., Siegel, 1979; Solomon, 1977; Vogel-Sprott and Sdao-Jarvie, 1989).

Against this backdrop of significant contributions to environmental interpretations of alcoholic disorders, the decade of the 1980s witnessed an upsurge in the vitality and maturity of alcohol research. The qualitative advance was undoubtedly the product of ten years of prior investment in alcohol-related research by the Federal government. Substantively, it was related to the excitement engendered in the early 1980s by new scientific developments represented in the rethinking or initiation of a profusion of psychosocial models and associated research (Blane and Leonard, 1987), the tremendous interest in the genetics of alcoholism (e.g., Cloninger, 1987; Schuckit, 1985), and a variety of methodological improvements and refinements. These latter included the increased availability of statistical tools that permit the testing of complex models; greater concern with antecedent-consequent relationships and a corresponding emphasis on planned longitudinal designs, thereby raising confidence in causal attributions; heightened attention to issues of population definition and sampling in order to enhance generalizability; and more emphasis on multimethod measurement and convergent/divergent findings to strengthen the stability of interpretations and to identify potentially important discrepancies.

From an environmental perspective one of the most fascinating and promising lines of inquiry with regard to the etiology of alcoholic disorders is represented by the tremendous outpouring of research on children of alcoholics (COA). Much of the impetus for this efflorescence has been the results of twin and adoption studies that showed higher concordance for alcoholism among monozygotic than dizygotic twins and a high incidence of alcoholism among offspring of alcoholics adopted into nonalcoholic families during infancy (for a critical review of this research, see Searles, 1988). These studies indicated a genetic basis for alcoholism. A concomitant determinant of the outpouring of research on COAs comes from the results of clinical research which has repeatedly shown the high incidence of alcoholic relatives in the histories of alcoholics in treatment.

A third but as yet subsidiary influence has been the highly popular, partly entrepreneurial movement within the provider community around child, adolescent, and adult COAs. This movement includes a national network of author-lecturers, workshops, regional and national meetings, and among adult COAs in particular an associated demand for services, especially group therapy. Research on COAs and family transmission of alcoholism has concentrated upon personality, temperamental, neuropsychological, and behavioral aspects and upon family processes facilitating or inhibiting transmission of outcomes.

Even though recent years have witnessed a tremendous growth in the quantity of research on COAs, it must be acknowledged that this area of investigation is just beginning to develop the conceptual-empirical basis for endeavors that may lead to major advances in our understanding of etiology. In summarizing a recent review of research on COAs, Windle and Searles (1990) conclude: "...COA research...is in its infancy..., many contradictory findings have been reported within each of the disciplinary domains,...relatively few theoretical approaches have been articulated formally with propositions tested to any degree of certainty, and...little evidence exists to suggest the kinds of preventions and interventions that are most likely to be helpful to COAs." (p.217). Part of the problem is that much COA research to date has compared late adolescent or young adult subjects with a family history of alcoholism (usually a parent, but a variety of schemes involving primary or secondary relatives have been used) to those without a family history on variables of convenience (e.g., drinking variables, personality and temperament measures, neuropsychological performance). The underlying assumption is that parental alcoholism (regardless of type, severity, length, course, etc.) will exert an effect (typically, an implicitly direct effect) on a behavior or domain of interest even though the nature of exposure to alcoholic family environment is unknown, cannot be inferred, and is undoubtedly highly variable across subjects. It is not surprising that "many contradictory findings have been reported."

This line of inquiry is nonetheless compelling because it serves to focus etiologic research, bringing to the fore the notion of risk and outcome within the context of human development. As the research has evolved, it has become evident that both risk and outcome are more complex than early studies and their rationales would suggest. Family history of alcoholic disorder may be best construed as a convenient and empirically useful starting point, an index of risks having to do with family processes and structure that affect child development. Outcomes have, as noted, been almost exclusively studied in adolescent and young adult samples; these distal outcomes implicitly assume some uniform and linear relationships between events in infancy, childhood, and early adolescence. Developmentalists would be quick to point out that such inferences, unless deeply embedded in theory and empirical evidence, are dubious at best. At this early stage of zeroing-in on the investigation of risk and outcome, then, there are not only needs for greater precision in our handling of the definition and measurement of risk and outcome, but a major need to conceptualize what occurs between risk and outcome. A more profitable route will be the emergence of concern with suboutcomes phenomenally unrelated to alcohol use that are more proximal to causal processes and which can be ultimately linked to alcoholic outcomes. Such an approach would be guided by conceptualizations of the developmental linkages between relevant suboutcomes and processes. This is to say, that before family history can confidently be linked to alcoholic disorders, the elucidation of mechanisms, processes, and behaviors that occur at various stages of development and the developmental connections among them is necessary.

One way of thinking about these issues is to assume that parental alcoholism creates disruption in family structure, function, and process, and that disruption affects the child negatively. The first proposition has substantial support in the alcohol literature (e.g., Jackson, 1954; Jacob and Leonard, 1988; Steinglass, Bennett, Wolin, and Reiss, 1987), although it is not clear whether disruptive effects are specific to parental alcoholism as contrasted to other parental psychopathology or other parental conditions that may disrupt the family. The case for the effects of disruption on the child is, of course, far less clear. If such effects do occur, they could assume a direct influence on the child (e.g., alcoholic father's aggression toward child) or an indirect influence through their effects on other family members (e.g., nonalcoholic mother assumes spouse's functions as well as her own, consequently neglecting child). The modes of influence can occur in at least three ways: (1) imitation or modeling, in which the child models itself after the alcoholic parent; (2) interaction with the index parent or nonaffected parent (e.g., positive interactions when alcoholic parent drinking and negative interactions when not drinking); and (3) bidirectional influences (e.g., family disruption affects child's school behavior; school performance elicits further family disruption).

The general implications of these considerations for methods include the adoption of developmental designs that articulate life stages beginning at birth, attention to underlying constructs that change phenomenally with growth (a case in point involves the relationships between activity levels, hyperactivity, attention deficit disorder, conduct disorder, and antisocial behavior or sociopathy), and the associated issue of employing measures appropriate to developmental level.

43

Of course the factors such a finer-grained approach must consider will depend upon the requirements of each investigation, but there are several factors that are important for any study falling within this line of inquiry. Key among these are (1) the nature of parental alcoholism and its effects on family function, (2) the development stage(s) of the child when parental alcoholism is active, and (3) sampling considerations. Specification of the nature of parental alcoholic disorder is particularly important: severity of alcoholism; aspects of family function that have been affected; whether drinking is steady or binge, occurs at home or outside the home; which parent is alcoholic; if the mother is the alcoholic, possible fetal alcohol effects on the child must be considered. Unfortunately, it is rare that these variations have been systematically taken into account. The effects of drinking on parental function (i.e., the question of disruption) requires specification: role function disruption; assumption of additional functions by the nonaffected spouse; parental conflict about drinking; behavioral-interactional differences between drinking and sober states as such differences relate to consistency or inconsistency of family climate or as they relate to the integrative influences of drinking noted by some observers; specifity of effects.

Knowledge concerning the developmental stage of the child when parental alcoholism is active is critical if we are to understand its impact on COA outcomes. Each developmental phase identifies areas of salient child function and growth, areas that may be adversely affected by disruption, and which in turn may affect later developmental stages. It is likely that the earlier the disruption, the more severe the effects; similarly, the longer the child is exposed to disruptive influences, the more severe the outcome. While the general thrust of COA research has been on alcoholic outcomes, it is equally important to identify nonspecific outcomes and the processes engendering them. Candidates include antisocial personality, depression, and poor social skills. The developmental precursors to both specific and nonspecific outcomes will vary according to developmental state of exposure. This issue has received virtually no attention in COA research. (For more detailed discussion of these issues, see Windle and Searles (1990), pages 227-229).

One source of the contradictory findings common in COA research relates to the nature of the samples that have been studied. Samples have for the most part been recruited from one of the three sources: children of alcoholics in treatment; adult COAs attending treatment; and adolescent and adult COAs drawn from populations of convenience or from defined population samples often recruited for other purposes. Generalizability is a problem for all but the general population samples. Further complications include measurement techniques for identifying parental alcoholism

44

that range widely in quality and the relevance and/or quality of measurement of key variables, especially those for general population samples. (See Tarter, Laird, and Moss, (1990), pages 75-76 for a more detailed discussion of sampling issues). Tentatively, it appears that COAs identified on the basis of their parents being in treatment are at higher risk for alcoholic and other negative consequences than those identified in general population samples. If this is the case it becomes important that both types of samples be studied, with the explicit caveat that the samples represent different populations. The question of sampling for very young COAs is a vexing but critical one in terms of the foregoing discussion. Perhaps general population samples can be recruited by screening attendees of prenatal clinics (a likely bias is underrepresentation of lower socio-economic status subjects) or obstetric delivery services. Young children (say, five years old or younger) of alcoholics in treatment could be recruited from alcoholism treatment units, with due attention to social class differences. Centering etiological alcoholism research early in life is rare indeed; except for some studies of fetal alcohol effect, our only example is Zucker's pioneering theoretical efforts (Zucker and Noll, 1982) and the research that has proceeded from them (Zucker, 1987).

In any event, environmentally-oriented research on the familial transmission of alcoholism, variously referred to as COA research or high-risk research, seems to have reached the endpoint of its initial ground-breaking stage. On the one hand, there appears to be some disarray in terms of a plethora of contradictory findings, lack of conceptual focus with an accompanying overflow of atheoretical descriptive studies, and weak methodologies. On the other, there are several syntheses of the work accomplished thus far that go a long way toward putting family transmission research on a much more solid and sophisticated foundation (e.g., Russell, 1990; Jacob, Seilhamer, and Rushe, 1989). These syntheses indicate the wealth of research opportunities that exist, propose methods and conceptualizations to realize these opportunities, and clarify issues in ways that further accentuate a focus on risk and outcome within a developmental framework.

This chapter suggests a family environment perspective based on the notion that disrupted alcoholic family function affects the child negatively not only with regard to alcohol use but in other psychological and social functions as well. It also suggests that a focus on interactional, modeling, and bidirectional influences in infancy and early childhood is a necessary step in deciphering the "environmental code" that underlies the etiology of alcoholic disorders.

45

REFERENCES

Barnes, G.M. (1990). Impact of the family on adolescent drinking patterns. In R.L. Collins, K.E. Leonard, and J.S. Searles (Eds.), *Alcoholism and the family* (pp. 137-161). Guilford: New York.

Blane, H.T. (1977). Acculturation and drinking in an Italian-American community. *Journal of Studies on Alcohol*, **38** 1324-1346.

Blane, H.T., and Leonard, K.E., Eds. (1987). *Psychological theories of drinking and alcoholism*. Guilford: New York.

Cloninger, C.R. (1987). Neurogenetic adaptive mechanisms in alcoholism. *Science*, **236** 410-416.

Donovan, J.E., Jessor, R., and Jessor, L. (1983). Problem drinking in adolescence and young adulthood: a follow-up study. *Journal of Studies on Alcohol*, **44** 109-137.

Fillmore, K.M. (1975). Relationships between specific drinking problems in early adulthood and middle age; an exploratory 20-year follow-up study. *Journal of Studies on Alcohol*, **36** 882-907.

Huba, G.J., and Bentler, P.M. (1982). A developmental theory of drug use: derivation and assessment of a causal modeling approach. In P.B. Baltes and O.G. Brim, Jr. (Eds.), *Life-span development and behavior* (Vol. 4) (pp.147-203). Academic Press: New York.

Jackson, J. (1954). The adjustment of the family to the crisis of alcoholism. *Quarterly Journal of Studies on Alcohol*, **15** 562-586.

Jacob, T., and Leonard, K. (1988). Alcoholic-spouse interaction as a function of alcoholism subtype and alcohol consumption interaction. *Journal of Abnormal Psychology*, **97** 231-237.

Jacob, T., Seilhamer, R.A., and Rushe, R. (1989). Alcoholism and family interaction: an experimental paradigm. *American Journal of Drug and Alcohol Abuse*, **15** 73-91.

Jones, M.C. (1968). Personality correlates and antecedents of drinking patterns in adult males. *Journal of Consulting and Clinical Psychology*, **32** 2-12.

Jones, M.C. (1971). Personality antecedents and correlates of drinking patterns in women. *Journal of Consulting and Clinical Psychology*, **36** 61-69.

Kammeier, M.L., Hoffmann, H., and Loper, R.G. (1973). Personality characteristics of alcoholics as college freshmen and at time of treatment. *Quarterly Journal of Studies on Alcohol*, **34** 390-399.

MacAndrew, C., and Edgerton, R.B. (1969). *Drunken comportment. A social explanation*. Aldine: Chicago.

McCord, W. and McCord, J. (1960). *Origins of alcoholism*, Stanford University Press: Stanford.

Russell, M. (1990). Prevalence of alcoholism among children of alcoholics. In M. Windle and J.S. Searles (Eds.), *Children of alcoholics: critical perspectives* (pp. 9-38). Guilford:New York.

Schuckit, M.A. (1985). Genetics and the risk for alcoholism. *Journal of the American Medical Association*, **254** 2614-2617.

Searles, J.S. (1988). The role of genetics in the pathogenesis of alcoholism. *Journal of Abnormal Psychology*, **97** 153-167.

Siegel, S. (1979). The role of conditioning in drug tolerance and addiction. In J.D. Keehn (Ed.). *Psychopathology in animals: research and treatment implications* (pp. 143-168). Academic Press: New York.

Solomon, R. L. (1977). An opponent-process theory of required motivation: the affective dynamics of addiction. In J.D. Maser and M.E.P. Seligman (Eds.). *Psychopathology: experimental models* (pp. 66-103). W.H. Freeman: San Francisco.

Steinglass, P., Bennett, L.A., Wolin, S.J., and Reiss, D. (1987). *The alcoholic family*. Basic Books: New York.

Tarter, R.E., Laird, S.B., and Moss, H.B. (1990). Neuropsychological and neurophysiological characteristics of children of alcoholics. In M. Windle and J.S. Searles (Eds.), *Children of alcoholics: critical perspectives* (pp.73-98). Guilford: New York.

Vogel-Sprott, M. and Sdao-Jarvie, K. (1989). Learning alcohol tolerance: the contribution of response expectancies. *Psychopharmacology*, **98** 289-296.

Windle, M. and Searles, J.S. (1990). Summary, integration, and future directions: toward a life-span perspective. In M. Windle and J.S. Searles (Eds.), *Children of alcoholics: critical perpectives* (pp. 217-238). Guilford:New York.

Zucker, R.A. (1987). The four alcoholisms: a developmental account of the etiologic process. In P.C. Rivers (Ed.), *Nebraska symposium on motivation, 1986: Alcohol and addictive behavior* (pp. 27-83). University of Nebraska Press: Lincoln.

Zucker, R.A., and Noll, R.B. (1982). Precursors and development influences on drinking and alcoholism: etiology from a longitudinal perspective. In *Alcohol consumption and related problems* (DHHS no. ADM 82-1190, pp. 289-330). U.S. Government Printing Office: Washington.

CHAPTER 6

Why We Should Reject The Disease Concept of Alcoholism*

Herbert Fingarette, Ph. D.

Why do heavy drinkers persist in their behavior even when prudence, common sense, and moral duty call for restraint? That is the central question in debates about alcohol abuse. In the United States, but not in other countries such as Great Britain (Robertson and Heather, 1982), the standard answer is to call the behavior a disease—"alcoholism"—whose key symptom is a pattern of uncontrollable drinking. This myth, now widely advertised and widely accepted, is neither helpfully compassionate nor scientifically valid. It promotes false beliefs and inappropriate attitudes, as well as harmful, wasteful, and ineffective social policies.

The myth is embodied in the following four scientifically baseless propositions: 1) Heavy problem drinkers show a single distinctive pattern of ever greater alcohol use leading to ever greater bodily, mental, and social deterioration. 2) The condition, once it appears, persists involuntarily: the craving is irresistible and the drinking is uncontrollable once it has begun. 3) Medical expertise is needed to understand and relieve the condition ("cure the disease") or at least ameliorate its symptoms. 4) Alcoholics are no more responsible legally or morally for their drinking and its consequences than epileptics are responsible for the consequences of their movements during seizures.

The idea that alcoholism is a disease has always been a political and moral notion with no scientific basis. It was first promoted in the United States around 1800 as a speculation based on erroneous physiological theory (Levine, 1978), and later became a theme of the temperance movement (Gusfield, 1963). It was revived in the 1930s by the founders of Alcoholics Anonymous (AA), who derived their views from an amalgam or religious ideas, personal experiences and observations, and the unsubstantiated theories of a contemporary physician (Robinson, 1979).

*This is a slightly edited version of an article in press to be published in The Harvard Medical School Mental Health Letter. By permission of Harvard University, copyright owner.

The AA doctrine won decisive support in the 1940s when a reputable scientist, E.M. Jellinek, published an elaborate statistical study of the "phases of alcoholism" (Jellinek, 1946). He portrayed an inevitable sequence of ever more uncontrollable drinking that led progressively to such symptoms as blackouts, tolerance, and withdrawal distress, until the drinker "hit bottom" as a derelict, became insane, or died. Jellinek's work seemed to put a scientific seal of confirmation on the AA portrait of the alcoholic. That was hardly surprising, since he had taken his data from questionnaires that were prepared and distributed by AA and answered by fewer than 100 self-selected members. Jellinek conscientiously acknowledged the source of his data and reservations about its scientific adequacy (Jellinek, 1946). Nevertheless, his dramatic-tragic portrait of the alcoholic became widely accepted and is now part of American folk beliefs.

Recent scientific literature shows that in reality the typical pattern of heavy drinking fluctuates. Some drinkers with numerous and severe problems deteriorate; others markedly improve, or develop different problems. Some claim loss of control; others do not. Many heavy drinkers report no serious social problems associated with their drinking and are not recognized as alcoholics by friends, colleagues, or even their families (Cahalan and Room, 1974; Rudy, 1986).

The idea that alcoholics are constantly drunk is quite false. One leading researcher points out that in any "given month one half of alcoholics will be abstinent, with a mean of four months of being dry in any one-year to two-year period" (Schuckit, 1984). During any ten to twenty-year period, about a third of alcoholics "mature out" into various forms of moderate drinking or abstinence. The rate of maturing out is even higher among heavy problem drinkers not diagnosed as alcoholics (Fillmore, 1988). Undoubtedly there is a small group who follow a pattern resembling Jellinek's four phases; one objection to the disease concept of alcoholism is that it focuses attention mainly on this marginal group.

It is now widely believed that a biological cause of alcoholism has been discovered; some people are said to have a biochemistry or a genetic predisposition that dooms them to be alcoholics if they drink. The truth is less dramatic. There are certain so-called biological markers associated with heavy drinking, but these have not been shown to cause it. One supposed marker is the metabolism of alcohol into acetaldehyde, a brain toxin, in the bodies of people who are independently identifiable as being at higher risk of becoming alcoholics (Lindros, 1978; Schuckit, 1984). Another proposed marker is the high level of morphine-like substances supposedly secreted by alcoholics when they metabolize alcohol (Schuckit, 1984). It is implausible that any residual effects, whether physical or psychological, could be so powerful as to override a sober person's ra-

49

tional, moral, and prudential inclination to abstain.

Recent studies have also been said to imply that alcoholism is a hereditary disease. But that is not what the genetic research shows. In the first place, these studies provide no evidence of a genetic factor in the largest group of heavy drinkers—those who have significant associated problems but are not diagnosable as alcoholics. Even among the minority who can be so diagnosed, the data suggest that only a minority have the pertinent genetic background. And even in this category, a minority of a minority, studies report that the majority do not become alcoholics (Goodwin, et al., 1973; Cloninger, et al., 1981; Deitrich and Spuhler, 1984).

It is not only misleading but dangerous to regard alcoholism as a genetic disorder. Heavy drinkers without alcoholism in their genetic backgrounds are led to feel immune to serious drinking problems, yet they have the greatest total number of problems. On the other hand, people who do have some hereditary disposition to alcoholism could easily become defeatist. Their risk is higher, and they should be aware of that, but their fate is still very much in their own hands.

The idea of a single disease obscures the scientific consensus that no single cause has ever been established, nor has any biological causal factor ever been shown to be decisive. Heavy drinking has many causes which vary from drinker to drinker, from one drinking pattern to another. Character, motivation, family environment, personal history, ethnic and cultural values, marital, occupational, and educational status all play a role. As these change, so do patterns of drinking, heavy drinking, and "alcoholism" (Fingarette, 1989). For example, alcohol is used in many so-called "primitive" societies, but their drinking patterns are not ours, and what we call alcoholism seems to be absent prior to contact with Europeans (Heath, 1989). That would not be true if alcoholism was a disease caused by chemical and neurological effects of drinking in conjunction with individual genetic vulnerability. The crucial role of psychology in alcoholics' drinking is demonstrated by experiments in which they are deceived about whether the beverage they are drinking contains alcohol. Their drinking patterns then reflect their beliefs; the actual presence or absence of alcohol is irrelevant (Marlatt et al., 1973).

Alcoholics do not "lack control" in the ordinary sense of those words. Studies show that they can limit their drinking in response to appeals and arguments or rules and regulations. In experiments they will reduce or eliminate drinking in return for money, social privileges, or exemption from boring tasks (Fingarette, 1989). To object that these experiments are invalid because they occur in protected settings is to miss the point, which is precisely that the drinking patterns of alcoholics can vary dramatically with settings, regardless of their previous patterns of drinking, and regardless of whether any alcohol is in their bodily systems or is accessible.

True, alcoholics often resist appeals to cease their alcohol abuse, and they ignore obvious prudential and moral considerations. The simplistic explanation that attributes this to an irresistible craving obscures a more complicated reality: they have developed a way of life in which they use drinking as a major strategy for coping with their problems (Fingarette, 1989). They have become accustomed to values, friends, settings, and beliefs that protect and encourage drinking. When they encounter drastically changed circumstances in a hospital, clinic, or communal group, they are capable of following different rules. Even some who "cheat" where abstention is expected nevertheless limit their drinking (Paredes et al., 1973). They do not automatically lose control because of a few drinks. Our focus on attention must shift from drinking per se to the meaning of drink for certain persons and the way of life in which its role has become central.

Responsible scientists who are familiar with the research but want to preserve the disease concept of alcoholism have had to redefine their terms. They define "disease" as whatever doctors choose to call a disease (Jellinek, 1960)! The point of using the word, they acknowledge, is "social" rather than medical. There is a lack of consistent self-control that leads to harmful consequences (Vaillant, 1990). Of course such sweeping uses of the term make almost every human and social problem into a "disease."

As for "loss of control", this phrase no longer coincides either with the ordinary meaning of those words or with what the public is encouraged to believe. Thus Mark Keller, one of the early leaders of the alcoholism movement, now reinterprets loss of control to mean that alcoholics who have decided to stop "cannot be sure they will stand by their resolution" (Keller, 1972). This is said to be compatible with anything from constant heavy drinking to remission in the form of permanent moderation or total abstention. Although the medical term "remission" is used, this is not a medical or scientific explanation: we all know that someone who resolves to change a long-standing way of life cannot be sure whether the promise will be kept. Similarly, craving, still popularly understood as an overwhelming and irresistible desire, has now been extended by researchers to include mild inclinations, although this makes nonsense of the supposed compulsion to drink (Hodgson et al., 1978).

The disease concept is sometimes rationalized on the ground that although scientifically invalid, it is a practical way of encouraging alcoholics to enter treatment (Fingarette, 1989). This argument is based on false assumptions and has harmful consequences. The many heavy drinkers who see themselves (often correctly) as not fitting the criteria of alcoholism under some current diagnostic formula are likely to conclude that they

51

have no cause for concern. Their inclination to deny their problems is thus encouraged. As for people who are diagnosable as alcoholics, the vast majority never became permanently abstinent, even after treatment or after they join AA (Polich et al., 1980; Fingarette, 1989: Peele, 1989). Yet the disease doctrine may cause them to develop a fatalistic conviction that even one slip is a disaster, since they have been led to believe, falsely, that occasional or moderate drinking is never possible for them.

When behavior is labeled a disease, it becomes excusable because it is regarded as involuntary. This is an important reason for its promulgation. Thus special benefits are provided to alcoholics in employment, health, and civil rights law, provided they can prove that their drinking is persistent and very heavy. The effect is to reward people who continue to drink heavily. This policy is insidious precisely because it is well intended, and those who criticize it may seem to lack compassion.

The United States Supreme Court, after reviewing detailed briefs pro and con, has consistently held in favor of those who say that alcoholics are responsible for their behavior, and has concluded that medical evidence does not demonstrate their drinking to be involuntary (Powell vs. Texas, 1968; Traynor vs. Turnage, 1988). Spokesmen for the National Council on Alcoholism (NCA) state publicity that they too believe alcoholics should be held responsible for their misdeeds, but they are being hypocritical. In the less visible forum of the federal courts, the NCA has repeatedly argued (Traynor vs. Turnage, 1988) that alcoholics should be protected from criminal and civil liability for their acts and excused from the normal regulatory requirements.

But the greatest scandal of the argument for the disease concept as a useful lie is the claim that it helps alcoholics by inducing them to enter treatment. On the contrary, both independent and government research shows expensive disease-oriented treatment programs to be largely a waste of money and human resources (Fingarette, 1989). Their apparent success proves illusory when they are compared in statistically rigorous studies with other programs, and with the rate of improvement in untreated alcohol abusers (which is a much higher rate than the disease concept has led the public to believe). Very often, perhaps always, brief outpatient counseling works just as well as a long stay in a hospital or other residential clinic costing thousands of dollars. Some studies conclude that professional intervention is slightly better than no treatment, although it makes no difference what the treatment method, duration, setting, or cost is. Other studies find no significant difference in results regardless of whether there is treatment.

We must refocus our compassion and redefine our policies on alcohol abuse. While continuing biological research, we should loosen the grip of physicians on the chief government agencies and research funding sources, and we should reject their deep bias in favor of the disease concept. Much greater resources must be shifted to psychological and sociocultural research. We should consider promising new approaches to treatment that are being used in other countries. The public should be better informed about the scientific facts and above all about our scientific ignorance. Our policies should reflect the fact that heavy drinking is not primarily a biochemical or medical problem but a human and social one.

REFERENCES

Cahalan, D. and Room, R. (1974) *Problem Drinking Among American Men.* Rutgers Center of Alcohol Studies: New Jersey.

Cloninger, C.R. et al. (1981). Inheritance of Alcohol Abuse: Cross-Fostering Analysis of Adopted Men. A*rchives of General Psychiatry,* **38** 861-868.

Deitrich, R.A. and Spuhler, K. (1984). Genetics of Alcoholism and Alcohol Actions. In Reginald Smart, et al. (Eds.). *Research Advances in alcohol and Drug Problems, Volume 8.* Plenum Press: New York.

Fillmore, K.M. (1988). Spontaneous Remission of Alcohol Problems. *Evaluating Recovery Outcomes.* University of California: San Diego.

Fingarette, H. (1989). *Heavy Drinking: The Myth of Alcoholism as a Disease.* University of California Press: Berkeley.

Goodwin, D.W. et al. (1973). Alcohol Problems in Adoptees Raised Apart from Alcoholic Biological Parents. *Archives of General Psychiatry,* **28** 238-243.

Gusfield, J.R. (1963). *Symbolic Crusade: Status Politics and the American Temperance Movement.* University of Illinois Press: Urbana.

Heath, D.B. (1989). Environmental Factors in Alcohol Use and Its Outcomes. In H.W. Goeddle and Dharam P. Agarwal (Eds.) *Alcoholism: Biomedical and Genetic Aspects.* Pergamon Press: New York.

Hodgson, R. et al. (1978). Craving and Loss of Control. In Peter E. Nathan et al. (Eds). *Alcoholism: New Directions in Behavioral Research and Treatment.* Plenum Press: NY.

Jellinek, E.M. (1960) *The Disease Concept of Alcoholism.* Hillhouse Press: New Haven.

Jellinek, E.M. (1946) Phases in the Drinking History of Alcoholics. *Quarterly Journal of Studies on Alcohol,* **7** 1-88.

Keller, M. (1972). On the Loss-of-Control Phenomenon in Alcoholism. *British Journal of Addiction,* **67** 155-166.

Levine, H.G. (1978). The Discovery of Addiction: Changing Conceptions of Habitual Drunkenness in America. *Journal of Studies on Alcohol*, **39** 143-174.

Lindros, K.O. (1978). Acetaldehyde—Its Metabolism and Role in the Action of Alcohol. In Y. Israel et al. (Eds.). *Research Advances in Alcohol and Drug Problems, Volume 4*. Plenum Press: New York.

Marlatt, G.A. et al. (1973). Loss of Control Drinking in Alcoholics: An Experimental Analogue. *Journal of Abnormal Psychology*, **81** 233-241.

Paredes, A. et al. (1973). Loss of Control in Alcoholism: An Investigation of the Hypothesis, with Experimental Findings. *Quarterly Journal of Studies on Alcohol*, **34** 1146-1161.

Peele, S. (1989). *The Diseasing of America*. D.C.Heath: Lexington, MA.

Polich, J.M. et al. (1980). *The Course of Alcoholism: Four Years After Treatment*. The Rand Corp.: Santa Monica.

Powell vs. Texas, 392 US 514 (1968).

Robertson, I.H. and Heather, N. (1982). A Survey of Controlled Drinking Treatment in Britain. *British Journal on Alcohol and Alcoholism*, **17** 102-105.

Robertson, D. (1979). *Talking Out of Alcoholism: The Self-Help Process of Alcoholics Anonymous*. Croom Helm: London.

Rudy, D.R. (1986). *Becoming Alcoholic*. Southern Illinois University Press: Carbondale.

Schuckit, M. (1984). *Drug and Alcohol Abuse*. Plenum Press: New York.

Traynor vs. Turnage, 99L.Ed 2d 618 (1988).

Vaillant, G. (1990). We Should Retain the Disease Concept of Alcoholism. *The Harvard Medical School Mental Health Letter*, (In press).

CHAPTER 7

The Biopsychosocial Model:
Application to the Addictions Field

Karol L. Kumpfer, Ph.D.,
Eric P. Trunnell, Ph.D., and
Henry O. Whiteside, Ph.D.

Introduction

A growing understanding that health and disease are determined by complex interactions among biological, psychological and sociological factors (Leigh and Reiser, 1980) has led some researchers (e.g., Engel, 1977; von Bertalanffy, 1974; Keye and Trunnell, 1986; Keye and Trunnell, 1988; Trunnell, White, Pederson, and Keye, 1989) to propose an alternative to the biomedical model. One of the authors (Kumpfer, 1987), after increased exposure to this mode of thinking among psychiatrists who had moved beyond the traditional medical model, proposed in 1987 the Biopsychosocial Model of Vulnerability to Substance Abuse. A biopsychosocial model is a reasonable way to incorporate most causes of alcohol and drug abuse into a single model. Our proposed biopsychosocial model is essentially a macro framework which can be used to integrate complementary and occasionally competing micro theories. This chapter reviews the biopsychosocial model and its historical roots in theory, specific application to addictions, guiding principles, and research and clinical advantages.

Historical Background

Researchers, primarily in behavioral medicine (Schwartz, 1982), have recently promoted biopsychosocial models applied to health sciences, in response to the need for more complex, interactional and contextual paradigms. Schwartz (1982) believes a major paradigm shift is moving the health sciences away from single-cause, linear models to multi-cause, interactive models.

Within the history of theory, Pepper (1942) has identified four different "world hypotheses" or approaches to explanations of nature. Gholson and Barker (1985) have linked these ways of thinking or constructing reality to Kuhn's "paradigms." These four paradigms include: 1) formistic or categorical "black- white" thinking, 2) **mechanistic** or single-cause, single-effect, or chains of single causes thinking, 3) **organicistic** or multi-causal, integrative and holistic thinking and 4) **contextual** or relational or transactional thinking.

Later, Pepper (1967) proposed a fifth world view, **selectivism**, to account for intentional, meaningful functioning, and goal-directed behavior. This view and contextualism are reflected in the transactional perspective as proposed by Altman and Rogoff (1987), which is based on the earlier distinctions made by Dewey and Bentley (1949) between interactional and transactional perspectives. Behavior is viewed as an integral part of the person and their environment. The unit of analysis is not just the person but an integration of elements in the environment and the person, resulting in his or her behavior.

Because of the multi-causal nature of addiction, understanding chemical dependency within a framework restricted to only a formistic and mechanistic world hypotheses offers little in the way of explanation or prediction. Unfortunately, the traditional biomedical model is primarily a mechanistic, linear model, which does not account for the complex experiences of individuals or their social context. Engel (1980) argued that the conceptual models used by clinicians to organize their knowledge strongly influence their interactions with patients, the data they collect, and their diagnoses and prescribed treatments. Because the dominant models guiding practice are rarely made explicit in clinical training, most clinicians are blind to the power such models exert on their thinking and behavior.

Where's the Person? Critics of the biomedical model argue that the biomedical model depends on a linear, single causal, physics model of science at the expense of the humanity of the patient (Engel, 1977; Engel, 1978; von Bertalanffy, 1974). This "robot or zoomorphic" model of man was a predominant view in the industrial age (von Bertalanffy, 1974). Ironically, this nineteenth century positivistic model was abandoned by the hard sciences early in the twentieth century, but has continued to dominate thinking in the social and behavioral sciences. Partly because of this "physics envy", even American psychology was dominated in the first half of this century by the concept of man as a reactive organism. Human behavior was thought to be completely predictable, or "trainable and conditionable." Even early treatments for alcoholism tried to condition patients to avoid alcohol. This mechanistic, conditioning approach simply did not work. Unmotivated patients "hot-wired" their conditioning by mixing the alcohol to which they had been deconditioned with different mixers or fruit juices, and continued drinking.

Humanistic Psychology. Considered a "third force" in the psychological study of humankind (after psychoanalysis and behaviorism), humanistic psychology tries to understand people in context, in total, or whole, as did Gestalt theory. Humanistic psychology proposed to study: 1) the **healthy** rather than the **sick** as the basic model, 2) people, developmentally over time and 3) people within their natural context. Humanistic psychology promoted the idea of an equal emphasis on protective or resiliency factors as compared to the primary emphasis on risk factors found in the biomedical model.

General System Theory. System theory (deRosnay 1979; Miller, 1978) provides a metatheoretical framework for more specific biopsychosocial models. Systems theory asserts that the behavior of any person or system can be understood only by the interaction of the many different hierarchical levels or systems impacting that person. A system is defined by deRosnay (1979) as a "set of elements in dynamic interaction, organized for a goal" (p.65). Weiss (1977) argued that systems theory is best understood as the logical ordering of nature into more and more complex systems. Each level or system of an organism (e.g., genes, cells, tissues, organs, nervous system, person, dyad, family, community, culture) is part of a more complex unit.

Schwartz (1982) identified different academic disciplines with each of these system levels. For instance, geneticists study chromosomes; cardiologists study organs; psychologists study individuals, dyads, and families; and sociologists study groups, communities, and cultures. He believes that systems theory can help break down the traditional boundaries between disciplines in the biomedical and behavioral sciences through biopsychosocial integration.

Need for An Integrated Theory. The need for a more integrated, interdisciplinary approach to the study of organisms is becoming more apparent. This need has reached critical mass in the "war on drugs", where the different "warriors" come from many different disciplinary fields. Within the interdisciplinary addictions field, no clear "paradigm shift" has occurred. The field appears to be in a "pre-paradigm phase." There are currently many different camps of devoted followers. Some genetic psychiatrists, for example, believe that genetic engineering will eventually solve the "drug problem"; AA-trained paraprofessionals believe that belief in a Higher Power and social support can cure alcoholics; doctors believe that drugs can cure drug dependency; and psychologists and social workers believe that psychotherapy will cure the patient.

Kuhn did not account for this lack of a single, mutually acceptable paradigm or way of thinking, but later writers have. Lakotas (1981) discussed a "pre-paradigm phase" as having several research programs and Laudan (1981) discussed the concept of "research traditions" consisting of families of theories that evolve gradually based on "core commitments" and empirical data (Gholson and Barker, 1985).

Biopsychosocial Model

The biopsychosocial model offers an integrated conceptual framework useful to all professionals and researchers in the addictions field. The authors' proposed biopsychosocial vulnerability model (Figure 7.1) is one potential macro theoretical framework helpful in organizing etiological factors for substance abuse.

Biological Factors. Several authors (Kumpfer, 1987; 1989; Goodwin, 1985) have reviewed the growing body of literature on the biological correlates of vulnerability to alcoholism and drug dependency. These reviews suggest that a large number of biological factors can predispose a person to alcohol or drug dependency. The authors' proposed biopsychosocial model includes three major cluster factors of biological variables:

1. genetic inheritance of different alcoholism syndromes (male-limited, milieu-limited, depression-sensitive), differences in metabolism and reactions to alcohol and other drugs, biochemical and neurological vulnerabilities, and temperament (ANS) differences, or cognitive (CNS) structural differences.

2. in utero damage to the fetus that could result in central or autonomic nervous system problems, and/or physical and biochemical damage that could make a child temperamentally or psychologically more vulnerable to alcohol or drug use, and

3. temperament or other physiological differences that could occur at anytime after birth due to sickness, accidents, physical trauma, improper diet, exposure to toxins, or alcohol or drug use.

These biological cluster variables are temporally ordered with genetic factors preceding in utero or later physiological damage to the child's biology. Additional biological cluster or individual variables could be added to the framework as discovered by empirical research.

The presence of any one of these biological conditions is generally not sufficient for the expression of alcoholism or drug dependency later in life. When a number of these biological factors converge and interact with non-supportive and negative environmental conditions, however, these "diseases of life-style" can emerge.

Psychosocial Factors. The major psychosocial environmental clusters included in the author's model are organized temporally into family, community\school, and peer\social cluster factors each containing an underlying cognitions, stress, coping process model (see Kumpfer and

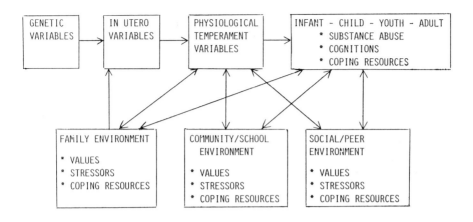

Figure 7.1 A bio-psychosocial vulnerability model.

DeMarsh, 1985) as follows:

1. family variables include family attitudes and values, which interact with family stressors (i.e., conflict, poverty, parent or sibling use of drugs), as buffered by positive family coping skills and resources (i.e., communication, problems solving skills, life skills, and external social and material support).

2. community\school variables including community\school attitudes and values towards prosocial activities and alcohol or drug use, which interact with community\school stressors (i.e., poverty, high crime rates, high population density, impersonal climate, discrimination, conflict or noncooperation and support, pressures to use drugs), as buffered by coping skills and resources (i.e., positive leadership, good problems solving skills, education, prevention and treatment resources).

3. peer\social variables including peer attitudes and values towards prosocial activities and alcohol and drug use, which interact with peer stressors (i.e., peer conformity pressure, developmental adjustment issues, poverty, lack of emotional or material support, depression and poor mental health, lack of opportunities, academic, job and social adjustment problems) as buffered by peer coping skills and resources (i.e., social support, effective group problem solving, conflict resolution and communication skills).

These cluster variables are also temporally ordered by major sources

59

of influence developmentally as the child matures. Family factors are primary and earliest in their sustained impact on the infant and youth. As the child matures and goes to school, school and community environmental factors have more impact. Eventually peer influences predominate, becoming the final common pathway to alcohol and drug use in youth (Dielman et al., in press; Elliott, Huizinga, and Ageton, 1985; 1989; Kumpfer and Turner, in press).

Literature reviews have also found research support for the impact of environmental factors on vulnerability to alcohol and drug dependency. Most researchers (Bry et al., 1982; 1987; Hawkins et al., 1987; Kumpfer, 1987) now accept the hypothesis that the more risk factors, the greater the vulnerability to drug abuse.

Principles of the Biopsychosocial Model. The explicit and implicit philosophical underpinnings and principles of the biopsychosocial model are the following:

1. Causation is multi-directional, multi-causal, probablistic, and sensitive to initial dependencies (as in chaos theory).
2. Changes in one aspect of the person-person or person-environment system can **reverberate** throughout the system.
3. Reciprocal transactions occur between the person and the environment.
4. The person is influenced by future events and is goal-directed (Bandura, 1989). Actions are purposive and intentional. People actively initiate events and try to minimize disruption to the system.
5. The person does not always move towards an ideal state, as in organicistic theory, but can also be self-destructive.
6. To be understood, the person must be pragmatically studied in relationship to his or her total unique context, including historical, current, and future factors.
7. Idiosyncratic events should also be studied.
8. The meaning of events to the person should be understood.
9. Attempts to study and measure the person\environment system change the system, hence there is no such thing as independent observation as proposed in positivistic theoretical research.
10. Longitudinal, developmental, ethnomethodological and anthropological research methods are needed to study such organicistic and transactional systems.
11. While a grand synthesis of general theory may occur, there are likely to be many exceptions based on the complexity of the system. Variability and novelty do occur, because each person and event is different in a transactionally related system.

Interactional vs. Transactional Aspects of the Model.

Before discussing the proposed biopsychosocial model, we would like to briefly make explicit the distinction between interactional and transactional views. This is based on the work of Altman and Rogoff (1987) and Dewey and Bentley (1949). Factors related to an individual's functioning, from an interactional view, are seen as separate and discrete entities, each impacting on the other in a unidirectional manner. Whereas, from a transactional view, these factors act on and are acted upon each other in a dynamic and reciprocal manner. The first view, interactional, is mechanistic; while the second view, transactional, is contextual and organicistic in nature (Altman and Rogoff, 1987).

Other authors in psychology, although not explicitly stated, have proposed similar views to the transactional view. For example, Bandura's (1978; 1986) *reciprocal determinism* views the "interaction" among behavioral, environmental, and person factors in a bidirectional, temporal manner.

The proposed biopsychosocial model is an organicistic model with transactional elements. As shown in Figure 7.1, there is considerable interaction between and within the biological and psychosocial factors. For example, family environmental factors, such as parenting style, family stressors, and family resources can have an "interactive" effect on the physiological and temperament characteristics in the child. This means that the child's temperament will also change the family environment. These proposed bi-directional influences have been substantiated in relational studies of children and their parents (Lewis and Lee-Painter, 1974). A temperamentally difficult child or, indeed, any child has an impact on his or her family, school, and peer environment.

Many biopsychosocial models have been criticized for still subordinating psychosocial factors to biological factors (Armstrong, 1987; Day, 1985). However, the proposed model places as great an emphasis on environmental factors as on biological factors.

The model incorporates all perceived and nonperceived aspects of the person's life. It is a "person-person and person- environment" system that is continuously changing over time and with critical events. This model goes beyond the interest of transactional models in *events* to an interest in the continuing interaction of the person with his or her biology and psychosocial environment. Developmental maturation principles apply as the person matures. The system operates by moving towards ideal states, homeostasis, and balance, but occasionally aberrant directions can occur, such as destructive tendencies. The meaning of the process should come from the perspective of the person, which the observer may never completely understand.

Another principle incorporated in the model is *self determinism*. Psychologists and sociologists are beginning to challenge the linear deterministic model of human behavior and replace it with notions of reciprocal determinism (Bandura, 1986) and a type of deterministic free choice in which people choose or shape environments to impact themselves in certain expected ways (Bandura, 1989). To support a drug habit, a high-risk child may drop out of school and get a job, working with other young drug users. Whereas a low-risk child may choose to save money to assure that he or she can attend a private religious college where alcohol and drug use are very low.

Likewise, the environmental realms of influence are not necessarily sequential or linear. Kumpfer has empirically tested this part of the model with the "Social Ecology Model of Adolescent Alcohol and Other Drug Use" using structural equations modeling (LISREL) statistics (Kumpfer and Turner, in press). After publication, the model was tested in reverse and found to almost be as good a fit. Since structural equations modeling analyses presume a linear order, it is not possible to simultaneously test interactive bi-directional models. Reversing the order of the variables produced suggestive evidence that youths' choices of peers were as likely to impact their relationships to school, community, and family as the family environment was to impact their school and peer environments.

Research methods and statistical techniques to test interactive and, eventually, transactional models are needed. Because of the complexity of the model and the requirements for a large data set with multiple time samples, empirical testing of the model will be difficult.

Implications for Prevention and Treatment

The major mandate of the biopsychosocial model is that the clinician understand the person in relation to his or her total biopsychosocial environment. The clinician should approach the collection of diagnostic data and development of a treatment protocol from this expanded framework. Without a complete understanding of the unique causes of addiction within a particular person, any proposed treatment regime is likely to be ineffective. A complete Patient Evaluation Grid (PEG) (Leigh and Reiser, 1980) as recommended by Schwartz (1982) would help the clinician to gather more complete data for diagnosis and treatment planning. The author has developed a risk assessment instrument for doctors' use that includes most of the major biopsychosocial risk and protective factors in the research literature. This instrument is based on the biopsychosocial model and can be found in Dr. Robert DuPont's recent OSAP Monograph (see Alta Institute Risk Assessment in Appendix in DuPont, 1989).

This approach could stimulate in clinical practice the gathering of a more comprehensive set of data and possibly improve empirical assessment and diagnosis. As pointed out by Schwartz (1982), however, there is little data to prove that taking this comprehensive, global approach will improve assessment. Some practitioners "miss the trees by focusing too hard on the forest." It would only seem logical, however, that systematically collecting data on the major known precursors of alcohol and drug abuse should increase the accuracy of prediction and diagnosis.

Many prevention specialists are currently attempting to develop methods for assessing the level of risk and protective factors in children and youth in order to target precious prevention services to those who need them most. This paper recommends that such risk and protective factor assessments include data on biological, psychological, and social factors— primarily family, school, and peer groups.

One major implication of this model for prevention is that prevention interventions targeting any part of the person- environment system or person-person system should also impact central determinants in many parts of the system. This reverberation concept of a transactional model makes the effectiveness of many different types of prevention interventions look more promising. Reverberation means that prevention specialists do not have to isolate a single, most influential cause that will prevent youth from using or abusing drugs. Many different types of prevention interventions targeted at different points in the person\environment system are likely to be effective. The more mutually reinforcing and coordinated the interventions, the more the impact. However, intervenors must understand the total impact of their prevention approach on the person and the total environmental context. In some cases, a particular prevention strategy could have negative impacts on other parts of the system and result in increased drug use.

Conclusion

A biopsychosocial model of addiction is a very useful conceptual framework for integrating the different causes of alcohol and drug abuse. Training in this framework should enhance communication and mutual respect between professionals in different disciplines working to prevent drug abuse. The biopsychosocial approach strengthens risk assessments for prevention programs and improves diagnosis and treatment of individuals likely to be chemically dependent.

It is unlikely that this model represents a clear "paradigm shift", although the postpositivistic and transactional philosophy contributing to this model may eventually have a major impact on theoretical and research paradigms in health sciences and behavioral sciences. The current model is primarily a macro "paradigms integration" framework in which many different theories can be integrated to approximate the complex reality of the etiology of addiction. For these reasons, the biopsychosocial model has much to offer professionals working in research, prevention, and treatment in the addictions field.

REFERENCES

Altman, I. and Rogoff, B. (1987). World views in psychology: Trait, interactional, organismic, and transactional perspectives. In D. Stokols, and I. Altman (Eds.), *Handbook of environmental psychology* (pp. 7-40). John Wiley and Sons: New York

Armstrong, D. (1987). Theoretical tensions in biophychosocial medicine. *Social Science Medecine*, 25 1213-1218.

Bandura, A. (1978). The Self System in Reciprocal Determinism. *American Psychologist*, 33 344-358.

Bandura, A. (1986). *Social Foundations of Thought and Action*. Prentice-Hall, Inc.: Englewood Cliffs, NJ.

Bandura, A. (1989). Human agency in social cognitive theory. *American Psychologist*, 44 1175-1184.

Bry, B., Pedraza, M., and Pandina, R. (1982). Extent of drug use as a function of number of risk factors. *Journal of Abnormal Psychology*, 9 273-279.

Bry, B., Pedraza, M., and Pandina, R. (1987). Number of risk factors predicts three year probabilities of heavy drug and alcohol use in adolescents. In Harris, L.S., (Ed.). *Problems of Drug Dependence*. Research Monograph 81. National Institute on Drug Abuse: Rockville, MD, 1988.

Day, S.B. (1985). The advance to biopsychosocial medicine. *Social Science Medicine*, 21 1335.

deRosnay, J. (1979). *The Macroscope*. Harper and Row: New York.

Dewey, J. and Bentley, A. F. (1949). *Knowing and the known*. Greenwood Press: Westport, CT.

Dielman, T.E., Butchart, A.T., Shope, J.T., Campanelli, P.C., and Caspar, R.A. (In press). A Covariance Structure Model Test of Antecedents of Adolescent Alcohol Misuse and Prevention Effort. *The Journal of Drug Education*.

DuPont, R.L. (1989). *Stopping Alcohol and Other Drug Use Before It Starts: The Future Prevention*. OSAP Prevention Monograph-1, DHHS Publication No. (ADM) 89-1645.

Elliott, D.S., Huizinga, D., and Ageton, S.S. (1989). *Understanding deliquency; A longitudinal multidisciplinary study of developmental patterns*. University of Colorado: Boulder, CO.

Engel, G.L. (1977). The need for a new medical model: A challenge for biomedicine. *Science*, **196** 129-136.

Engel, G.L. (1978). The biopsychosocial model and the education of health professionals. *Annuals New York Academy of Sciences*, **310** 169-181.

Engel, G.L. (1980). The clinical application of the biopsychosocial model. *The American Journal of Psychiatry*, **137** 535-544.

Gholson, B. and Barker, P. (1985). Kuhn, Lakatos, and Laudan. Applications in the History of Physics and Psychology. *American Psychologist*, **40**,7 755-769.

Goodwin, D.W. (1985). Is alcoholism hereditary? A review and critique. *Archives of General Psychiatry*, **6** 171-174.

Hawkins, J.D., Lishner, D.M., Jenson, J.M., and Catalano, R.F. (1987). Delinquents and drugs: What the evidence suggests about prevention and treatment programming. In Brown, B.S., and Mills, A.R., (Eds.). *Youth at High Risk for Substance Abuse*. National Institute on Drug Abuse: Rockville, MD, 81-131.

Keye, W. R. and Trunnell, E. P. (1986). A biopsychosocial model of premenstrual syndrome. *International Journal of Fertility*, **31** 259-262.

Keye, W. R. and Trunnell, E. P. (1988). A biopsychosocial model. In W. R. Keye (Ed.), *The premenstrual syndrome* (pp. 201-219). W.B. Sanders: Philadelphia.

Kumpfer, K.L. (1987). Special populations: Etiology and prevention of vulnerability to chemical dependency in children of substance abusers. In Brown, B.S. and Mills, A.R., (Eds.). *Youth at High Risk for Substance Abuse*, DHHS Publication No. (ADM) 87-1537 Alcohol, Drug Abuse and Mental health Administration. U.S. Government Printing Office: Washington, DC.

Kumpfer, K.L. (1989). A Critical Review of Risk Factors and Prevention Strategies. In Shaffer, D., Philips, I., and Enzer, N., (Eds.). *Prevention of Mental Disorders, Alcohol and Other Drug Use in Children and Adolescents*, OSAP Prevention Monograph-2, DHHS Publication No. (ADM) 89-1646; 309-372.

Kumpfer, K.L. and DeMarsh, J. (1985). Family, environmental, and genetic influences on children's future chemical dependency. In Ezekoye, S., Kumpfer, K., and Bukoski, W., (Eds.). *Childhood and Chemical Abuse: Prevention and Intervention*. Hayworth Press: NY.

Kumpfer, K.L. and Turner, C.W. (In press). The Social Ecology Model of Adolescent Substance Abuse: Implications For Prevention. *International Journal of Addictions*.

Lakatos, I. (1981). History of Science and its Rational Reconstructions.

Scientific Revolutions. Oxford University Press: New York, 107-127.

Laudan, L. (1981). *Science and Hypothesis*. Reidel: Boston.

Leigh, H. and Reiser, M.F. (1980). Approach to patients: The systems-contextual framework and the Patient evaluation grid. *The Patient: Biological, Psychological, and Social Dimensions of Medical Practice*. Plenum Medical Book Company: New York, 185-200.

Lewis, M. and Lee-Painter, S. (1974). An interactional approach to the mother-infant dyad. In Lewis, M., and Rosenblum, L.A., (Eds.). *The Effect of the Infant on its Caretaker*. Wiley and Sons: New York.

Miller, J.G. (1978). The need for a general theory of living systems. *Living Systems*. McGraw-Hill Book Company: New York, 1-8.

Pepper, S.C. (1942). *World Hypothesis: A Study in Evidence*. University of California Press: Berkeley, CA.

Pepper, S.C. (1967). *Concept and Quality: A World Hypothesis*. Open Court: LaSalle, IL.

Schwartz, G.E. (1982). Testing the biopsychosocial model: The ultimate challenge facing behavioral medicine? *Journal of Consulting and Clinical Psychology*, **50** 1040-1053.

Trunnell, E. P., White, G. L. Jr., Pedersen, D. M., and Keye, W. R. (1989). Biopsychosocial model for premenstrual syndrome: An alternative approach. *Physician Assistant*, **13** 45-52.

von Bertalanffy, L. (1974). General system theory and psychiatry. In Arieti, S. (Ed.). *American Handbook of Psychiatry, Volume 1*: The Foundations of Psychiatry. Basic Books, Inc.: New York, 1095-1117.

Weiss, P. (1977). The system of nature and the nature of systems: empirical holism and practical reductionism harmonized. In Schaefer, K.E., Hensel, H., and Brody, R., (Eds.). *Toward a Man-Centered Medical Science*. Futura Publishing Co.: Mount Kisco, New York.

Section B

DO WE NEED A VARIETY OF PUBLIC POLICIES TO PREVENT ALCOHOL ABUSE?

CHAPTER 8

Thinking About Alcohol Controls

Robin Room, Ph.D.

The Inevitability of Alcohol Controls

By alcohol controls is meant governmental structuring of/or intervention in the market for alcohol beverages (Mäkelä et al., 1981). This intervention can take many forms, including taxation and other interventions in the pricing of alcohol; subsidization of the production of alcoholic beverages or of their raw materials; regulation of the time, place, and manner of alcohol sales; full or partial monopolization of sales; and regulation of the contents, packaging, and advertising of alcoholic beverages. In modern industrial states, some form of alcohol controls is almost inevitable. There are only two alternatives to alcohol controls: a complete laissez-faire policy, in which the state takes no interest in the alcohol market; or total prohibition, where the state outlaws the alcohol market. Neither alternative is likely or politically palatable in the modern industrial state. The rule of the state in regulating the market is by now well accepted for foodstuffs and hazardous commodities—both of which alcohol could be considered as being. A laissez-faire policy for alcohol would thus be an anomaly. On the other hand, prohibition has proved unenforceable for a psychoactive drug as deeply entrenched and readily produced as alcohol. A strong argument for alcohol controls rather than prohibition, in fact, is that a legal industry is more amenable than an illegal one to state influence, and becomes the state's ally against illegal production and marketing.

Controls on alcohol production, marketing, and consumption have been imposed for many reasons. Government agricultural policies, providing subsidies to farmers, frequently affect the price of the alcoholic beverages made from the subsidized grapes or grain. On the other hand, alcohol taxes are an important source of state revenues; they were particularly important prior to the advent of the income tax. In hierarchical societies, alcohol controls have often functioned as sumptuary laws keeping alcohol out of the hands of those who are powerless or thought to be dangerous. Desires to maintain public order or increase productivity have lain behind such measures as restrictions on alcohol sales on election days or paydays, embargoes on serving those in working clothes before noon, and bans on serving the already intoxicated.

68

Historically, public health considerations have played a relatively small role in alcohol controls. Perhaps the earliest forms of control motivated by such considerations were regulations of beverage contents, prescribing the ingredients and forbidding adulterants. In the second half of the 19th century, an explicit ideology of alcohol control emerged, as an alternative to prohibition. At least in part, the alcohol controls proposed under this ideology—state monopoly, high license fees and taxes, alcohol rationbooks, etc.—were motivated by considerations of public health.

Though it is interesting to examine the overt rationales for alcohol controls, the motivation are often mixed, with covert rationales also at stake. In any intervention in a profitable market, someone is likely to be gaining and someone losing. Control measures often have the effect of limiting competition, creating a partial monopoly, and potentially increasing the profits for those who remain in the market. Along with such considerations as public health, public order, productivity and family protection, vested economic interests are thus often at stake in any change in alcohol controls.

Alcohol controls are thus almost inevitable in the modern industrial state, but many motivations and interests underlie the particular structuring of alcohol controls in any jurisdiction. A realistic debate about alcohol controls needs to be couched not in terms of an abstract argument for or against such controls but rather in terms of the rationale and the effects of particular changes from the existing structure of controls.

Effects of Alcohol Controls

In recent decades, a substantial literature evaluating the effects of alcohol controls has emerged. A number of reviews of this literature have appeared (e.g., Smith, 1988; Room 1984a). We may draw a number of conclusions about the effects of alcohol controls:

> • Under all circumstances so far measured, raising the price of alcoholic beverages reduces the consumption, when other factors are unchanged. Since alcoholic beverages, and particularly the most popular type of beverage in a given society, are often not very price-elastic, raising the alcohol taxes will usually both add to government revenues and modestly reduce the level of consumption. It appears that the effect on heavy drinkers' consumption is at least as strong proportionately as the effect on light drinkers' consumption.
>
> • Other alcohol control measures which limit alcohol's availability in terms of time, place, and manner of sale or in terms of the buyer's eligibility (e.g., minimum purchase age, alcohol rationing) often—though not always—affect the level of consumption. The effects seem to

69

be stronger in situations of restricted availability than in situations of relatively free availability.

• There is little concrete evidence of an effect of controls on the advertising or presentation of alcoholic beverages (e.g. warning labels on bottles, warning signs in stores) on levels of consumption.

• From a policy perspective, the effects of alcohol controls on rates of health and social problems is arguably more important than the effects on consumption levels. The rates of various alcohol-related problems— alcohol-related traffic casualties, cirrhosis deaths, violent crime rates— are often affected by alcohol controls. The effect of price and availability controls on rates of alcohol-related problems is often stronger than the effects on consumption levels. This suggests that some alcohol controls may have an especially strong effect on vulnerable subpopulations (e.g., those at risk of death from cirrhosis) or may push consumption into less risky locales or forms (it may be that the main effect of raising the U.S. drinking age has been in partly separating teenage drinking from driving).

These conclusions are based on a wide-ranging and multinational literature. Rather than drawing on cross-sectional comparisons and other study designs which offer only weak evidence of casual connections, they rely on much stronger designs studying changes over time in given societies or localities, often with a comparison of changes in control societies or localities. But the limitations of the literature evaluating the effects of alcohol controls should be kept in mind:

• Most of the studies have been carried out in societies with a strong tradition of concern about alcohol problems—notably in Nordic and English-speaking countries. These are societies in which there is a long tradition of state oversight of the alcohol supply, and in which home production of alcoholic beverages is much less important than in many developing countries. There is reason to believe that the relations of alcohol controls with some alcohol problems is affected by the cultural position of alcohol and the level of concern about drinking—e.g., the relation of consumption levels with violent crime may be stronger in societies that define alcohol as a powerful and criminogenic substance.

• The most broad-ranging segment of the literature concerns the effects of prices and taxes on consumption levels. The literature on the effects of raising and lowering drinking ages is very well-developed, but is almost entirely based on North American experience. More generally, the literature relies heavily on "natural experiments": on studying changes in alcohol availability and controls which occur as policy decisions, rather than an experimental interventions. This means that alcohol control measures are only studied when and to the extent they are politically feasible somewhere. The general trend towards liberalizing alcohol controls in the last 40 years means that, except for taxes and minimum drinking ages, there are more studies of the effects of loosening than of tightening alcohol controls. Thus, too, the literature on unpopular restrictive measures, even those, such as alcohol rationing, which seem likely to affect alcohol-problems rates, is not very developed. An exception to this are the studies of the effects of liquor-store strikes and other perturbations in the alcohol supply. But, although these studies give dramatic and important evidence of the effects on health and social problems rates of restricting alcohol supplies, they reflect special and relatively short-term situations.

• As is true more generally for evaluation studies, studies of the effects of alcohol controls provide much stronger evidence on short-term than on long-term effects. An effect which is immediate and discontinuous is more measurable than an effect which is delayed and gradual. This limitation of the technology of evaluation tends to favor measures where the postulated connection between control and consumption is immediate and mechanical over measures where the postulated connection is more distal and diffuse. Thus, for instance, we might expect the effects of a price rise or the closing of the liquor store on the corner to be inherently more detectable than the effects of a change in advertising regulations.

Competing Interests In Alcohol Controls: Symbolism, Consumer Convenience and Public Health Effects

As Gusfield's classic interpretation (1963) of the temperance movement as a "symbolic crusade" suggests, alcohol policies have long been a favored arena for symbolic policymaking. Public health interests must also be balanced against competing interests, including such considerations as the convenience of the consumer. The research evidence on the practical effects of alcohol controls is thus relevant to discussions of alcohol control policy, but is by no means determinative. This is true even in the Nordic societies, despite their commitment to an ideology of rational social experimentation. Thus the Norwegian parliament failed to make permanent a year-long experiment in closing state alcohol stores on Saturdays, despite evaluative evidence that casualty and social problems were thereby reduced.

Alcohol control policies have often been the medium of symbolic statements about social status, about norms for behavior, and about the cultural position of alcohol in American society. Thus the lowering of the

71

minimum drinking age in the early 1970s was a part of a general shift in the definition of the age of majority, while the raising of the minimum drinking age in the 1980s can be seen as in part reflecting general societal worries and fears about youth. In the debates over restricting alcohol advertising and requiring warning labels which have been gathering steam in the U.S. and in many other countries in the last decade, it is often acknowledged that the primary issue is not the measurable effects of advertising or labels on behavior, but rather the statement which the advertising or the label makes about the cultural position of alcohol (e.g., Wallack, 1983). Is alcohol to be viewed as just another consumer product, between soap and cereal on the supermarket shelves, or it is to be set apart as a special and problematic commodity? (see Mäkelä et al., 1981, pp. 95–96). Behind the answers to such questions often lie deep convictions about what kind of society we want.

Such symbolic concerns should not necessarily be viewed as unrelated to practical concerns about the effects of alcohol controls. Often, indeed, the immediate pragmatic concerns of public health work run up against such symbolic issues: providing birth control to prevent teenage pregnancy is seen as condoning disapproved sexuality, providing sterile needles to IV drug users is seen as condoning illicit drug use. Quite often, however, symbolic concerns can be translated into concerns about long-term effects, as opposed to the short-term effects which are more easily measured by evaluations. In this view, the effects of alcohol advertising, for instance, are seen as played out not so much in individual impulsive choices to start drinking or to have a drink, but rather through a general "wettening" of the society, for instance through establishing the idea that drinking is an intrinsic component of glamour, romance, and having fun.

Such arguments about the symbolism of government actions are important and relevant, but we should be wary of accepting assertions about long-term effects uncritically. It can be argued, for instance, that in the long run, national Prohibition in the U.S. had a paradoxical effect. Instead of entrenching an anti-drinking ideology, as its proponents intended, it provided an attractive target for the generational revolt of the youth of the 1920s, and thus provided the foil for the eventual establishment of a "wet" ideology (Room, 1984b).

In present-day industrial societies, the main resistance to applying the lessons of the alcohol control evaluations (other than from production and marketing interests) comes not from symbolic concerns but rather from a consumer convenience ethic, which demands that almost all commodities be readily accessible in unlimited quantities to the individual consumer, subject only to the consumer's ability to pay. In the postwar period, the strength of this expectation has swept away Sunday "blue laws" and other general restrictions on shop hours, despite labor union opposition, and it is now providing some of the impetus for system change in eastern Europe. Political decisions about alcohol control measures must therefore balance the potential good effects of the measure on public health or order against the consumer inconvenience it creates. Respondents in general population surveys are noticeably more enthusiastic about alcohol controls that are seen as affecting only others than about controls that are seen as also affecting themselves (Cameron, 1981). The effect of this consumer convenience ethic can be seen in the fact that such measures as advertising restrictions and warning labels and signs are everywhere more politically feasible than new restrictions on the hours of sale or rationing of alcohol sales. Given that the consumer convenience ethic is conditioned on the customer's ability to pay, raising alcohol taxes has also proved more feasible than direct limitation of availability.

Alcohol Controls and Alcohol Policies

The idea that governments should have a coherent alcohol policy, including provision for treatment, education and other prevention measures as well as alcohol controls, has spread from Scandinavia quite widely in recent years (e.g., Moore and Gerstein, 1981; Moser, 1985). As argued above, alcohol controls are, nearly inevitably, a part of any general alcohol policy. But it would be as counterproductive to rely entirely on alcohol controls in such a policy as to ignore them completely. Like other legislative and regulatory measures, alcohol controls are only effective in a free society when they enjoy a wide measure of popular support. For many control measures—e.g., advertising restrictions and warning labels—the societal debate about the measure, and the education this entails, may well be more important in its effects than the measure itself.

Even for alcohol controls with wide popular support, there are limits to their effectiveness. As recent Soviet experience has reaffirmed, if the price of alcohol rises too high, or if the supply is sufficiently restricted, an illicit market will supply part of the shortfall, carrying with it the social costs Americans know only too well from the present-day illicit drug market.

From a governmental perspective, alcohol controls have some unique advantages. In the form of taxes and license fees, they generate rather than cost revenue (though they thereby create a governmental interest in the level of alcohol sales). In the form of controls on availability, they are cheaply and efficiently administered. The main target of regulation is not the consumer but the commercial producer, distributor, or seller, and the fundamental enforcement sanction is not penal but the threat to close down or seize the business. Such commercial controls are more effective and

73

easily enforced than criminal laws (Room, 1983). Often, indeed, business competitors will assist in the enforcement process. On the other hand, as heavily regulated industries, the alcoholic beverage industries inevitably become heavily involved and often powerful in the political process, in an attempt to control their fate.

In the whole spectrum of alcohol policies in the modern industrial state, then, alcohol controls are destined to play a unique but not dominant role. Unlike treatment, incarceration, or other interventions, alcohol controls require no expensive establishment of service providers, and only a relatively small enforcement staff. If taxes are counted in, alcohol controls are a net source of revenue to the state. But the content and stringency of alcohol controls, even as they affect the extent and nature of alcohol problems in the society, are very much formed and constrained by the society's concerns about the attitudes to those problems.

REFERENCES

Cameron, T. (1981). *Alcohol and Alcohol Problems: Public Opinion in California, 1974–1980*, Alcohol Research Group: Berkeley, Report C31.

Gusfield, J. (1963). *Symbolic Crusade: Status Politics and the American Temperance Movement*. University of Illinois Press: Urbana, IL.

Mäkelä, K. Room, R., Single, E., Sulkunen, P., Walsh, B., with 13 others. (1981). *Alcohol, Society, and the State: 1. A Comparative Study of Alcohol Control*. Addiction Research Foundation: Toronto, Ont.

Moore, M. and Gerstein, D., eds. (1981). *Alcohol and Public Policy: Beyond the Shadow of Prohibition*. National Academy Press: Washington, DC.

Moser, J., ed. (1985). *Alcohol Policies in National Health and Development Planning*. World Health Organization: Geneva. Offset Publication No. 89.

Room, R. (1983). Legislative Strategies and the Prevention of Alcohol Problems, pp. 152–164 In: Grant, M. and Ritson, B., eds., *Alcohol: The Prevention Debate*. Croom Helm: London.

Room, R. (1984a). Alcohol Control and Public Health. *Annual Review of Public Health*, **5** 293–317.

Room, R. (1984b). A "Reverence for Strong Drink": The Lost Generation and the Elevation of Alcohol in American Culture. *Journal of Studies on Alcohol*, **45** 540–546.

Smith, D.I. (1988). Effectiveness of Restrictions on Availability as a Means of Preventing Alcohol Problems. *Contemporary Drug Problems*,

15 627–684.

Wallack, L. (1983). Alcohol Advertising Reassessed: The Public Health Perspective, pp. 243–248 In: Grant, M., Plant, M., and Williams, A., eds., *Economics and Alcohol: Consumption and Controls*. Croom Helm and Gardner Press: London, Canberra and New York.

CHAPTER 9

Flawed Policies from Flawed Premises: Pseudo-Science about Alcohol and Drugs

Dwight B. Heath, Ph.D

Public health policies are often influenced by political considerations that are extraneous, or even counterproductive, in terms of the scientific and humanitarian criteria that ideally would apply. We all recognize that economic necessity, unrelenting pressures of time, lack of personnel or facilities, the unavoidable need for compromise, emotional reactions, or various other reasons can be invoked to account for some such discrepancies, although unalloyed political expediency is doubtless also a consideration in at least some instances. An increasingly influential factor in recent years has been the promulgation of quasi-scientific "data" and "principles" that come to be accepted as justification for a variety of policies that have little factual basis.

In this paper, I will briefly discuss different kinds of representation and misrepresentation that occur concerning alcohol and drugs; although the issue is undoubtedly relevant elsewhere, I will focus on agencies of the United States and the United Nations.

The Fallacy of "the Control Model" of Prevention
Throughout the world, people are increasingly being told by public health "authorities" and "experts" that it is necessary to reduce everyone's drinking if we are to reduce a wide range of alcohol-related problems. For example, within the context of a W.H.O. publication, it is baldly asserted that "because of the overwhelming evidence that consumption levels are closely related to the extent of alcohol-induced harm, the cornerstone of primary prevention must be the control and, where necessary, the reduction of national *per capita* alcohol consumption" (Walsh, 1982:79).

Unfortunately, the evidence is by no means overwhelming, so such a simplistic formula is grossly distorted and far removed from what is often cited as a factual basis. The intellectual cornerstone of the recent wave to control the availability of alcohol, cited as such by all of those who have any scholarly credentials or pretensions in the field of alcohol studies, is a monograph compiled by an international group who met in Finland some years ago (Bruun et al., 1975). The crucial wording of their original report is extremely tentative. What they said, after comparing historical trends concerning death from liver cirrhosis in various countries was simply that "... changes in the overall consumption of alcoholic beverages have a bearing on the health of the people in any society. Alcohol control measures can be used to limit consumption: thus control of alcohol availability becomes a public health issue" (Bruun et al., 1975:90).

Successive attempts to find out just what kind of "bearing" such changes in consumption have on public health and social welfare have met with a remarkable lack of uniformity. Lest it appear that I selectively emphasize the views of colleagues who are outspoken critics of increasing legislative and regulatory controls, I will first cite people who had been co-authors with Bruun in the original study. For example, a multinational study by Mäkelä et al., (1981), including four of Bruun's co-authors, offers the following generalization: "as each society has its peculiar drinking habits, the mixture of problems varies accordingly and, in cross-sectional comparisons, there are few positive relationships between consumption level and the incidence of problems..." (Mäkelä et al., 1981:62). Similarly, "relations of alcohol consumption level and patterns to casualties and social problems associated with drinking are far less clear and universal.... correlations of these problems with consumption level are frequently negligible or negative" (ibid: 90). A close inspection of the case-studies reveals those inconsistencies. For example, both Poland and Finland had "very low" overall consumption but both had high rates of social conflicts related to drinking, crimes of violence, arrests for drunkenness, and fatal alcohol poisoning. The Netherlands, with "very similar" consumption, showed "few signs of disruptive drinking, " while Switzerland, with "the highest level of aggregate consumption" among the seven societies studied, had "few signs of social conflicts related to disruptive drunken comportment" (ibid: 45–46).

Despite such evidence and their own apparently contradictory generalizations, they asserted at the end that "one of the basic findings of our study, however, is that the growth in alcohol consumption was accompanied by an increase in a broad variety of problems related to drinking. When all the case studies are taken together, this holds true not only for consequences of prolonged drinking, but for social and health problems related to single-drinking episodes" (Mäkelä et al., 1981: 109).

That kind of oversimplification has tended to recur in a variety of contexts, and to influence legislators, administrators, and others who are not familiar in detail with the studies. For example, addressing an international policy-oriented readership, "...alcohol-related health problems can be expected to vary with the level of overall consumption" (Sulkunen,

1985: 123). Writing to a broad lay readership in the U.S., to introduce a set of policy recommendations: "while only a fraction of all alcohol users—the alcoholics—have most of the alcohol related illness, there is a distinct correlation between the total consumption of alcohol by a society and the prevalence of all alcohol related problems and diseases including alcoholism per se" (West, 1984: 4). When the Director General of the World Health Organization asserted unequivocally that "any reduction in per capita consumption will be attended by a significant decrease in alcohol related problems" (W.H.O., 1978: 4), too many journalists, bureaucrats, and other non-specialists unquestioningly accepted that apparently authoritative judgment.

One might well wonder how it can be that such cautious and nuanced conclusions as those originally offered by Bruun et al. (1975) became converted or "translated" into such dogmatic and slanted premises, which now serve as guides to policy-making.

Whereas the premises of "the control model" appear, in cross-cultural perspective, to be flawed, the alternative "sociocultural model" (Heath, 1988a) fits with the experience of many populations throughout history and around the world. That is, teaching young people honestly about the nature and effects of alcohol, and instilling them with norms about the limits of appropriate and inappropriate behavior, serves as a kind of "immunization" against alcoholism and drinking problems. No immunization is foolproof, but the reactions against prohibition when it was tried in India, Britain, Sweden, Russia, the United States, and elsewhere, or the "forbidden-fruit" appeal among American adolescents today, suggest that increasing emphasis on social control—peer-pressure, adherence to norms, etc. —is likely to be more effective in the long run than increasing emphasis an legal and regulatory controls—such as shorter hours of sale, higher purchase-age, server-liability, and so forth.

Playing the Numbers: How Many Alcoholics?

A recent article in *Science* took testimony before the U.S. Senate Committee on Governmental Affairs as a distressing example that "government research institutes and individual scientists are generally careful to include the best information in their reports to Congress, but occasionally the data are not statistically sound or are extrapolated beyond the limitations of the survey" (Barnes, 1988: 1729). It has been a standing joke among researchers that, during the two decades since Congress (in a unanimous vote) established the National Institute on Alcohol Abuse and Alcoholism, through which hundreds of millions of dollars have been channeled for treatment, prevention, and research, the estimated number of alcoholics has continued to rise at a rapid rate. Rather than question the efficiency and effectiveness of the agency, let us consider the basis for such estimates.

Robin Room provides an anecdotal account of how the original "9 million" was extrapolated, on the basis of a survey that included no questions about alcoholism (quoted in Barnes 1988:1729). Don Cahalan, Kaye Fillnore, Mark Keller, Selden Bacon, and other knowledgeable researchers have, in diverse contexts, provided variant, but similarly plausible, versions of what might be viewed as an origin myth for this quasi-scientific pseudo-statistic.

Over the years, successive publications by NIAAA have revised the number upward, usually with no source cited, or with reference to an un-published survey that was not available through the Institute.The terminology has changed often in succeeding years, so that, in the most recent report, "an estimated 18 million adults 18 years old and older currently experience problems as a result of alcohol use" (NIAAA, 1987:12). Repeated efforts by several interested epidemiologists and social scientists to ascertain an empirical basis for the rapidly evolving estimates of prevalence have been unsuccessful.

The Fabrication of "Consensus Documents"

Levine (1984) described his concern, based on first-hand experience in which he found many discrepancies between the so-called "consensus document" that was promulgated by the organizers of an international transdisciplinary conference on alcohol, and what had actually transpired at the conference. As a fellow participant in the same conference, I share his consternation that the document stressed some things that had never been mentioned during the conference, distorted much of what had been said, and proposed generalizations that virtually all of the speakers had explicitly warned were unwarranted (Heath, 1988b,c). Delegates to the World Health Assembly who saw the "consensus document" but not the proceedings could not have avoided misunderstanding, as the document that purported to summarize our scientific deliberations went in very different directions from what actually transpired.

Propaganda in the "War on Drugs"

In attempting to muster support for his tough enforcement-oriented policies, the Director of the Office of National Drug Control Policy provided "...terrible proof that our current drug epidemic has far from run its course. Estimated 'frequent' use of cocaine in any form (measured by the number of survey respondents who report ingesting that drug one or more times each week, and calculated as a percentage of the total cocaine-using population) has doubled since 1985" (Bennett, 1989:3). That statistic is not nearly so alarming when one remembers that, citing the same survey just 2 pages earlier, he had noted that "current use" of cocaine was down 48 percent in the same time. This means that only about half as many people were using cocaine in any given month (in 1989, as compared with 1985). Halving the denominator—a far more important index of a diminishing "drug epidemic" —would automatically double the *rate* of "frequent use," even with no change in the actual number of those confirmed addicts. If our concern is with the prevalence of drug use and its related problems, the significantly smaller number of "current users" is, as he himself noted, "good news—very good news" (Bennett: 1989:1). That kind of numerical shell-game may be effective as propaganda in a "Drug Czar's" declared "war on drugs," but it grossly distorts the findings of the ninth periodic Notional Household Survey on Drug Abuse, and is seriously flawed as a basis for developing or justifying any kind of policy.

A Warning about Warning Labels

Recent federal legislation that mandates the inclusion of a health-warning label on every container of alcoholic beverages illustrates another instance in which a policy was instituted on the basis of virtually no scientific evidence, although media coverage and political pronounce-ments often implied the opposite. Senator Strom Thurmond had repeat-edly proposed such labeling since 1967, and had repeatedly failed to gain sufficient support. Part of the hesitancy on the part of many Congressper-sons may well have been the fact that testimony in successive years demonstrated that there was no support for assertions that such labels would prevent alcohol-related problems by educating consumers. Finally, in 1986, Congress charged the Public Health Service to conduct a search of the literature on this controversial subject. The project was contracted to Micro Systems, Inc., who concluded: "The literature search did not discover any empirical research studies which examined the impact of product labeling upon the *health consequences* associated with [any kind of] product use. [Furthermore,] the literature search did not identify any studies of the effects of alcohol warning labels in countries that currently require such labels" (D.H.H.S 1987: Appendix B(1)). In short, no immediately relevant data exist in print!

But they went on to review the literature that was available on other aspects of warning labels: 2 studies of warnings on soft drinks about sac-charin, and one study of warnings on cigarette packages (in Sweden). On the basis of those 3 cases—none on alcohol, and one in another country—they did not hesitate to make policy recommendations. They concluded that "health warning labels *can* have an impact on the consumer if. . .certain conditions be met, so the review of the research literature on health warning labels suggests the following major implications for alcohol warning labels: ..." (D.H.H.S. 1987:3–5). The ensuing web of conjecture was treated as if it comprised substantive findings of the sort that had been sought but could not be found.

The Dangers of Pseudo-Science

Presumably the P.H.S.'s report to Congress was interpreted as "proving" the efficacy of labeling. The Omnibus Drug Act of 1988 (P.L. 100–610: Title VIII) included, with no fanfare, a provision that drinks packaged after November 1989 carry a warning from the Surgeon General about possible fetal damage and about risk while driving or operating machinery.

It seems unlikely that anyone seriously believes a warning-label would deter an alcoholic from taking a drink, but there does appear to be a widespread belief that "it wouldn't do any harm, so why not require a label just on the off-chance that it might do some good?" The answer to that question is that taking ineffective—or, at best, untested—action seems likely to divert our attention from the need for tested and effective action.

Instead of gaining a false sense of security from having mandated warning-labels, legislators might better have supported further research on why it is that a small portion of those who drink encounter various drinking problems, how young people can be taught to abstain (like fully one-third of the adult population in the U.S. today), or to drink moderately (like fully 90% of the rest), thereby avoiding such problems. Or another appropriate action would be to learn more about how those who have such problems can be helped to overcome them.

It is not that we lack such knowledge today. We do not have all the answers, but great progress has been made on all of these subjects. Perhaps more to the point is the fact that such knowledge is being effectively channeled into appropriate programs of prevention and treatment, but at a distressingly slow rate. In recent years, such practice efforts are, ironically, increasingly hampered by the diversion of funds to support an increasingly militant but ineffectual "war on drugs." As in this country's several previous attempts at stemming drug-use by military, police, and judicial actions (Brecher, 1987), drugs are becoming not scarcer but rather more widely available, not more attenuated but ever stronger, and not more expensive, but cheaper yet, as government expenditures on countermeasures escalate and as abuses of civil liberties (in the name of law-enforcement) proliferate.

Similarly, the fallacy of the control model of prevention offers the illusion of providing a sure solution to alcohol-related problems far more quickly and easily than could be done with the sociocultural model.

Revision of norms is a slow and gradual process, requiring education in the broadest sense, and involving all sectors of the community. But the contrasts between Spaniards who drink every day and Swedes who do so only occasionally, Jews who are taught at an early age to drink ceremonially, and Irishmen whose convivial drinking starts much later in life, Camba who praise drunkenness and East Indians who fear it, all show that problems stem less from how much one drinks than from how one drinks and what one expects the outcomes to be (Heath, 1982).

Inflated estimates of the prevalence of alcoholism, or of the "growing" use of cocaine, are crude appeals to the compelling quality of numbers. They should neither distract us from addressing the far more important qualitative dimensions of public and private harms that are suffered nor should they be taken as quantitative justification for continuing policies that have proven to be flawed.

Perhaps the most tragic risk in all such manipulations is that the growing use of pseudo-science might eventually discredit the scientific enterprise itself. We would all be poorer if policy-makers came to view science as irrelevant and empirical evidence as unimportant. Let us hope that more people will learn to recognize the difference.

REFERENCES

Barnes, D.M. (1988). Drug: Running the numbers. *Science*, 240 1729–1731

Bennett, W.J. (1989). Introduction, *National Drug Control Strategy* (Office of National Drug Control Policy), U.S. Government Printing Office: Washington.

Brecher, E.M. (1987) Drug laws and drug law enforcement: A review and evaluation based on 111 years of experience. *Drugs and Society*, 1 (1) 1–27.

Bruun, K, Edwards, G, Lummio, M, Mäkelä, K., Pan, L., Popham, R.E., Room, R., Schmidt, W., Skog, O.J., Sulkunen, P., and Österberg, E. (1975). *Alcohol Control Policies in Public Health Perspective*. Finnish Foundation for Alcohol Studies: Helsinki.

Department of Health and Human Services (June, 1987). *Review of the Research Literature on the Effects of Health Warning Labels: A Report to the United States Congress (pursuant to P.L. 99–570, sec. 4017, Anti-Drug Abuse Act of 1986)*, [D.H.H.S.: Washington].

Heath, D.B. (1982). Sociocultural variants in alcoholism. *Encyclopedic Handbook of Alcoholism* (Eds. E.M. Pattison and E. Kaufman). Gardner Press: New York.

Heath, D.B. (1988a). Emerging anthropological theory and models of alcohol use and alcoholism. *Theories on Alcoholism* (Eds. C.D. Chaudron and D.A. Wilkinson). Addiction Research Foundation: Toronto.

Heath, D.B. (1988b) Alcohol control policies and drinking patterns: An international game of politics against science. *Journal of Substance Abuse*, **1** 109–115.

Heath, D.B. (1988c) Quasi-science and public policy: A reply to Robin Room about details and misrepresentations in science. *Journal of Substance Abuse*, **1** 121–125.

Levine, H.G. (1984). What is an alcohol-related problem? (Or what are people talking about when they refer to alcohol problems?). *Journal of Drug Issues*, **14** 45–60.

Mäkelä, K., Room, R., Single, E., Sulkunen, P., and Walsh, B. (1981). *Alcohol, Society and the State, Vol. 1: A Comparative Study of Alcohol Control.* Addiction Research Foundation: Tronoto.

National Institute on Alcohol Abuse and Alcoholism (1987). *Sixth Special Report to the U.S. Congress on Alcohol and Health*, (D.H.H.S. Publication (ADM) 87–1519), N.I.A.A.A.: Rockville, MD.

Sulkunen, P. (1985). International aspects of the prevention of alcohol problems: Research experiences and perspectives. *Alcohol Policies* (Ed. M. Grant). World Health Organization Regional Publications, European Series 18: Copenhagen.

Walsh, D. (1982). *Alcohol-Related Medicosocial Problems and their Prevention.* World Health Organization Regional Publications, Public Health in Europe 17.

West, L.J. (1984). *Alcoholism and Related Problems: Issues for the American Public.* The American Assembly, Columbia University, and Prentice-Hall, Inc.: Englewood Cliffs, NJ.

World Health Organization (1978). Report by the Director General, Executive Board, Sixty-third Session, *Alcohol Related Problems: The Need to Develop Further the WHO Initiative* (Provisional Agenda Item 23, Attachment E). World Health Organization: Geneva, (27 Nov).

SHOULD THE MINIMUM DRINKING (PURCHASE AGE) BE LOWERED?

CHAPTER 10

The Drinking Age Should Be Lowered ✓

David J. Hanson, Ph. D.

The Drinking Age Should Be Lowered

There is extensive evidence that the consumption of alcoholic beverages has occurred in most societies throughout the world and has probably occurred since the Paleolithic Age and certainly since the Neolithic Age (Knupfer, 1960). The records of all ancient civilizations refer to the use of alcoholic beverages. Such accounts are found on Egyptian carvings, Hebrew script, and Babylonian tablets (Patrick, 1952). The Code of Hammurabi (cir 2225 B.C.) devoted several sections to problems created by the abuse of alcohol and in China, laws that forbade making wine were enacted and repealed forty-one times between 1100 B.C. and 1400 A.D. (Alcoholism and Drug Research Foundation of Ontario, 1961). These and other sources of evidence indicate that concern over alcohol use and abuse are not unique to present societies.

The place of alcohol in American society since the colonial period has clearly been ambivalent. "Drinking has been blessed and cursed, has been held the cause of economic catastrophe and the hope for prosperity, the major cause of crime, disease and military defeat, depravity and a sign of high prestige, mature personality, and a refined civilization" (Straus and Bacon, 1953). This ambivalence is reflected in the changing drinking age laws and drinking ethos as indicated in Table 10.1.

Organized efforts to limit drinking or the role of alcoholic beverages have existed in the United States since the early 1800s. However, alcohol has been the only substance whose proposed prohibition has provoked strong controversy and conflict. On one hand, the prohibition of narcotics has met little organized resistance while the prohibition of cigarette, coffee or cola beverages sales has not attracted significant political support. Gusfield (Gusfield, 1962; 1963) contends that alcohol has been a symbolic issue through which a struggle for primacy in social status has been fought between differing life styles—small town versus city, "old American" versus recent immigrant, the South and Midwest versus the Northeast. An alternate explanation is that while alcohol is clearly associated with numerous personal and social problems (thus motivating the prohibition impulse), its use is widespread and widely accepted (thus motivating its

Table 10.1

A Schemata of Drinking Age Laws in the United States from 1700 to 1987 Relative to Drinking Ethos and Social Climate

Time	Age Law	Drinking ethos	Social climate
1700-1800	No age laws except in a few locales very young.	Colonial North America thrives on drinking. Men, women and children all use alcohol. Moderation is a cultural norm.	Rural life in the colonies. Close family ties. Parents had absolute authority to define children's rights and restrictions.
1800-1850	Isolated state and local age laws began to evolve. The age varied, but usually was 16 or younger.	Drinking was beginning to change. Moderation was waning, and young (especially college youth often drank heavily and sometimes engaged in delinquent behavior).	Industrial revolution. Temperance movement emerging.
1850-1920	Many local and state laws began to "protect youth" by age laws which varied from 16 to 20.	Temperance movement flourishing and is not a major political force. Heavy drinking also continued.	16- to 20-year olds now being treated as preadolescents. Industrial development and job specialization put youth out of labor market.
1920-1930	Prohibition for all by constitutional amendment.	Drinking illegal, consumption moves underground. Mobster control of manufacture and distribution. Drinking continues in contempt of the law.	Nightlife flourishes in hidden bars and ballrooms. Unsettled period leading to economic depression.
1934-1960	Age 21 established for postprohibition alcohol use.	Drinking continuing with alcohol now legal. Underage drinking now "a problem" as teenagers drink outside adult sanction.	Recovery from economic depression. World War II and baby boom of postwar period.
1960-1972	Many states lower drinking age to 18.	Alcohol use flourishes along with use of marijuana and other drugs.	Youth participation in economy and society very evident. Issues made over 18 as age of majority with all rights expected. Vietnam. "Hippie movement."
1972-1987	States began moving drinking age back to 21. In 1986, Congress passes a law requiring all states to set 21 as legal age or lose highway funds.	Alcohol use flourishes with 75% of teenagers declaring that they use in national studies.	Negative reaction to high rate of youth involvement in drinking related auto accidents. Republican administration and conservative movement in U.S. society.

(Lotterhos et al., 1988, pp. 631-632).

defense). In either case, the consequence is often intense emotion and struggle.

Following the repeal of the Eighteenth Amendment in 1933, prohibition efforts have largely been age-specific. In 1970, Congress passed the Twenty-Sixth Amendment, which grants the right to vote in Federal elections to citizens between the ages of 18 and 21. A movement then began to extend other rights and privileges of adulthood to those aged 18; between 1970 and 1975, 29 states reduced their minimum legal drinking age (Wagenaar, 1983). However, by the late 1970s controversy over minimum drinking age laws became widespread and this pattern was reversed. Much of the concern arose over the number of young people involved in automobile accidents, many of which were alcohol-related (Wechsler and Sands, 1980).

A common response to the need to "do something" about a perceived problem has been to seek a legal solution through legislation and it appears that laws in the United States are among the most stringent in the world (Mosher, 1980). Of course, raising the drinking age to reduce drunk driving is an indirect and incomplete way to attack the problem. "No doubt raising the drinking age to 25, 30 or even 50", as one house of the Mississippi legislature recently passed, would also tend to reduce drunk driving. The youngest age group is being chosen as a symbolic gesture because of its political impotence and because...there are no major economic consequences..." (Mosher, 1980, p. 31). A more direct and effective approach might be to address the problem of intoxicated drivers *regardless* of their age or social status.

Mosher has pointed out that

> "these modern youthful-drinking laws and enforcement priorities contrast with trends in youthful-drinking patterns. In the abstract, one would predict that increasingly stringent controls on availability and emphasis on enforcement would lessen the actual amount of alcohol consumed. Indeed, for all the problems associated with national Prohibition, use did decline during that period. Such is not the case for youthful drinking. Statistics show that under-aged persons increased their use of alcohol steadily form the 1930s to the 1960s, when legislation to curtail sales was most active. Ironically, a plateau was reached both in the prevalence of teenage drinking and in legislative action to restrict availability to teenagers at approximately the same time. " (Mosher, 1980, p. 25).

Both up-dating and corroborating Mosher's observation is the fact that following the reduction of drinking age laws in the 1970s, the proportion of collegians who drink has trended downward (Engs and

Hanson, 1988).

An unresolved issue underlying minimum drinking age laws is determining the age at which young people are mature enough to assume adult responsibilities. The lack of consensus regarding this issue in general is reflected in the diverse and changing minimum ages for other behaviors. These include age of consent for sexual intercourse, to purchase contraceptive devices, to marry without parental approval, to drive a car, to serve on a jury, and to buy and use tobacco (Wechsler and Sands, 1980).

Some studies (Perkins and Berkowitz, 1987; Engs and Hanson, 1986) have found little differences between drinking patterns of young people legally able and not legally able to drink. One reason for this lack of differentiation might be the pervasive informal supply networks and mechanisms whereby underage individuals generally experience little or no difficulty in obtaining alcohol. Another reason may be the ease with which many underage people were able to drive to neighboring states (or provinces) to purchase or consume alcohol. In any case, it would appear that legislation generally has had virtually no impact on alcohol behaviors and problems.

Drinking patterns are governed by the common fabric of values, symbols, and meanings shared by a group (Globetti, 1976). Legislation designed to prohibit customs embedded in a group risk failure, as did national prohibition in such countries as Iceland (1915-1922), Russia (1916-1917), Finland (1919-1932) and the United States (1920-1933) (Ewing and Rouse, 1976). National prohibition does not seem to be attainable except in those countries in which, by far, the large majority of inhabitants practice a religion prohibiting the use of alcohol (Tongue, 1976).

Underlying minimum age legislation are the assumptions of American prohibitionism: alcohol consumption is sinful and dangerous; it results in problem behavior; and drinking in any degree is equally undesirable because moderate social drinking is the forerunner of chronic inebriation (Sterne et al., 1967). Naturally, young people, if not everyone, should be protected from alcohol, according to this view.

Attempts to legislate behavior often lead to unintended and undesirable consequences. For example, Australian laws closing bars at six o'clock got the working men out of the establishments and possibly home to their families in time for dinner. However, they also produced the undesirable custom known as the six o'clock swill, which involves consuming as much beer as possible between the end of work and the six o'clock closing time (Room, 1976). Sterne and her colleagues (1967) concluded that minimum age laws not only fail in their intent but also produce very questionable consequences:

1. "The consumption of alcohol in automobiles is clearly undesirable, yet in denying the right of the older teenager to its public purchase and consumption, we unwittingly suggest this combination."
2. "The practice of patterned evasion of stringent liquor laws is a poor introduction of youth to adult civic responsibility, suggesting adult roles which incorporate neither respect for nor conformity to the law."
3. "As Prohibition amply demonstrated, liquor laws which do not meet with public acceptance provide illicit business opportunities. While taverns have not been found to be an important factor producing delinquency, a small minority of them capitalize on this opportunity for illicit business, catering to questionable entertainment and an outlet for drugs." (Sterne et al., 1967, pp. 58-59).

Alcohol legislation is often passed with less concern for the law's actual impact (or lack thereof) on drinking behavior than with its political value for the legislators; that is, with how their constituents will perceive their votes and how future opponents might be able to attack their voting records[1] (Room, 1976, p. 269). Furthermore, with over two-thirds of the adult American population being drinkers, rigorous enforcement of restrictive legislation is not viewed as a priority by the general population, by the police, or by the courts.

Even if enforcement of prohibitive legislation were vigorously pursued, there is little evidence that it would be successful. The widespread demand for alcohol and the ease with which a large variety of products can be converted into alcoholic beverages easily lead to "home brew" and other illicit manufacture. Ease of distribution gives natural rise to bootlegging and smuggling under such circumstances.

Not surprisingly, age-specific prohibition does not appear to be effective in reducing either the proportion of drinkers or their drinking problems. A study of a large sample of young people between the ages of 16 and 19 in Massachusetts and New York after Massachusetts raised its drinking age revealed that the average, self-reported daily alcohol consumption in Massachusetts did not decline in comparison with New York (Hingson et al., 1983). Comparison of college students attending schools in states that had maintained for a period of at least ten years a minimum drinking age of 21 with those in states that had similarly maintained minimum drinking ages below 21 revealed few differences in drinking problems (Engs and Hanson, 1986).

Comparison of drinking before and after the passage of raised minimum age legislation have generally revealed little impact upon behavior (Perkins and Berkowitz, 1985; Hanson and Hattauer, n.d.). For example, a study that examined college students' drinking behavior before and after an increase in the minimum legal drinking age from 18 to 19 in New York State found the law to have no impact on under-age students' consumption rates, intoxication, drinking attitudes, or drinking problems (Perkins and Berkowitz, 1985). These findings were corroborated by other researchers at a different college in the same state (Hanson and Hattauer, n.d.). A similar study at Texas A & M examined the impact of an increase of the minimum drinking age from 19 to 21. There was no increase in consumption or alcohol problems among under-age students. However, there was a significant increase among such students in attendance at events where alcohol was present. There were also significant increases in the frequency of their requests to legal-age students to provide alcohol and in their receipt of illicit alcohol from legal-age students (Mason et al., 1988).

A longitudinal study of the effect of a one-year increase of the drinking age in the province of Ontario found that it had a minimum effect on consumption among 18 and 19 year-old high school students and none among those who drank once a week or more (Vingilis and Smart, 1981). A similar study was conducted among college students in the State University System of Florida to examine their behavior before and after an increase in the drinking age from 19 to 21. While there was a general trend toward reduced consumption of alcohol after the change in law, alcohol-related problems increased significantly. Finally, an examination of East Carolina University students' intentions regarding their behavior following passage of a new 21-year age drinking law revealed that only 6% intended to stop drinking, 70% planned to change their drinking location, 21% expected to use a false or borrowed identification to obtain alcohol, and 22% intended to use other drugs. Anecdotal statements by students indicated the belief of some that it "might be easier to hide a little pot in my room than a six pack of beer." (Lotterhos et al., 1988, p. 644).

Over the past four decades it has been demonstrated that the proportion of collegiate drinkers increases with age (Straus and Bacon, 1953; Wechsler and McFadden, 1979; Perkins and Berkowitz, 1987). However, in July of 1987 the minimum purchase age became 21 in all states. Because drinking tends to be highly valued among collegians, because it is now illegal for those under 21 to purchase alcohol, Engs and Hanson (1989) hypothesized that reactance motivation (Brehm and Brehm, 1981) would be stimulated among such students, leading more of them to drink. Their data from 3,375 students at 56 colleges across the country revealed that, after the legislation, significantly more under-age students drank compared to those of legal age. Thus, the increase in purchase age appears to have been not only ineffective but actually counter-productive, at least in the short run.

There is extensive evidence that while an abstinence religious environment is associated with a lower proportion of people drinking, alcohol-related problems are much more common among those in such milieu who do drink (Hanson, 1972). This appears to result from several factors. First, such individuals have typically not learned how to drink. Thus, they have not learned how to use alcohol in moderation. Secondly, they are more likely to drink in a secretive manner or in environments free of moderating or restraining social control over their drinking. Thirdly, abstinence groups often portray the person who drinks as one who misuses alcohol. Thus, they inadvertently present a negative role model which can guide behavior of those who do drink (Globetti, 1976, p. 166). Fourthly, for young people, abstinence teaching may encourage rather than deter use by making alcohol use a symbol or tool of rebellion against authority. The nature of the rebellion can gain further strength and intensity from disapproval and repression (Globetti, 1976, p. 167).

Conversely, most Jews, Chinese, and Italians drink, yet those groups have low rates of drunkenness and other forms of problem drinking. In all three groups, children begin drinking at an early age in the home and they observe alcohol being used in an unemotional and controlled manner. They learn that alcohol is a natural and normal part of life, do not view its use as a sign or symbol of adulthood, nor associate it with intoxication. To the contrary, they learn that alcohol abuse is taboo. Importantly, they are provided with role models for the appropriate use of alcohol (Plaut, 1967; Wilkinson, 1970; Hanson, 1972).

It is clear that much formal alcohol education is unrealistic, alienates young people, and tends to be ineffective if not counterproductive (Hanson, 1982). Cisin has stated the problem very well:

"In our values as parents and educators, we have a responsibility for the socialization of our children, a responsibility for preparing them for life in the world. Part of our job is teaching children how to handle dangerous activities like driving, swimming, drinking, and sex. We behave toward our children as though there were really two different kinds of dangerous activities. Driving and swimming fall into the first type: we carefully teach our children that these are dangerous activities, and we deliberately set out to be sure that they know there is a right way and a wrong way to participate in these activities."

" On the other hand, when we look at the other kind of dangerous activities, exemplified by drinking and sex, we seem to know only one word: 'Don't.' We do not bother to say there is a right way and there is a wrong way; we just say 'Don't!' We do not really want to produce abstainers; we have the illusion that they will follow our advice and be abstainers (in the case of sex, until marriage; and in the case of alcohol, until maturity) until they reach the magic age at which they can handle these activities. But as to the rights and wrongs of handling it when the great day comes, we choose to keep them in the dark. Now this is sheer hypocrisy. We are slowly awakening to the fact that we owe our children sex education in the home and in the school—education not dominated by the antisex league. We should be brave enough to tell them the truth; that drinking is normal behavior in the society, that moderate drinking need not lead to abuse; that drinking can be done in an appropriate civilized way without shame and guilt. Perhaps greater socialization in the direction of moderate drinking is part of the program we need for prevention of alcohol problems in the future" (1978, p. 154).

In a major publication generated by the work of the Cooperative Commission on the Study of Alcoholism, Wilkinson (1970) proposed that the minimum age for the purchase or consumption of alcohol on commercial premises, or to have them in public possession, should be eighteen rather than twenty-one. However, with meals in bona fide restaurants serving alcohol, those under eighteen should be permitted to order alcoholic drinks, provided they are accompanied by their parents or guardians who approve. Unless a college has a specific ethos against drinking, it should provide supervised places enabling students to drink wine or beer with their meals. On the other hand, drinking at home should be free of any minimum legal age restriction (Wilkinson, 1970).

Clearly, the basic assumption underlying the above proposals is that most people who are going to drink as adults should learn to manage alcohol at an early age and with their families. Retrospective studies of the early drinking experiences of problem and non-problem drinkers support the hypothesis that early drinking experiences may influence subsequent drinking behavior. Problem drinkers appear to begin their drinking at a later age than others, to have their first drinking experience outside the home, to become intoxicated the first time they drink, and to drink as an act of rebellion (open or secret) against parental authority (Plaut, 1967).

It has been said that if there is one universal characteristic that pervades humanity, it may be the urge to manipulate and control the behavior of others (Cisin, 1978) and nowhere is this more apparent than in the effort to control drinking behavior through legislative edict. The minimum drinking age laws in the United States have undergone over 100 modifications since their introduction in the 1930s (Wechsler and Sands, 1980, p. 2). The most recent series of increases in the minimum age will be no more successful than were those of the past. What we need are not more laws but the wisdom and courage to move beyond such simplistic answers to a complex social problem.

Footnote

[1]For example, as governor of Massachusetts, Michael Dukakis vetoed
two bills to lower the drinking age. His vetoes became a campaign issue
that apparently contributed to an unexpected defeat in his bid for reelection
in 1978 (Mosher, 1980).

REFERENCES

Alcoholism and Drug Addiction Research Foundation of Ontario (1961).
   "It's best to know". Alcoholism and Drug Addiction Research Foundation of Ontario: Toronto, Ontario.

Brehm, S. and Brehm, J.W. (1981). *Psychological reactance: A theory of
   freedom and control.* Academic Press: New York.

Cisin, I.H. (1978). Formal and informal social controls over drinking. In
   Ewing, J.A. and Rouse, B.A. (Eds.). *Drinking: alcohol in American
   society—issues and current research.* Nelson-Hall: Chicago, IL.

Engs, R.C. and Hanson, D.J. (1986). Age-specific alcohol prohibition and
   college student drinking problems. *Psychological Reports,* **59** 979-
   984.

Engs, R.C. and Hanson, D.J. (1988). University students' drinking patterns and problems: examining the effects of raising the purchase age,
   Public Health Reports, **103** 667-673.

Engs, R.C. and Hanson, D.J. (1989). Reactance theory: a test with
   collegiate drinking. *Psychological Reports,* **64** 1083-1086.

Ewing, J.A. and Rouse, B.A. (1976). Drinks, drinkers, and drinking. In
   Ewing, J.A. and Rouse, B.A. (Eds.). *Drinking: alcohol in American
   Society—issues and current research.* Nelson-Hall: Chicago, IL.

Globetti, G. (1976). Prohibition norms and teenage drinking. In Ewing,
   J.A. and Rouse, B.A. (Eds.). *Drinking: alcohol in American society—
   issues and current research.* Nelson-Hall: Chicago, IL.

Gonzalez, G.M. (1989). Effects of raising the drinking age among college
   students in Florida. *College Student Journal,* **23** 67-75.

Gusfield, J.R. (1962) Status conflicts and the changing ideologies of the
   American temperance movement. In Pittman, D.J. and Snyder, C.R.,
   (Eds.). *Society, culture and drinking patterns.* Wiley: New York.

Gusfield, J.R. (1963). *Symbolic Crusade: status politics and the American
   Temperance movement,* University of Illinois Press: Urbana, IL.

Hanson, D.J. (1972). *Norm qualities and deviant drinking behavior.*
   Syracuse University: Syracuse, NY, unpublished Ph. D. dissertation.

Hanson, D.J. (1982). The effectiveness of alcohol and drug education.
   Journal of Alcohol and Drug Education, **27** 1-13.

Hanson, D.J. and Hattauer, E. (n.d.). Effects of legislated drinking norms on college students' behaviors. Potsdam College: Potsdam, New York, unpublished paper.

Hingson, R., Merrigan, D., and Heeren, T. (1985). Effects of Massachusetts Raising its Legal Drinking Age from 18 to 20 on Deaths from Teenage Homicide, Suicide and Nontraffic Accidents. *Pediatric Clinics of North America*, **32** 221-233.

Knupfer, G. (1960). Use of alcoholic beverages by society and its cultural implications. *California's Health*, **18** 17-21.

Lotterhos, J.F., Glover, E.D., Holbert, D. and Barnes, R.C. (1988). Intentionality of college students regarding North Carolina's 21-year drinking age law. *International Journal of Addiction*, **23** 629-647.

Mason, T., Myszka, M., and Winniford, J. (1988). Assessing the impact of the 21-year old drinking age: the Texas A & M study. Paper presented at annual meeting of New York State Sociological Association, Oswego, New York, October 7-8.

Mosher, J.F. (1980). The history of youthful-drinking laws: implications for current policy. In Wechsler, H. (Ed.). *Minimum-drinking-age laws*. Lexington Books: Lexington, MA.

Patrick, C.H. (1952). *Alcohol, Culture and Society*. Duke University Press: Durham, NC.

Perkins, H.W. and Berkowitz, A.D. (1985). College students' attitudinal and behavioral responses to a drinking-age law change: stability and contradiction in the campus setting. Paper presented at the Annual Meeting of the N.Y. State Sociological Association, Rochester, October 18-19.

Perkins, H.W. and Berkowitz, A.D. (1987). Stability and contradiction in college students' drinking following a drinking law change. Paper presented at the Joint Meeting of the American College Personnel Association and the National Association of Student Personnel Administration, Chicago, March 15-18.

Plaut, T.F. (1967). *Alcohol problems: a report to the Nation by the Cooperative Commission on the Study of Alcoholism*. Oxford University Press: New York.

Room, R. (1976). Evaluating the effect of drinking laws on drinking. In Ewing, J.A. and Rouse, B.A., (Eds.). *Drinking: alcohol in American society—issues and current research*. Nelson-Hall: Chicago, IL.

Sterne, M.W., Pittman, D.J. and Coe, T. (1967). Teenagers, drinking and the law: study of arrest trends for alcohol-related offenses. In Pittman, D.J. (Ed.). *Alcoholism*. Harper & Row: New York.

Straus, R. and Bacon, S.D. (1953). *Drinking in College*. Yale University Press: New Haven, CT.

Tongue, A. (1976). 5,000 years of drinking. In Ewing, J.A. and Rouse, B.A. (Eds.). *Drinking: alcohol in American society—issues and current research.* Nelson-Hall: Chicago, IL.

Vingilis, E. and Smart, R., (1981). Effects of raising the legal drinking age in Ontario.*British Journal of Addiction,* **76** 415-424.

Wagenaar, A.C. (1983). *Alcohol, young drivers, and traffic accidents.* Lexington Books: Lexington, MA.

Wechsler, H. and McFadden, M. (1979). Drinking among college students in New England. *Journal of Studies on Alcohol,* **40** 969-996.

Wechsler, H. and Sands, E.S. (1980). Minimum-age laws and youthful drinking: an introduction. In Wechsler, H. (Ed.). *Minimum-drinking-age laws.* Lexington Books: Lexington, MA.

Wilkinson, R. (1970). *The prevention of drinking problems: alcohol control and cultural influences.* Oxford University Press: New York.

CHAPTER 11

Why We Need A Minimum-Purchase Age of 21

Richard J. Goeman, B.S.

With a current legal minimum-purchase age of 21 in the United States there has been, and continues to be, controversy. There are valid points concerning both sides of this issue, with either side offering fair grounds for debate. However, based on the literature, I have chosen to support the legal minimum-purchase age of 21. Available research appears to indicate this is the desired position and the current laws should remain unchanged. Although correct terminology states: "legal minimum-purchase age", for reasons of practicality, minimum age, minimum-drinking age, and legal age apply the same meaning. For this chapter these terms will be used interchangeably throughout.

For hundreds of years alcohol has been used for a variety of reasons. These include celebration, relaxation, and recreation (Wechsler, 1980). Also, before the practice of modern medicine alcohol was used incessantly as a medication to cure illness, as a vehicle for other drugs and potents, and for anesthesia.

Over the course of history beverage alcohol (i.e., beer, wine, and spirits) has been readily available and frequently misused, although it was rarely deemed hazardous. In fact, dating back as early as the eighteenth century some authorities considered alcohol wholesome and good for the soul. During this period of time, purchase and consumption of alcohol by young people were loosely governed. The majority of young persons drank while experiencing little opposition from authorities. Even during the temperance movement there were no restrictions placed solely on youth regarding their use of beverage alcohol. Instead, the entire population experienced restrictions through regulation of hours of sale, location of alcohol outlets, and high license fees (Wagenaar, 1983). Early in the twentieth century, laws were enacted to govern the sale of beverage alcohol to youth. This became one way in which the state could gain limited control over adolescent behavior. However, it was not until after the repeal of Prohibition in 1933 that strict minimum-age laws were implemented. At that time all fifty states passed laws concerning the legal

96

minimum-purchase age; most states set the age at 21 (Wagenaar, 1983). Beyond that point little else took place for nearly four decades regarding the minimum-age law.

In 1970, the Twenty-Sixth Amendment to the United States Constitution was passed by Congress. This Amendment granted the right to vote in Federal elections to citizens between the ages of 18 and 21. Shortly thereafter, a movement began that would allow other rights and privileges to the new "citizens of legal age." Over the next five years (1970-1975) twenty-nine states lowered their legal minimum-purchase age (Engs and Hanson, 1988).

Effects of the Reduced Drinking-Age Law

With the reduction of these laws, controversy within the realms of academia, politics, law-enforcement, and industry quickly arose regarding the wisdom of such choices (Works, 1973; Distilled Spirits Council of the United States, 1973; Bowen and Kagay, 1973; Zylman, 1973). Some individuals in the political arena argued that huge increases in alcohol-related automobile accidents involving youth occurred immediately after lowering the minimum age (Michigan Council on Alcohol Problems, 1973). Other arguments surfacing during that time indicated these increases were due to changes in police-reporting techniques, increases in the number of young drivers, and long-term trends concerning alcohol consumption and the incidence of automobile accidents (Zylman, 1974). However, by the mid-1970s, controlled studies of the effects of reduced minimum-age laws were becoming available in the United States and Canada. Although the degree of magnitude varied among the states and provinces studied, the majority of research concluded that lowering the minimum legal- purchase age led to significant increases in alcohol-related automobile accidents among young drivers (Wagenaar, 1983).

Research was accomplished concerning the rate of fatal automobile accidents among fifteen-to-seventeen-year-old and eighteen-to-twenty-year-old drivers in Michigan, Wisconsin, and Ontario where the minimum drinking-age had been lowered. The rate of fatal accidents in those states and province, for 36 months prior to and 12 months after the law change, was compared with the rate of fatal accidents in the bordering states of Indiana, Illinois, and Minnesota where the minimum-age law was not lowered. Significant increases in the number of fatal automobile accidents were found among all the ages previously listed in the states and province that chose to lower their minimum-drinking age. The rate was considerably higher for Michigan and Ontario than for Wisconsin. The lower rate in Wisconsin may have been due to a less drastic change in availability of alcohol. In Wisconsin, eighteen-to-twenty-year- olds had always been able to purchase beer and wine (Williams, Rich, Zador, and Robertson, 1974).

Studies conducted with the state of Massachusetts reported identical results. Research on automobile accidents using a "time series" method measured the rate of accident involvement of individuals aged fifteen-to-seventeen, eighteen-to-twenty, twenty-one-to-twenty-three, and twenty-four and over. After the minimum-age was reduced, eighteen-to-twenty-year-old drivers experienced significant increases in total fatal automobile accidents, alcohol-related fatal automobile accidents, and alcohol-related property damage accidents. However, there were no significant changes for drivers aged twenty-one-to-twenty- three and twenty-four and over (Cucchiaro, Ferreira, and Sicherman, 1974). Monthly time series was also the method used to compare data collected from Maine, Michigan, and Vermont where the minimum age was lowered, with Louisiana, Pennsylvania, and Texas, where the minimum-age remained constant over the study period. These results revealed a significant increase in the rate of involvement in alcohol-related automobile accidents among young drivers in Maine and Michigan. It was suggested that lack of significant change in rates of automobile accidents in Vermont was due to the eighteen-year-old drinking age in the bordering state of New York (Douglass, Filkins, and Clark, 1974).

Three years later, Douglass and Freedman (1977) replicated parts of the above study. Results produced from that effort showed that the alarming rate of automobile accidents involving alcohol and young drivers had persisted over the first four years after the minimum-age was lowered (1972-1975). In yet a third study done in the state of Michigan, researchers using an entirely different analytical technique than Douglass were able to observe the same significant increase in alcohol-related automobile accidents among young drivers (Flora, Filkins, and Compton, 1978).

One of the most startling discoveries in opposition to reducing the legal age evolved from a study done in London, Ontario. Here, researchers examined the rates of automobile accidents in drivers aged sixteen-to-twenty and twenty-four years old for a six year period (1968 through 1973). Following a minimum-age reduction in Ontario, alcohol-related automobile accidents among drivers aged eighteen-to-twenty increased 150 to 300 percent. In the twenty-four-year-old age group, only a 20 percent increase in alcohol-related automobile accidents was noted (Whitehead et. al., 1975). After an additional two years of examining accident data, Whitehead (1977) was able to show a permanently higher rate in this type of automobile accident among young drivers after reducing the minimum drinking age.

In the province of Saskatchewan, researchers were able to document that after the legal-age was lowered from twenty-one to nineteen in April

1970, drivers aged sixteen-to-twenty experienced a 20 to 50 percent increase in automobile accidents involving alcohol. After the legal age was again reduced, this time to eighteen, in June 1972, this same group of drivers experienced further increases in automobile accidents where alcohol was the major contributing factor (Shattuck and Whitehead, 1976).

Researchers studying the effect of allowing young people to drink alcohol in Alberta, Canada examined the rate of drivers with blood-alcohol concentrations of 0.08 percent or greater who had been fatally injured in automobile accidents. Alcohol related automobile accidents increased 118 percent among drivers aged fifteen-to-nineteen after the legal age was lowered (Bako, MacKenzie, and Smith, 1976).

The Economic and Other Costs to Society

The cost to society regarding the effects of the minimum-age law and use of alcohol in general has been insurmountable. The author here is not opposed to drinking alcohol. However, the manner and degree to which it is consumed in this country indicates a serious dilemma.

In the span of time since the legal-age was lowered, the United States has spent billions of dollars annually in health care, social services, property damage, and lost production (Berry and Boland, 1977; Schifrin, Hartsog, and Brand,1980). Unfortunately, the trend continues.

During a subcommittee hearing of the U.S. House of Representatives in October 1983, a bill was introduced which favored prohibiting the sale of alcoholic beverages to persons under 21 years of age. It reads: "Each year, 25,000 people are killed by drunken drivers. In disproportionate numbers, these drivers appear to be young people. The twenty-year old age category is a particular problem. Each year, highway accidents involving alcohol create economic losses of over $20 billion, and incalculable losses in terms of human suffering, wasted potential, social dislocation, and death" (Florio 1983).

A recent study done by the Insurance Institute for Highway Safety noted that when there was an increase in fatal automobile accidents for teenage drivers, especially accidents involving alcohol, a direct correlation existed between the legal minimum- drinking age and the incidence of these accidents.

In 1984, in New York state alone, the State Division of Alcoholism and Alcohol Abuse projected that a 21-year-old minimum drinking-age would save on an annual basis 60-70 lives, 1,200 serious injuries, and 75 million dollars in societal costs (Padavan, 1984). The organization, Mothers Against Drunk Drivers (MADD, 1983) reported that 25 cents of every auto insurance premium dollar goes to pay for damage done by drunk drivers.

These figures are astronomical when one considers a state such as Michigan, where only high-price "No-Fault" insurance is permitted. What our society pays in human suffering, wasted potential, and death is beyond anyone's comprehension.

Positive Outcome Studies

Contrasting all the studies reporting negative results, there are many that report positive after states and provinces raise the legal-age. For example, Maine experienced, between 1974 and 1979, a reduction from 14 to 20 percent in automobile accidents involving alcohol after raising their legal-age (Klein, 1981). Research completed in the state of Illinois revealed a 9 percent decrease in nighttime single-vehicle accidents among nineteen-to-twenty-year-old drivers after raising their legal-age from nineteen to twenty-one in January 1980 (Maxwell, 1981). One investigation examined fatal automobile accident involvement from 1975 to 1980 in nine states that chose to raise their minimum-age. Bordering states were used in comparison which did not raise their minimum-age. Eight of the nine states experienced decreases in young driver involvement in nighttime fatal automobile accidents after the minimum-age was raised; accident reductions ranged from 6 to 75 percent. Averaging across the nine states studied, the researchers concluded that increasing the legal minimum-purchase age in any given state should result in a 28 percent reduction in nighttime fatal automobile accidents among the age group affected by the legal change (Williams, Zador, Harris, and Karpf, 1981). It should be noted here that Cook and Tauchen (1982) estimated the effect of allowing youth access to alcohol by reducing the drinking-age, using nationwide United States data on the number of young people killed in automobile accidents. Results of the fatality data pooled across states and years revealed that a 7 percent increase in the number of youth killed in automobile accidents was correlated with reductions in the legal minimum- purchase age.

Other studies have shown that when minimum-age laws are lowered, there is an increase in alcohol-related problems other than driving while intoxicated. For example, Engs and Hanson (1986) report that in states with under 21 minimum-age laws, a higher percentage of students reported drinking an alcoholic beverage while driving, missing classes due to drinking, receiving lower grades due to drinking, and indicating they thought they had a drinking problem. In other research, it may be noted that among New England college students, 29 percent of the men and 11 percent of the women were classified as heavy drinkers (Wechsler and McFadden, 1979). Half of these students reported experiencing problems related to drinking, such as blackouts, fighting, and trouble with authorities (Wechsler and Rohman, 1981).

The apparent relationship between age and unsafe and irresponsible behavior while drinking or drunk driving is fairly easy to document. During adolescence and early adulthood (15 to 24), accidents, homicides, and suicides account for 75 percent of all fatalities. However, the activity generating the highest number of deaths in this age group is automobile accidents. Whatever the cause of death, alcohol is clearly implicated in at least 50 percent of the fatalities for this age population. During late adolescence and early adulthood, male and female alike have a higher risk of incurring some negative consequence(s) associated with use of alcohol than during any other point in their lifetime. Many individuals, professional or otherwise, acknowledge that a reduction in alcohol consumption by persons under the age of 21 is a necessary and effective means for reducing alcohol-related automobile accidents and other problems associated with the use of alcohol. These individuals cite data showing that when the legal minimum-purchase age is lowered, there is a significant increase in the rate of automobile accidents and cases in which young people operated a motor vehicle while intoxicated (Wechsler, 1980).

In summary, the information in review here indicates that the majority of studies concerning the impact of lower legal drinking-ages on involvement in automobile accidents and other alcohol-related problems continue to show significant increases. Person most often involved with these increases are those who under the new law become eligible to purchase alcohol; usually eighteen-to-twenty-year-old individuals. Therefore, to prevent further drinking and other related problems among youth in our society, the current legal minimum purchase age of 21 should continue.

REFERENCES

Bako, G., MacKenzie, W.C., and Smith, E.S.O. (1976). "The Effect of Legislated Lowering of the Drinking Age on Total Highway Accidents among Young Drivers in Alberta, 1970-1972." *Canadian Journal of Public Health*, **38** 161-163.

Berry, R.E., Jr. and Brand, J.P. (1977). *The Economic Cost of Alcohol Abuse*. Free Press: New York.

Bowen, B.D. and Kagay, M.R. (1973). *Report to the White House Conference on Youth: The Impact of Lowering the Age of Majority to 18.* White House Conference on Youth: Washington, DC.

Cook, P.J. and Tauchen, G. (1982). *The Effect of Minimum Drinking Age Legislation on Youthful Auto Fatalities 1970- 1977.* Unpublished manuscript.

Cucchiaro, S., Ferreira, Jr., and Sicherman, A. (1974). The Effect of the 18-year-old Drinking Age on Auto Accidents. Massachusetts Institute of Technology, Operations Research Center. Cambridge, MA.

Distilled Spirits Council of the United States. (1973). "Survey of Minimum Age Law Experience on Drinking/Driving." *DISCUS Newsletter*, 330.

Douglass, R.L., Filkins, L.D., and Clark, F.A. (1974). The Effect of Lower Legal Drinking Ages on Youth Crash Involvement. *The University of Michigan, Highway Safety Research Institute*. Ann Arbor, MI.

Douglass, R.L. and Freedman, J.A. (1977). Alcohol-related Casualties and Alcohol Beverage Market Response to Beverage Alcohol Availability Policies in Michigan. *The University of Michigan, Highway Safety Research Institutes*. Ann Arbor, MI.

Engs, R.C. and Hanson, D.J. (1986). Age-Specific Alcohol Prohibition and College Students' Drinking Problems. *Psychological Reports*, **59** 979-984.

Engs, R.C. and Hanson, D.J. (1988). University Students' Drinking Patterns and Problems: Examining the Effects of Raising the Purchase Age. *Public Health Reports*, **103** (6) 667-673.

Flora, J.D., Filkins, L.D., and Compton, C.D. (1978). Alcohol Involvement in Michigan Fatal Accidents: 1968-1976. *The University of Michigan, Highway Safety Research Institute*. Ann Arbor, Michigan.

Florio, J.J. (1983). *Prohibit the Sale of Alcoholic Beverages to Persons Under 21 Years of Age*. H.R. 3870. U.S. House of Representatives, Committee on Energy and Commerce, Subcommittee on Commerce, Transportation, and Tourism. Washington, DC.

Klein, T. (1981). *The Effect of Raising the Minimum Legal Drinking Age on Traffic Accidents in the State of Maine*. U.S. National Highway Traffic Safety Administration. Washington, DC.

Maxwell, D.M. (1981). *Impact Analysis of the Raised Legal Age in Illinois*. U.S. National Traffic Safety Administration: Washington, DC.

Mothers Against Drunk Drivers (MADD). (1983). *Striking Back at the Drunk Driver*, pp. 582-583.

Padavan, F. (1984). *"21"—It Makes Sense/Education, Prevention, Enforcement, Raising the Drinking Age*. New York, New York.

Schifrin, L.G., Hartsog, C.E., and Brand, D.H. (1980). "Costs of Alcoholism and Alcohol Abuse and Their Relation to Alcohol Research." In *Institute of Medicine, ed., Alcoholism, Alcohol Abuse and Related Problems: Opportunities for Research*, pp.165-186. National Academy Press: Washington, DC.

Shattuck, D. and Whitehead, P.C. (1976). *Lowering the Drinking Age in Saskatchewan: The Effect on Collisions among Young Drivers*. Department of Health: Saskatchewan, Canada.

Wagenaar, A.C. (1983). *Alcohol, Young Drivers, and Traffic Accidents.* Lexington Books, Lexington, Massachusetts.

Wechsler, H. and McFadden, M. (1979). Drinking among College Students in New England. *Journal of Studies on Alcohol,* **40** 969-996.

Wechsler, H. and Rohman, M. (1981). Extensive Users of Alcohol among College Students. *Journal of Studies on Alcohol,* **42** 149-155.

Wechsler, H. (1980). *Minimum - Drinking - Age Laws.* Lexington Books: Lexington, MA.

Whitehead, P.C., Craig, J., Langford, N., MacArthur, C., Stanton, B., and Ferrence, R.G. (1975). "Collision Behavior of Young Drivers: Impact of the Change in the Age of Majority."*Journal of Studies on Alcohol,* **36** 1208-1223.

Whitehead, P.C. (1977). *Alcohol and Young Drivers: Impact and Implications of Lowering the Drinking Age.* Non-medical use of Drugs Directorate. Department of National Health and Welfare, Health Protection Branch, Research Bureau: Ottawa, Ontario.

Williams, A.F., Rich, R.F., Zador, P.L., and Robertson, L.S. (1974). The Legal Minimum Drinking Age and Fatal Motor Vehicle Crashes. *Insurance Institute for Highway Safety*: Washington, DC.

Williams, A.F., Zador, P.L., Harris, S.S., and Karpf, R.S. (1981). "The Effects of Raising the Legal Minimum Drinking Age on Fatal Crash Involvement." *Insurance Institute for Highway Safety*: Washington, DC.

Works, D.A. (1973). "Statement on 18-Year Old Drinking." *Journal of Alcohol and Drug Education,* **18** 14.

Zylman, R. (1974). "Drinking and Driving after It's Legal to Drink at 18: Is the Problem Real?" *Journal of Alcohol and Drug Education,* **20** 48-52.

Zylman, R. (1973). "When It is Legal to Drink at 18: What Should We Expect?" *Journal of Traffic Safety Education,* **20** 9-10.

SHOULD WE HAVE MANDATORY DRUG TESTING AT THE WORKSITE?

CHAPTER 12

Mandatory Random Testing Needs To Be Undertaken At The Worksite

Robert L. DuPont, MD

Introduction

In the late 1980s the workplace took center stage in the national drug abuse prevention effort with the focus being the drug test. No other aspect of the War on Drugs involved such a broad segment of the nation as the drug test at work. Urine tests for abused drugs had previously been limited to forensic, drug abuse treatment, and criminal justice settings (DuPont and Saylor, 1989). The drug test at work became the most controversial aspect of drug abuse prevention efforts.

Drug testing technology and practice evolved rapidly throughout the 1980s at the pinnacle of modern biotechnology, becoming effective, inexpensive, and reliable as a means of detecting recent use of specific drugs, including drugs that cause impairment in the workplace (Schotten-feld, 1989). The application of this technology in the workplace was justified by the rapid rise in the percentage of workers who used illicit drugs. In 1988, for example, the National Institute on Drug Abuse (NIDA) estimated that 12% of full-time employed Americans between the ages of 20 and 40 used an illicit drug in the previous month (National Institute on Drug Abuse, 1989). Among high school seniors entering the workforce, the levels of drug use were even higher; in 1988, 18% reported current use of marijuana and 3% use of cocaine. High school dropouts had even higher rates of illicit drug use (University of Michigan, 1989).

Drug use had many serious costs in the workplace, including the estimated $1,000 paid by each worker each year because of the effects of drug and alcohol abuse, whether or not that worker used drugs or alcohol. Included in this estimate are the costs of lost productivity, accidents, and health cost of drug-and alcohol- abusing workers. This involuntary Chemical Dependence Tax has grave impacts on the nation's productivity and competitiveness (DuPont, 1989a). Cutting that tax by preventing drug problems is the goal of drug testing in the workplace with benefits in increased wages, improved health, lowered product costs, and improved product quality.

When the drug test came to the workplace there were intense controversies over any form of testing. For example, there were charges that the
tests were inherently unreliable and that they identified as drug users
people who were merely in the vicinity of someone using marijuana. It was
also claimed by critics of testing at work that common over-the-counter
and health food supplements would be misinterpreted as drug positive
results (Hawks and Chaing, 1986). The publication of guidelines for
workplace drug testing by the US. Department of Health and Human
Services (1988), federal requirements for drug testing within the federal
workforce and among many federally regulated workplaces, and a series
of court cases all occurring between 1987 and 1989, shifted the controversy about drug testing away from the question of the reliability or
legality of testing.

By 1990 most opponents of testing conceded that when done properly,
drug tests were able to accurately and reliably identify recent drug use. The
new battleground in workplace drug testing focused on two critical, unresolved areas. The first was whether testing was warranted for workers
where there was no "safety or security" risk in their work. In the view of
the critics of testing, drug tests at work might be justified for transportation
or nuclear power workers, but not for most workers whose jobs were not
safety-sensitive. The second battleground in the early 1990s about drug
testing at work was whether testing should be required for workers on a
"random" basis, that is, without individualized suspicion that the particular employee was impaired by drugs at the time the drug test was requested.
This paper addresses the second of these two points, arguing that random,
unindicated, drug testing at work is desirable.

About the Author

The reader of a chapter on so controversial and personal a subject as
random drug testing in the workplace deserves to know something about
the author. I am a medical doctor, a psychiatrist, who has worked for over
two decades in drug abuse prevention and treatment.

The only drug users who have recovered from their addiction, in my
experience, have recovered because someone else cared enough about
them to insist that they become drug free. Surely the process of recovery
requires that the former drug users ultimately adopt drug-free values and
goals themselves, but the beginning of recovery is almost always the
insistence of one or more people in the drug users' lives to end their drug
use.

With reference to the specific topic of this chapter, I have seen
hundreds of drug abusers who have recovered control of their lives
because their employers put their employment on the line in what is called

"job jeopardy." Bluntly, that means, "You work here, you don't use drugs; you use drugs, you don't work here." This new and, for most people, still unfamiliar approach has become known as Tough Love. It happens in the workplace just the way it does in families (DuPont, 1984). Even more personally, I have been drug tested at work for two decades. All staff members of the two organizations I work with are randomly tested for drugs. I am a "survivor" of random drug tests at work, and so are all the people with whom I work.

My views about drugs in the workplace, including my support for random drug tests at work, have been published in a variety of professional and general books, journals, and newspapers (DuPont, 1984, 1989a, 1989b, 1989c, 1989d, 1989e).

"Random" Drug Testing Defined

A drug test in the workplace today means a urine sample collected in a private, but secure, medical environment similar to routine urine collection at a doctor's office. The sample is tested to be sure it comes from the tested employee and has not been adulterated. Direct observation of the urine collection is not required in the workplace unless there is reason to believe the employee will falsify the drug test. The drug test is analyzed by a two-step process in a high-technology clinical laboratory. This drug test process includes careful collection, chain-of-custody, medical review, and retention of all positive samples for one year after collection. This total system, which is now standard in workplace drug testing, permits retest if an employee claims to have been falsely identified as a drug user. Using this system there are no false positives (US. Department of Health and Human Services, 1988; DuPont, 1989a, 1989b).

This system does not detect use of medicines, except for those that are on occasion abused by drug users. Thus, the workplace drug testing system does not identify use of birth control pills, heart medicines, or antidepressants. Workplace drug tests only detect use of "controlled substances," or drugs that are either purely illegal (such as marijuana and PCP), or drugs that can be used either medically or nonmedically (such as painkillers, antianxiety medicines, and sleeping pills). Medical use is separated from nonmedical use of these substances by a medical review officer, a trained physician who sees the drug tests before they are reported to the employer. Only urine drug tests taken at work that show recent use of potentially impaired drugs, for which there is no medical prescription for that employee, are reported to the employer as positive. Medical use of substances, such as Valium or codeine, are reported as "negative" tests.

"Random testing" needs to be contrasted to the other two common types of drug tests in the workplace. The first is "pre-employment" testing;

that is, urine tests for recent drug use taken at the time a person applies for a new job. The second common form of drug test at work is "for-cause" testing. These are tests of a particular person because he or she shows some particular signs of possible drug use. Examples of causes for drug tests at work include appearing to be under the influence of a drug, being repeatedly late for work, or having an accident. Other causes justifying a drug test for a particular employee are a past history of treatment for drug abuse, and abnormal behavior at work (e.g., fighting or falling asleep). Neither pre-employment nor for-cause testing is now either particularly uncommon or controversial in the American workplace.

In contrast to pre-employment and for-cause testing, random testing remains controversial in nonmilitary workplaces in the United States. Random testing for drugs means that a particular worker is chosen at random to be tested at a particular time. Usually this selection is done by computer with a small percentage of workers being selected to be tested each day with only a few hours of notice. With random drug testing, every worker is subject to being drug tested every day the worker is at work regardless of how the worker is performing on that day.

The Uses of Random Drug Testing in the Workplace

If all drug users were obviously impaired at work, random testing would not be needed because supervisors could be trained to detect drug-caused impairment. They could, having identified a potentially impaired worker, request a for-cause drug test. Unfortunately, there is clear evidence that most illicit drug users do not appear to be impaired at work, even when drugs are having a profound effect on their performance. After 20 years working with drug abusers, I always insist on drug testing my patients simply because I cannot tell when they are using drugs, even when I spend 50 minutes talking with them in my office. If I cannot identify recent drug use, how can even the most highly trained supervisor?

Why should someone who has never used an illegal drug welcome a random drug test at work? Unless those non-using employees are tested, employees who do use illicit drugs will not be tested. The non-user of illicit drugs who is drug tested at work is in the same situation as those who have no intention of ever hijacking an airplane when they walk through metal detectors at airports; if they do not submit to the slight inconvenience of going through the detector, then hijackers will not be deterred or, failing deterrence, detected.

Although most drug use does not produce easily detected symptoms, some drug use causes such flagrant symptoms of impairment that supervisor training is worth the investment. Supervisors, and co-workers, can identify the most outrageous examples of drug-caused impairment on the job. Even when signs of recent drug use are identified, such as irritable mood or the appearance of fatigue, these behaviors are often caused by other factors in the employees' lives. Thus, many for-cause tests for drugs will be negative. Supervisors are usually reluctant to ask for a drug test if there is any doubt that the abnormal behavior is caused by drug abuse. Employees are usually not pleased when a supervisor singles them out for a drug test. Supervisors are generally not pleased when the requested for-cause drug test comes back showing no recent drug use. Thus, when a company has a for-cause drug test program they typically do few drug tests, even when high percentages of their employees are using illicit drugs. This means that for-cause testing is a weak deterrent to drug use in the workplace because it is seldom used. Drug users in the workforce typically have a high level of confidence that their drug use will not be detected because they do not feel impaired and they do not believe they will be drug tested. All too often they are wrong in believing they are not impaired, but right in believing that they will not be tested.

On good reason to do random tests is that most drug-caused impairments are not identified when companies rely on for-cause tests. Another good reason is that such tests are routine and do not require a supervisor to confront an employee with the suspicion that he or she is using drugs. The military experience using random tests since 1982 and the smaller civilian experience with random testing over the last few years have established these two central points: Random testing is fair and it is effective. Random drug testing at work achieves its primary goal of preventing drug use and drug-caused problems, without demoralizing workers or forcing large numbers of workers either to leave their jobs or to enter treatment. It does this by making the drug-free workplace a reality. Random testing at work give workers at all levels a strong, practical reason to stop using illicit drugs: If they do not stop using illicit drugs they will lose their jobs (National Institute on Drug Abuse, Office of Workplace Initiatives, 1989; Walsh and Gust, 1989).

Throughout this chapter I have focused on employees in safety and security positions, emphasizing that they are the most appropriate employees to be subjected to random drug testing. The same arguments that apply to these employees apply to all others: Random testing is the best, fairest, and most cost-effective way to prevent illicit drug use. Focusing on only those industries with safety-related jobs discriminates against all other employees. All workers stand to gain equally from random drug testing. The reason for beginning with safety and security roles is not because they are more important or because the employees in their other jobs are not equally benefited by random testing, it simply reflects the controversies over the use of random testing in the workplace today.

It is my strong belief that any employee subject to drug testing is helped by that testing. That randomly tested employee is not harmed by testing, whether or not that employee is in a safety-related job, and whether or not that employee uses illicit drugs. Anyone concerned for employee welfare should be arguing for random drug tests in the workplace today. Despite this belief, however, I recognize that many people are unfamiliar with random drug tests. These sometimes fearful people may even believe that such tests are a threat to them. Much of the media and many apologists for illicit drug use as well as many opponents of testing actively fuel these fears. Out of consideration for these fears, and the political and legal conflicts they support, I am respectful of the necessity of time passing before random drug testing is universally applied in the American workplace.

Random drug testing, still unfamiliar in the civilian workplace, is not for everyone. There are important contractual and financial issues in many workplace settings when it comes to random testing. There is an important educational requirement before beginning random testing to be sure everyone in the company understands the system and how it works. Particular concern needs to be shown to non-using employees who inappropriately but understandably may fear identification of their use of legitimate medicines. Concerns about the reliability of the entire drug testing system need to be dealt with fully.

Societal Implications of Random Drug Tests at Work

After two decades of dealing with the drug abuse epidemic, it is becoming increasingly clear that the drug abuse epidemic will end only when the demand for drugs dries up. The recent calls for drug legalization again point out the terrible incentive provided for illicit drug traffickers by the huge demand of the 14.5 million Americans who now use illicit drugs on a regular basis. Seventy percent of these current American users of illicit drugs are employed (DuPont, 1989c; DuPont and Goldfarb, 1990). If this nation is to achieve the goal of drug abuse prevention and dry up the demand for drugs, the first and best place to act is in the workplace. We can give a clear signal to Americans of all ages, races, and social classes: Using illicit drugs is incompatible with work. Random drug testing in the workplace is the best way to make this point.

REFERENCES

DuPont, R.L. (1984). *Getting Tough on Gateway Drugs: A Guide for the Family.* American Psychiatric Press: Washington, DC.
DuPont, R.L. (1989a). Drugs in the American workplace: Conflict and

opportunity. Part I: Epidemiology of drugs at work. *Social Pharmacology*, **3** 133-146.

DuPont, R.L. (1989b). Drugs in the American workplace: Conflict and opportunity. Part II: Controversies in workplace drug use prevention. *Social Pharmacology*, **3** 147-164.

DuPont, R.L. (1989c). Never trust anyone under 40: What employers should know about drugs in the workplace. *Policy Review*, Spring 1989, 52-57

DuPont, R.L. (1989d). Workplace urine tests will cut drug use. *Newsday*, March 14, 1989.

DuPont, R.L. (1989e). A doctor's case for random drug tests. *The Washington Times*, March 27,1989.

DuPont, R.L. and Goldfarb, R.L. (1990). Drug legalization: Asking for trouble. *The Washington Post*, January 26, 1990.

DuPont, R.L. and Saylor, K.E. (1989). *Urine Testing in Drug Treatment: Harnessing Technology to Promote Recovery*. Institute for Behavior & Health, Inc.: Rockville, MD. (unpublished).

Hawks, R.L. and Chaing, C.N. (1986). *Urine Testing for Drugs of Abuse*. Research Monograph #73. National Institute on Drug Abuse: Rockville, MD.

National Institute on Drug Abuse (1989). Highlights of the 1988 National Household Survey on Drug Abuse. *NIDA Capsules*, August 1989.

National Institute on Drug Abuse, Office of Workplace Initiatives. (1989). *Drugs in the Workplace: Research and Evaluation Data*. DHHS publication number (ADM)89-1612, NIDA Research Monograph 91. National Institute on Drug Abuse: Rockville, MD.

Schottenfeld, R.S. (1989). Drug and alcohol testing in the workplace — objectives, pitfalls, and guidelines. *Am J Drug Alcohol Abuse*, **15** 413-527.

University of Michigan. (1989). Teen drug use continues decline, according to U-M survey. Cocaine down for second straight year; crack begins decline in 1988. University of Michigan, News and Information Services, Institute for Social Research: Ann Arbor. February 24, 1989. (News release jointly with the Alcohol, Drug Abuse and Mental Health Administration and the National Institute on Drug Abuse.)

US. department of Health and Human Services. (1988). Mandatory guidelines for federal workplace drug testing programs. *Federal Register*, April 11, 1988.

Walsh, J.M. and Gust, S.W. (Eds). (1989) *Workplace Drug Abuse Policy*. DHHS publication number (ADM)89-1610. National Institute on Drug Abuse, Office of Workplace Initiatives: Rockville, MD.

CHAPTER 13

Drug Testing: Probable Cause Only

Thomas J. Delaney Jr., CEAP

In July, 1983, President Ronald Reagan established a "President's Commission on Organized Crime." President Reagan picked a long-time Federal Judge from New York City, Irving R. Kaufman as Chairman. On April 3, 1986, the Commission issued its reports. One of its four reports was devoted to drug abuse. It was widely reported at that time (Panner and Christakis, 1986) that the Commission called for wide spread urine testing of employees to determine the presence of "drugs" in their bodies. Interestingly enough, Judge Kaufman wrote an article (*New York Times,* October 26, 1988) seeming to distance himself from this thrust only months later. Two quotes by Judge Kaufman himself should have given pause to the rush of drug testing. They were:

> On September 15, President Reagan signed an executive order
> calling for drug testing of broad range of the Federal Government's 2.8
> million civilian employees earmarking about $56 million for the under-
> taking in the first year. The increased use of drug testing by government
> agencies and private employers—more than a quarter of the Fortune 500
> companies test job applicants—is part of a larger trend in society's war
> on drug abuse, with a pronounced shift of emphasis to the drug user. But
> to inquire whether someone is for or against drug testing in the workplace
> is really to pose a question without content, the variables are so great. Is
> the drug test to be administered to Government workers—in which case
> the Fourth Amendment's protection from unreasonable searches and
> seizure must be satisfied—or to employees in private industry? Does a
> given company intend to test its employees at random or will a worker
> be asked to submit to urinalysis only when he exhibits some sign of drug
> abuse? Are employees to be included in the screening or only job
> applicants? (1988, p.52).

After a lengthy article, Judge Kaufman then concludes:

> Unfortunately, the debate on drug screening has been rich in
> emotion and hyperbole. Not all proposals for drug testing are the brain-

child of Big Brother or a knee-jerk reaction to saturation media coverage of drug abuse. Some screening programs may genuinely represent an effort to keep the workplace drug-free in order to insure safety and improve performance. But, heightened sensitivity to concerns about privacy, accuracy and legality are indispensable. (p. 69).

Perhaps Judge Kaufman was a minority on his own commission. Perhaps, as a long time jurist who committed his career to justice for all Americans, he was shocked how this one part of the Commission report was being used to turn a disease into a moral problem, embarking on a dangerous course of mixing private business with government law enforcement or to promote the worst motives of vengeance and greed of the rich and mighty over the every day working person. No matter what his motives, he was too late and "the horse was out of the barn." Attorney General Meese was on the eve of recommending that employers search lockers and send corporate snitches to bars to root out the drug using fiends from factories and offices. The First Lady was playing her best role in acting out grandmotherly fantasies to school children throughout the country with one line, i.e., "Just Say No." And, in a greater Washington tradition of every"war", the profiteers and opportunists had smelled the opportunities available in the urine testing business. Government careers and private fortunes have flourished in the insuring madness to impose random testing on American workers (only the alert lobbying of the Canadian Ambassador to the United States has thus far prevented efforts to export this hysteria to their countries)

Perhaps the content of the Organized Crime Commission Report would have not even made a difference as long as drug use was defined as a criminal justice issue. The history of public health is filled with successful examples of cooperation between health and police professionals to control plagues and other communicable diseases. But a sense of history and balanced efforts are not ingredients of public policy making in an era of "spin doctors" and fifteen second TV "bits" back to the voters.

In his October 1988 quotation, Judge Kaufman cites the number of Fortune 500 companies doing applicants testing. He fell for a favorite ploy of the urine testing cartel. In the second Reagan term, the government bureaucrats and the drug testing merchants were forever bombarding the press with announcements of Fortune 500 companies who were doing urine testing. What kind of testing, how often, company wide or one small group, what happened to the results? None of this mattered. Clearly, the game plan was to stampede American industry to get on board. They were told that this was war against a foe that threatened the very existence of our society. One call from the White House or Defense Department to the CEO

113

of a government contractor usually communicated the message. Can we say that you are testing employees? One or ten thousand did not make any difference, we will just announce that another Fortune 500 company has agreed to do drug testing. If that did not quite do the trick, how would the CEO and his wife like to be considered for invitation to an upcoming function at the White House?

Of course, there were a few left-wing extremists who thought that there might be some legal or constitutional objections to drug testing. This was the other reason for the push to panic public opinion that urine testing was essential if the Republic was to survive. Some of them still cling to the widely regarded as naive assumption that courts dispassionately apply the appropriate laws to the facts of a particular case and render a politically neutral decision. But to listen to TV anchors and drug testing enthusiasts tell it, there is apparently some undefined point in the public opinion polls where the courts are to disregard rights and render the decision demanded by the masses. So, government spokespeople tell us that 80+% of Americans favor drug testing with the implication that this is supposed to mean something in applying the law.

Judges, Senators, and Congressmen read papers, too. The true believers in the urine testing crowd certainly were not going to pass up the opportunity to influence them. The Attorney General would certainly appreciate the chance to tell his side of the story to your editorial board!

In the latter half of the 1980s, there was an all out offensive to institute all kinds of drug testing in the American workforce. (By the way, there was an interesting reaction in the State Legislatures where a number of bills were passed to assure that drug testing that was being pushed from Washington would be done fairly in their states. The "test them all—what do they have to be afraid of" crowd in Washington is now pushing for a Federal law that would take away power of the States to enact safeguards in drug testing). Although, American industry is increasingly questioning the utility of such tests, the drug testing advocates have not given up. There is an awful lot of money still to be made from this. However, a reader may legitimately ask, "What are the alternatives? Isn't there a drug abuse problem in the country and isn't drug testing the way to get drugs out of the workplace?"

There is not one but several drug problems in the country. On of these is a major law enforcement problem. It involves not only the arrest of people who are violating drug laws but large numbers who violate other laws while under the influence of drugs or who commit crimes to support their habit. But the criminal justice issues are beyond the scope of this paper. They should also be beyond the role of employers and labor unions. Those who suggest that there be random testing of employees are giving

114

support to those who would make employers and unions into arms of law enforcement. Not only does that violate a long standing tradition in this country, but it opens up a "Pandora's Box" that will let out a police state in the United States. Simple solutions to complex problems often produce more complex problems. This would certainly be the case in random drug testing of employees. As long as drug use is perceived as a law enforcement issue in this country, employers will do well to avoid random drug testing. If not, the criminal justice system will want access to test results.

In a letter printed in the *New York Times* of October 4, 1986, Professor Leonard H. Glantz of Boston University well stated the problem with mixing law enforcement and job performance:

> "You also confound two separate issues when you introduce public safety concerns regarding the ability of certain individuals in delicate positions, such as air traffic controllers, to competently perform their jobs. Random testing for illegal drugs is being sold as a public safety measure, but it, in fact, is a law enforcement measure.
>
> ...the proposed tests are for **illegal** drugs only. . .
>
> ...It should not be forgotten that the stimulus for the Federal Government's recent fervor for random urinalysis come from the President's Commission on Organized Crime. It is a bad idea as a matter of both law and policy to turn employers, either public or private, into arms of law enforcement agencies.
>
> ...the recent drug-testing craze turns our attention away from the essential and more complex issue of how accurately it assesses job performance."

Indeed, the "Achilles' heel" of random testing is the lack of a sound basis to link drug use with impaired job performance. In the *Washington Post* on September 24, 1986, nationally syndicated columnist Judy Mann, quoted the legal director of the American Civil Liberties Union, Arthur Spitzer, as saying:

> "If employers and the government were really concerned, they'd be developing performance-related tests so that when an air traffic controller shows up to work, he'd have to pass a five minute test on hand-eye coordination, vision-tests that tell us whether a person can perform. If he can't, then he shouldn't be performing that day regardless of whether he's used drugs in his life. Maybe he was up all night or fighting the flu."

What Mr. Spitzer is describing is just plain, good management, A worker should be hired, compensated, and disciplined based on whether he or she can do his/her job. The score on a urine test is irrelevant. Good management is practiced by supervisors in many organizations. That is why, contrary to the pronouncements for the White House and its neighbor across Lafayette Park (where federal agents lured a young man in order for President Bush to show seized cocaine to a national television audience), and the United States Chamber of Commerce, most supervisors and employers are ignoring the pressure to drug test. A very good "front line" explanation is contained in an article in the magazine *Inc.* (Maltby, 1987). Here are some quotes from that article:

> "Instead of testing for what really matters—impairment—drug testing looks for the presence of drug metabolites in the employees urine, which remain in the body for up to two months. So, an employee who fails a drug test may not be impaired at all. Firing good, sober employees for something they might have done last Saturday does not increase safety.
> ...Drug testing may even **decrease** safety. Any experienced manager knows that a safe quality product and a safe work environment do not come from a demoralized, unhappy workforce. But this is exactly what drug testing produces.
> ...we try to screen out the drug abusers. Not by telling us directly, of course, but by learning about which applicants had chronic absenteeism, inconsistent quality, and bad work habits at their former job. And we find out with much more accuracy than we could with a hit-or-miss drug test.
> ...Most of our supervisors have taken a 36-week intensive management-training course to help them (judge job performance). If an employee's performance consistently falls short of our expectations, then the supervisor sits down with him or her and discusses the problem. When employees are open with supervisors—as is often the case—and the problem is drugs or alcohol, we help get them into a treatment program."

Many readers who are knowledgeable of the evolution of efforts to identify and rehabilitate workers with alcohol and drug problems, will recognize much of what Mr. Maltby does as elements of an employee assistance program (EAP). Although Mr. Maltby does not identify himself as the EAP coordinator at Drexelbrook, he probably is because a small (300 employee) company can have a trained human resource expert take on the EAP duties in conjunction with other duties. It is necessary that the person have the commitment and training that he obviously does. In most cases, a company of that size will contract with an EAP service firm. In any

116

case, this type of EAP approach is much more effective and less disruptive than a program of random drug testing.

The senior EAP authority in American universities is Dr. Harrison Trice of the School of Industrial and Labor Relations at Cornell University. He has been studying the phenomenon of alcohol and drug use in the American workplace for over 40 years. In the 1970s, he and Dr. Paul Roman (now at the University of Georgia) authored the seminal text "Spirits and Demons at Work." This book should be required reading for would-be drug policy makers in Washington. More recently, Trice co-authored the article "Lessons from EAPs for Drug Screening" with his Cornell colleague Dr. William J. Sonnenstuhl, which appeared in the *ILR Review*. The following excerpts from the article should amply demonstrate that random urine screening for drugs in workers is misguided, at best.

"A well-run EAP is sufficient for the identification of drug users in companies where there are few or no dangerous jobs—for example, universities, Wall Street firms, factories, service occupations, broadcasting, and retail stores. This is possible because supervisors properly trained in constructive confrontation are equipped to break through the denial systems of users, abusers and addicts—regardless of the drug in question" (1989).

REFERENCES

Glantz, L.H. (1986). Employers Should Not Be Law Enforcers. *The New York Times*.

Kaufman, I.R. (1988). The Battle Over Drug Testing. *The New York Times*, October 26, pp. 52–69.

Maltby, L.L. (1987). Why Drug Testing Is A Bad Idea. *Inc.*, pp. 152–53.

Mann, J. (1986). Politicians' Handy Drug War. *The Washington Post*.

Panner, M.J. and Christakis, N.A. (1986). The Limits of Science in On-The-Job Drug Screening. *Hastings Center Report*, pp. 7–12.

Sonnenstuhl, W. and Trice, H. (1989). Lessons from EAPs for Drug Screening. *ILR Review*, pp. 25–29.

SHOULD THERE BE MORE REGULATIONS AND RESTRICTIONS ON ALCOHOL BEVERAGE ADVERTISEMENTS?

CHAPTER 14

Alcohol Advertising: Regulation Can Help

Kimberly A. Neuendorf, Ph.D.

Introduction

Alcohol is a drug, its use tolerated by virtue of its long history. But if one's exposure to alcohol use was limited to media images, one would be left with the impression that alcohol provides a useful medium for making and keeping friends, for handling problems, and or relaxing. Particularly in advertising, and generally in other fictional representations of alcohol use, the images are overwhelmingly positive. Treatment of alcohol related problems is avoided, as is any discussion of appropriate drinking contexts.

A History of Self-Regulation. There is a double-edged public perception of alcohol use—innocuous or even healthful in moderation[1], destructive in excess and for youthful users. This duality makes regulation in this area notably controversial. Completely prohibited in some nations, alcohol advertising in the U.S. has enjoyed a long history of self-regulation. Younger (1987) provides a review of this history, citing codes of practice for industry organizations such as the Distilled Spirits Council of the United States, the United States Brewing Association ("Beer advertising should neither suggest nor encourage overindulgence...drinking by individuals below the legal age of purchase... drunk driving..." p. 1146), and the Wine Institute ("Any advertisement which has an appeal to persons below the legal drinking age is unacceptable," p. 1147).

Self-regulation in media industries has also played a role. For example, prior to 1982, the National Association of Broadcasters (NAB) Radio and Television Codes effectively kept hard liquor ads off the air in most markets via self-monitoring (National Association of Broadcasters, 1978a;b). Ironically, the U.S. Justice Department's concern that such uniform standards constituted a violation of anti-trust statutes resulted in the elimination of the Codes. This has been followed by isolated cases of hard liquor ads on TV and radio (Tucker, Hovland and Wilcox, 1987; Wilcox, Hovland and Fletcher, 1988), while broadcast network standards and practices units voluntarily keep hard liquor ads off national television.

While many would claim that self-regulation is working and is the optimal method of maintaining a fair marketplace of ideas while exercising some social control, others argue that such voluntary guidelines are easily sidestepped. For example, hard liquor advertising has aired for years (even prior to 1982) on Hispanic broadcast services, and has withstood a number of critical challenges[2].

Alcohol Advertising as Commercial Speech. Since the mid-1970s, commercial speech has been afforded First Amendment protection. Case law has supported a laissez faire information environment, in which audiences serve as juries deciding the fate of propositional statements in ads. Theoretically, pro-alcohol messages will be balanced by cautionary messages in public service announcements (PSAs), news reports, etc. However, there is compelling evidence from the case of cigarette advertising that such an informational mix is difficult to achieve (Bagdikian, 1983). Weis and Burke (1986) cite a litany of examples of the tobacco industry's financial pressure on media institutions to suppress information that would threaten tobacco sales, even to the point of censoring news reports. As recently as 1984, a *Time* magazine health news supplement, written "in cooperation with the American Academy of Family Physicians," was excised of all negative references to smoking, much to the chagrin of the surprised AAFP (p. 62). While there is less direct evidence that such a conspiracy of silence exists for alcohol issues, at least two social scientific studies have found a relationship between the amount of alcohol advertising in a magazine and a lack of editorial content critical of alcohol (Tankard and Peirce, 1982; Minkler, Wallack and Madden, 1987).

The Supreme Court refined its stand on commercial speech in the 1980 *Central Hudson* case, in which the New York State Public Utilities Commission sought to promote energy conservation by banning electric utility advertising. This groundbreaking case established a four-part test for government regulation of advertising: a) the advertising must be for a lawful activity and must not be false or misleading (otherwise, the speech is unprotected, already illegal), b) the regulation must directly advance, c) a substantial state interest, and d) the regulation must be no more extensive than necessary (*Central Hudson Gas and Electric Corp. vs Public Service Commission of New York*, 1980; Curtis, 1985; Younger, 1987; Hovland and Wilcox, 1987; Trauth and Huffman, 1987; Schuster and Powell, 1987). In the 1986 Posadas case, the Supreme Court applied this four-part test to a Puerto Rican law prohibiting locally-aimed advertising for the commonwealth's gambling casinos (*Posadas de Puerto Rico Associates vs. Tourism Company*, 1986). In a novel interpretation of the second part of the *Central Hudson* test, Justice Rehnquist found "reasonable" the legislators' mere *belief* that such advertising would increase gambling by locals (Trauth and Huffman, 1987).

A "Direct" Advancement of a State Interest. Thus, it is no longer incumbent upon the regulating body to show a definitive, causal impact of the advertising upon the public. The presence of a legislative "belief" that restrictions on the commercial speech will advance the state interest is enough—in the case of alcohol advertising, the belief that regulating alcohol ads will decrease consumption and/or abuse would be sufficient. Prior to *Posadas*, it was generally assumed that alcohol advertising regulation was an impossibility, due to a lack of definitive evidence for a *causal*, negative impact of alcohol advertising on the public.

The probabilistic nature of social scientific research methods has prohibited a conclusion that exposure to alcohol ads *causes* individuals to a) drink more, b) abuse alcohol, or c) begin drinking at an earlier age. However, a reasonable belief that alcohol advertising *tends to contribute* to each of these might be supported by social scientific evidence (Neuendorf, 1987). Let us briefly consider each.

Does alcohol advertising increase consumption? Econometric studies have found no substantial, consistent relationship between amount of advertising and aggregate alcohol sales in a given state or nation (Simon, 1969; Borgeois and Barnes, 1979; Wilcox, 1985; Ornstein and Hanssens, 1985; Smart, 1988). The strongest set of relationships was found by Franke and Wilcox (1987), who discovered spot TV wine advertising and distilled spirit advertising in magazines to predict relevant consumption, with no prediction for beer consumption. When the *individual* is the unit of analysis, the results are still mixed. Experimental studies have failed to identify a link between a single exposure to alcohol ads and subsequent drinking among adults (McCarty and Ewing, 1983; Kohn, Smart and Ogborne, 1984; Kohn and Smart, 1984; Sobell et al., 1986). Surveys designed to gauge correlations between self-reported long-term alcohol ad exposure and alcohol consumption have provided little evidence of effects. The only national survey, conducted a decade ago by Michigan State University researchers, found no relationship for adults, but did find a small, significant relationship between advertising exposure and beer and liquor consumption for the 665 teens in the sample (Atkin and Block, 1981; Atkin, Hocking, and Block, 1984).

Does alcohol advertising contribute to alcohol abuse? Analyzing the same MSU data cited above, Atkin, Neuendorf, and McDermott (1983) found two types of alcohol abuse—drinking to excess and drinking and driving— significantly related to self-report alcohol ad exposure among the national sample of teens and young adults[3]. In a median split, high exposure subjects reported an average consumption of 4.5 drinks during an evening at a bar or party, with 33% reporting a five-drink-plus bout at least weekly, and 39% reporting drinking and driving in the last month. Low exposure subjects reported averages of 2.9 drinks, 16%, and 25%, respectively. Other studies have found meager contributions of alcohol

121

exposure, but strong effects for peer influence among teens (Strickland, 1983) and weak but statistically significant effects of alcohol advertising among adults (Neuendorf, 1987).

Does alcohol advertising encourage young people to start drinking? Strickland's (1983) survey of 772 "current drinker" teens found that although exposure to alcohol advertising was significantly related to consumption, its effect was eclipsed by that of peer association[4]. The MSU group found small but statistically significant correlations between advertising exposure and both beer and liquor consumption for teens, which held even when controlling for peer and parental influence, age, gender, and church attendance (Atkin, Hocking and Block, 1984)[5].

There is growing evidence that alcohol advertisers use special appeals to reach youthful audiences (Jacobson, Atkins, and Hacker, 1983; Neuendorf, 1987), by down-playing the alcohol content of such products as wine coolers and marketing such related products as Spuds MacKenzie stuffed animals and T-shirts (Ehrlich, 1987). In a study of adolescent responses to liqueur ads in magazines (Neuendorf and Pearlman, 1988), one-third of all product identifications were wrong, mistaking the liqueur for a non-alcoholic beverage or food. Compared to hard liquor ads, the liqueur ads were seen as promoting products that were significantly more healthy and appropriate for a younger clientele. A 1987 national poll of fourth-graders by *My Weekly Reader* found only 26% thought a wine cooler a day was harmful; 26% said "many" of their peers had tried coolers (Ehrlich, 1987).

It also seems clear that youngsters pay close attention to alcohol ads, in some cases paying greater attention than do adults (Atkin et al., 1988). Of 100 children aged 10-14 asked to name their three favorite TV commercials, 20% named at least one beer or wine spot (Neuendorf, 1985). Experimental findings by the MSU group concluded that two types of appeals used widely in alcohol advertising—celebrity endorsement and sexual appeals—significantly enhanced a number of adolescents' positive impressions of the ads and the products advertised, but did not correspondingly influence adults' evaluations. In fact, the older the respondent, the more negative the response to sex (Atkin and Block, 1981).

In summary, there is little evidence that alcohol advertising contributes to aggregate or individual consumption, there is some evidence that alcohol ad exposure is related to a greater likelihood of drinking to excess or drunk driving. Alcohol ads do seem to attract and persuade a youthful audience, although peer influences are generally more powerful. With the evidence to date, it is impossible to pinpoint the causal direction of these relationships—e.g., perhaps those with a predilection to drink dangerously are attracted to alcohol ads as reinforcement for their actions.

Alcohol Advertising: False and Misleading? Of course, the four-part *Central Hudson* test is irrelevant if the advertising is false or misleading, in which case the authority of the FTC and BATF comes into play. Just as social science's probabilistic nature has historically limited the legal application of its findings, the *receiver* orientation of behavioral research often stands at odds with the definitional dogma of regulation. That is, regulators hope to find a flaw in the *ad* that makes it false and misleading, while a behavioral scientist would examine the *audience's* perceptions of the ad.

For example, there is no doubt in this researcher's mind that most children are misled by Saturday morning puffery and fail to understand most TV spot disclaimers (Bryant and Anderson, 1983; Alwitt and Mitchell, 1985). Even adults are prone to cognitive and attitudinal impacts. Gerbner's oft-supported cultivation theory states that repeated exposure to consistent media images will create beliefs and expectations about the real world. This effect is maximized when the individual has few real life comparative models, and when the individual strongly identifies with the media models. Heavy TV viewers, for example, are found to be more fearful of what they perceive to be a crime-wracked real world (Gerbner, Gross, Morgan, and Signorielli, 1980). In this light, much of what the ad industry calls "lifestyle" advertising (Nathanson-Moog, 1984) could be construed as false and misleading, as could virtually all alcohol advertising aimed at youngsters[6].

What implicit promises are commonly found in alcohol advertising? A content analysis by Finn and Strickland (1982) found TV ads to emphasize sociopsychological themes—70% of the sampled ads associated consumption with "camaraderie", 41% with "relaxation", and 38% used humor. The MSU group also found the presentation of many favorable contexts of consumption—social camaraderie (in 54% of TV ads and 10% of magazine ads), escape (32% and 14%), romance (19% and 16%), and elegance (16% and 18%) (Atkin and Block, 1981). Strickland and Finn (1984) concluded that magazine alcohol ads are highly likely to include characters that demographically match the target audience, inviting stronger acceptance of the implicit claims.

Positive images of drinking in alcohol ads are supported by a consistent media message environment of condoned social imbibing (Greenberg et al., 1980; Neuendorf, 1990). Gerbner and colleagues (1982) found over one-third of prime-time TV characters were alcohol users, but only 1% were abusers. A 1975 content analysis counted 8.5 alcohol beverages per hour vs. 7.4 soft drinks per hour in soap operas (Lowery, 1980). And, 62% of all beverages were identified as alcoholic in a 1977 study of TV sitcoms and dramas (Breed and DeFoe, 1981).

Drinking in fictional media is often depicted as a means of dealing with stress or as a way to relax in conversation with friends (Pfautz, 1962; Lowry, 1981; Neuendorf, 1985), though images of alcoholics, specifically, are quite negative (Cook and Lewington, 1979; Signorielli, 1987). Amazingly, one analysis found drinking occurred during or just before work in 25% of cases; heavy drinking was excused or rationalized in 39% of sitcom cases, with humor the usual mechanism (Breed and DeFoe, 1981). A recent study reports a steady increase in TV drinking since 1969, with no significant increase in the proportion mentioning harmful effects (Signorielli, 1987). TV drinkers are also more likely to be involved in a romantic relationship (57% of drinkers vs. 35% of non-drinkers).

Only a couple of studies have linked exposure to such positive images to audience perceptions, however. Atkin and Block (1981) found that respondents heavily exposed to alcohol ads perceived the typical drinker as more fun-loving, happier and more good-looking. A survey of 100 adolescents found heavier TV viewers to be significantly more likely to think "all people who drink are happy" and "you have to drink to have fun at a sporting event" (Neuendorf, 1985).

Advertising agencies that handle alcohol products admit that consumers are "buying a symbol" (Message in a bottle, 1988), but thus far the glamorization of liquor has not qualified as "misleading." In Oklahoma and Mississippi cases, ads that identified alcohol consumption with "the good life" (Trauth and Huffman, 1987, p. 417) and that projected "an image of wine drinkers as successful, fun-loving people, without warning of the dangers of alcohol" (Younger, 1987, p. 1173) were deemed by federal courts to *not* be misleading. But deceptive communication is defined as a message "having the tendency or capacity to deceive a significant portion of the audience to whom the message is addressed" (Younger, 1987, p. 1151). This capacity is *testable* using survey and experimental methods, and could readily be put to the test[7].

Conclusion

In the current U.S. legal environment, alcohol advertising regulation is feasible, a major turnaround from the pre- Posadas era. Probabilistic evidence from social science could provide legislators with a reasonable belief that action would help reduce alcohol abuse and/or use by youngsters, or would help counteract a media view of alcohol consumption as useful and glamorous. Regulation is unlikely to result in a dramatic drop in overall consumption, but could assist in making alcohol consumption safer and in better preparing users for the negative aspects of alcohol use.

Evidence from the case of cigarette advertising leads us to believe that the most effective *type* of regulation would involve enforced counteradvertising, rather than a prohibition against alcohol ads[8]. In the 1960s the requirement that TV tobacco ads be matched by PSAs warning of the dangers of smoking was accompanied by a drop in smoking rates; the 1971 ban on tobacco advertising on TV and radio was followed by a rise. Cultivation theory *would* predict such an outcome—when the message environment is homogeneously pro-alcohol, public perceptions are likely to follow. A message mix would limit this type of "mainstreaming."

While it may be that "price, overall availability and social influences are likely to be the most potent influences on . . . consumption" (Smart, 1988, p. 315), alcohol advertising is a socially controllable influence, one that seems to reinforce alcohol abuse and youthful consumption, and offers oblique, unrealistic images of a safe and happy drinking world.

Footnotes

1. Citing a series of medical studies, Younger (1987) concludes that "the danger of alcohol arises only from its abuse, not from mere consumption" (p. 1151). Moderate drinking may in fact be associated with some positive health benefits—e.g., lower levels of coronary heart disease.
2. The Telemundo network resisted pressure to drop liquor advertising during a 1987 attack from the Center for Science in the Public Interest (Colford, 1987).
3. Multiple regression analyses controlled for self-reported family and peer drinking patterns, interpersonal encouragement to drink, and demographics (age, gender, social status, community size and religiosity). For both excessive consumption and hazardous drinking, the Contribution of alcohol advertising exposure held significant after these controls, at $p < .05$.
4. The partial correlation between self-reported exposure and drinking was .32, controlling for age, sex, race and total TV viewing. After the addition of peer influences, the partial fell to .18.
5. Beta weights of .10 and .34, respectively, both $p < .05$.
6. It should be kept in mind that in an alternate legal light, this potentially misleading nature of alcohol advertising could serve as an additional impetus for legislators to "believe" in injurious results.
7. One additional unique way in which alcohol ads may use covert tactics to make implicit sexual promises is through subliminal embeds. This controversial view has been supported by two studies in recent years, which indicate that subliminal cues do exist in magazine liquor ads and that they can affect attitudes and sexual motives (Ruth and Mosatche, 1985; Kilbourne, Painton, and Ridley, 1985).
8. Alcohol advertising bans in European nations and Canadian provinces have *not* been accompanied by decreased overall consumption (Smart, 1988).

REFERENCES

Aitken, P.P., Eadie, D.R., Leathar, D.S., McNeill, R.E.J., and Scott, A.C. (1988). Television advertisements for alcoholic drinks do reinforce under-age drinking. *British Journal of Addiction*, **83** 1399-1419.

Alwitt, L.F., and Mitchell, A.A. (Eds.). (1985). *Psychological processes and advertising effects: Theory, research and applications.* Lawrence Erlbaum: Hillsdale, NJ.

Atkin, C., and Block, M. (1981). *Content and effects of alcohol advertising.* National Technical Information Services:Springfield, VA.

Atkin, C., Hocking, J., and Block, M. (1984). Teenage drinking: Does advertising made a difference? *Journal of Communication*, **34**(2) 157-167.

Atkin, C.K., Neuendorf, K., and McDermott, S. (1983). The role of alcohol advertising in excessive and hazardous drinking. *Journal of Drug Education*, **13** 313-325.

Bagdikian, B. (1983). *The media monopoly.* Beacon Press: Boston, MA.

Borgeois, J.C. and Barnes, J.G. (1979). Does advertising increase alcohol consumption? *Journal of Advertising Research*, **19** (4) 19-29.

Breed, W. and DeFoe, J.R. (1981). The portrayal of the drinking process on prime-time television. *Journal of Communication*, **31**(1) 58-67.

Bryant, J. and Anderson, D.R. (Eds.). (1983). Children's understanding of television: Research on attention and comprehension. Academic Press: New York.

Central Hudson Gas and Electric Corp. vs. Public Service Commission of New York, 447 U.S. 557 (1980).

Colford, S.W. (1987, Oct. 12). Hispanic TV stations under fire. *Advertising Age*, p. 12.

Cook, J. and Lewington, M. (Eds.). (1979). *Images of alcoholism.* British Film Institute: London.

Curtis, J.M. (1985). Advertising regulated products. *1985 Annual Survey of American Law*, **3** 621-638.

Ehrlich, E. (1987, Oct. 26). Are wine coolers leading kids to drink? *Business Week*, p. 38.

Finn, T.A. and Strickland, D.E. (1982). A content analysis of beverage alcohol advertising: II. Television advertising. *Journal of Studies on Alcohol*, **43** 964-989.

Franke, G. and Wilcox, G. (1987). Alcohol beverage advertising and consumption in the United States, 1964-1984. *Journal of Advertising*, **16** (3) 22-30.

Gerbner, G., Gross, L., Morgan, M., and Signorielli, N. (1980). The "mainstreaming" of America: Violence profile no. 11. *Journal of Com-*

munication, **30** (3) 10-29.

Gerbner, G., Morgan, M., and Signorielli, N. (1982). Programing health portrayals: What viewers see, say, and do. In D. Pearl, L. Bouthilet, and J. Lazar (Eds.), Television and behavior: *Ten years of scientific progress and implications for the eighties, Vol. II, Technical reviews,* (pp. 291-307). U.S. Department of Health and Human Services: Rockville, MD.

Greenberg, B.S., Fernandez-Collado, C., Graef, D., Korzenny, F., and Atkin, C.K. (1980). Trends in use of alcohol and other substances on television. In B.S. Greenberg (ed.), *Life on television: Content analyses of U.S. TV drama,*(pp. 137-195). Ablex: Norwood, NJ.

Hovland, R., and Wilcox, G.B. (1987). The future of alcoholic beverage advertising. *Communications and the Law,* **9** (2) 5-14.

Jacobson, M., Atkins, R., and Hacker, G. (1983). The booze merchants: The inebriating of America. CSPI Books: Washington, DC.

Kilbourne, W.E., Painton, S., and Ridley, D. (1985). The effect of sexual embedding on responses to magazine advertisements. *Journal of Advertising,* **14** (2) 48-55.

Kohn, P.M., and Smart, R.G. (1984). The impact of television advertising on alcohol consumption: An experiment. *Journal of Studies on Alcohol,* **45** 295-301.

Kohn, P.M., Smart, R.G., and Ogborne, A.C. (1984). Effects of two kinds of alcohol advertising on subsequent consumption. *Journal of Advertising,* **13**(1) 34-40, 48.

Lowery, S.A. (1980). Soap and booze in the afternoon: An analysis of alcohol use in daytime serials. *Journal of Studies on Alcohol,* **41** 829-838.

Lowry, D.T. (1981). Alcohol consumption patterns and consequences on prime time network TV. *Journalism Quarterly,* **58** 3-8.

McCarty, D., and Ewing, J.A. (1983). Alcohol consumption while viewing alcoholic beverage advertising. *The International Journal of the Addictions,* **18** 1011-1018.

Message in a bottle. (1988, Oct. 13). *Marketing,* pp. 34-37.

Minkler, M., Wallack, L., and Madden, D. (1987). Alcohol and cigarette advertising in Ms. magazine. *Journal of Public Health Policy,* **8** 164-179.

Nathanson-Moog, C. (1984, July 26). Brand personalities undergo psychoanalysis. *Advertising Age,* p. 18.

National Association of Broadcasters. (1978a). *The Radio Code, Twenty-First Edition.*

National Association of Broadcasters. (1978b). *The Television Code, Twentieth Edition.*

Neuendorf, K.A. (1985). Alcohol advertising and media portrayals. *Journal of the Institute for Socioeconomic Policy*, **X** (2) 67-78.

Neuendorf, K.A. (1987). Alcohol advertising: Evidence from social science. *Media Information Australia*, **43** 15-20.

Neuendorf, K.A. (1990). Health images in the mass media. In E. Berlin Ray and L. Donohew (Eds.), *Communication and Health: Systems and Applications,* (pp. 111-135). Lawrence Erlbaum: Hillsdale, NJ.

Neuendorf, K.A., and Pearlman, R.A. (1988). Alcohol as good food: Adolescents' responses to liqueur ads. Paper presented to the Advertising Division of the Association for Education in Journalism and Mass Communication, Portland, OR.

Ornstein, S.I., and Hanssens, D.M. (1985). Alcohol control laws and the consumption of distilled spirits and beer. *Journal of Consumer Research*, **12** 200-213.

Pfautz, H.W. (1962). Image of alcohol in popular fiction: 1900-1904 and 1946-1950. *Quarterly Journal of Studies on Alcohol*, **23** (1) 131-146.

Posadas de Puerto Rico Associates vs. Tourism Company, 106 S. Ct. 2968 (1986).

Ruth, W.J. and Mosatche, H.S. (1985). A projective assessment of the effects of Freudian sexual symbolism in liquor advertisements. *Psychological Reports*, **56** 183-188.

Schuster, C.P. and Powell, C.P. (1987). Comparison of cigarette and alcohol advertising controversies. *Journal of Advertising*, **16** (2), 26-33.

Sheppard, M.A. and Lockhart, D. (1988). Alcohol advertising on television: Should we be worried? *The International Journal of the Addictions*, **23** 429-432.

Signorielli, N. (1987). Drinking, sex, and violence on television: The cultural indicators perspective. *Journal of Drug Education*, **17** 245-260.

Simon, J.L. (1969). The effect of advertising on liquor brand sales. *Journal of Marketing Research*, **VI** 301-313.

Smart, R.G. (1988). Does alcohol advertising affect overall consumption? A review of empirical studies. *Journal of Studies on Alcohol*, **49** 314-323.

Sobell, L.C., Sobell, M.B., Riley, D.M., Klajner, F., Leo, G.I., Pavan, D., and Cancilla, A. (1986). Effect of television programming and advertising on alcohol consumption in normal drinkers. *Journal of Studies on Alcohol*, **47** 333-340.

Strickland, D.E. (1983). Advertising exposure, alcohol consumption and misuse of alcohol. In M. Grant, M. Plant, and A. Williams (Eds.). *Economics and Alcohol: Consumption and Controls* (pp. 201-222).

Gardner Press, Inc.: New York.

Strickland, D.E. and Finn, T.A. (1984). Targeting of magazine alcohol beverage advertisements. *Journal of Drug Issues*, **14** 449-467.

Tankard, J. and Peirce, K. (1982). Alcohol advertising and magazine editorial content. *Journalism Quarterly*, **59** 302-305.

Trauth, D.M. and Huffman, J.L. (1987). Policy considerations for the control of alcoholic beverage advertising. *Journal of Broadcasting and Electronic Media*, **31** 409-426.

Tucker, L., Hovland, R., and Wilcox, G. (1987). Consumer response to Seagram's equivalency ad campaign on TV. *Journalism Quarterly*, **64** 834-838, 946.

Weis, W.L. and Burke, C. (1986). Media content and tobacco advertising: An unhealthy addiction. *Journal of Communication*, **36** (4) 59-69.

Wilcox, G.B. (1985). The effect of price advertising on alcoholic beverage sales. *Journal of Advertising Research*, **25** (5) 33-38.

Wilcox, G.B., Hovland, R., and Fletcher, D. (1988). Consumer response to a TV liquor spot. *Journalism Quarterly*, **65** 195-196.

Younger, S. (1987). Alcohol beverage advertising on the airwaves: Alternatives to a ban or counteradvertising. *UCLA Law Review*, **34** 1139-1193.

CHAPTER 15

Alcohol Advertising Restrictions Without Due Cause

Harold Shoup, B.A.
and
Christine Dobday, M.B.A.

Introduction

Alcoholism and drunk-driving gained national awareness as two of society's primary ills during the tenure of the former United States Surgeon General C. Everett Koop. Alcohol advertising was condemned as the alleged root of these evils by those who subscribe to a simple, lineal theory: alcohol advertising increases alcohol abuse which increases drunk-driving. But the theory has a basic flaw: it's wrong. It is not supported by research data, empirical evidence, or previous studies. Despite the compelling evidence, country after country has tried to affect alcohol consumption by limiting alcohol advertising; and has found such restrictions to have little, if any effect. In the United States, the fallacies surrounding alcohol advertising persist much to the detriment of the consumer. Although the movement to combat alcohol abuse is admirable, the measures undertaken must be proven effective when the freedom of commercial speech is at risk.

Ad Restrictions Do Not Solve the Problem

A study conducted by the Federal Trade Commission determined that, "... a review of the literature regarding the quantitative effect of alcohol advertising on consumption and abuse found no reliable basis to conclude that alcohol advertising significantly affects consumption, let alone abuse" (Crawford, 1985).

The University of Texas at Austin reinforced these findings. Over a twenty-one year period from 1964 to 1984, they examined the effect of alcohol advertising expenditure level on alcoholic beverage consumption in the U.S. "The findings indicate that advertising expenditure levels have no important relationship with aggregate consumption" (Wilcox, 1985). Anti-alcohol interests would have the public believe that alcohol advertising plays a major role in prompting abusive behavior but the

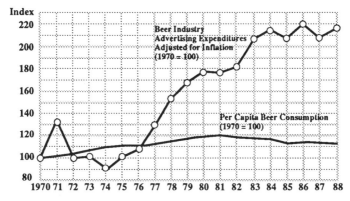

Figure 15.1 Advertising and Consumption 1970-1988. *Source: Beer Institute*

statistics prove otherwise.

In British Columbia and Manitoba, Canada and The U.S.A. the effects of alcoholic beverage restrictions showed no substantial link between advertising and consumption (Waterson, 1983; Smart and Cutler, 1976; Ogbourne and Smart, 1980). In France, imports of whiskey actually rose from 157,000 proof gallons in 1957 — the year whiskey advertising was banned — to 6,294,000 proof gallons in 1979. The ban, having proven ineffective, was then lifted (Waterson, 1983). This lack of a correlation cannot be overlooked when the dissemination of information on a legal product is in jeopardy.

Over the past few years, alcohol advertising expenditures have increased; however, alcohol-related traffic fatalities have decreased. (See chart below).

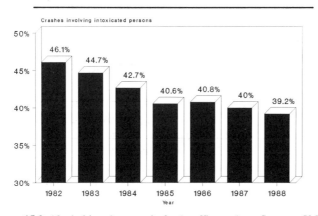

Figure 15.2 Alcohol involvement in fatal traffic crashes. *Source: U.S. Dept. of Transportation. Data released: August 1988*

131

Thus, the evidence indicates that other factors, such as society's intolerance of alcohol abuse, stronger law enforcement, educational programs, and public service initiatives are responsible for the decline in alcohol abuse and that the volume of product advertising is irrelevant.

The statistics are equally impressive among teenage drivers. In the 16-19 year old range, fatal crashes involving teenage drivers declined to 18.7% in 1987, down from 21% in 1986, and 28.4% in 1982. (Federal Register, 1988). These significant decreases were achieved with no restrictions on commercial speech.

The Role of Alcohol Advertising

It may seem illogical or counter-intuitive that alcohol advertising does not significantly affect overall consumption of the product. However, a careful review of the data reflects an intense inter-brand rivalry, not an attempt to attract new drinkers to that product. Alcohol is a "mature" product category, which means that consumers are aware of the product and its basic characteristics; therefore, the overall level of consumption is not affected significantly by the advertising of specific brands.

In this latter regard, it is significant to note that the Health and Human Services Department in its *Seventh Special Report to the U.S. Congress on Alcohol and Health* (1989), concluded that "research has yet to document a strong relationship between alcohol advertising and alcohol consumption." This same report also makes no recommendation to ban or restrict alcohol advertising.

Marketing strategists in mature product categories realize that the over-riding objective of advertising is to promote brand loyalty and encourage brand switching. In the same way that manufacturers of laundry detergent and tooth paste promote their brands, producers of alcoholic beverages advertise their brands to protect and expand their share of the available market.

An examination of the nature of the beer industry illustrates the very practical reasons why market share is so critical to every participant in this market.

The domestic annual retail market for beer is roughly $40 billion. Thus, an advertising campaign that would gain just one point of additional market share would produce $400 million in increased sales for the brewer advertising the product. On the other hand, if total beer consumption increased one percent (and that would be a quantum leap forward for this relatively static category), a brand with a 10% share would only gain $40 million in sales.

Attempts by any one brand to "grow" the total market simply don't make sense. The potential return for any single brand would be in the

Scenario I: Increase Total Market	
Total beer market is:	$ 40,000,000,000
Brand A's share is 10 percent, or:	$ 4,000,000,000
Total market increases by one percent to:	$ 40,400,000,000
Brand A's 10 percent share is now:	$ 4,040,000,000
Scenario II: Increase Market Share	
Total beer market remains flat at:	$ 40,000,000,000
Brand A's share increases by one percent, or:	$ 400,000,000
Brand A's 11 percent share is now:	$ 4,400,000,000

Table 15.1 Money differences between increasing total market versus increasing market share.

approximate proportion to its existing share of the market. Small wonder, then, that brand managers target their advertising dollars on established consumers of their products in a effort to reinforce brand loyalty or encourage trial by users of other brands. Brand managers realize that the name of the game is share of market, not size of market.

The Constitutional Right to Advertise

It is also illogical and inappropriate to deny consumers access to truthful information that helps them make informed purchase decisions. Approximately two-thirds of Americans consider themselves drinkers according to the U.S. Surgeon General (Press conference, May 5, 1989). For the consumer, advertising plays an important role in providing information about alcoholic beverages. It communicates information on new products such as wine coolers and low-alcohol beer, as well as information on pricing and packaging. Just as alcohol producers have the right to distribute information via advertising, the consumer has the right to receive it. In this sense, it is fundamental to both our government and our economy that people can be trusted to make wise decisions if they have access to all relevant information. Proposed restrictions to limit commercial speech have a resultant diminution of the First Amendment rights of both alcoholic beverage advertisers and consumers.

Recognizing this fundamental danger, the Supreme Court has ruled that such restrictions on commercial speech must advance a specific

133

government interest and be narrowly tailored in its method of doing so. (Central Hudson, 1980) Thus, freedom of commercial speech cannot be swept aside by advertising bans and restrictions that would have an unsubstantiated effect on product abuse and simultaneously deprive responsible consumers of their right to truthful information.

Conclusion

The problems of alcohol abuse are complex and cross all sections of society. The only successful way to address alcoholism is to confront the socio-economic, psychological, and possibly genetic factors which can be directly linked to the behavior. The subjective and arbitrary singling out of advertising as a major controlling cause of abuse is unsupported by research. Alcohol advertising already is regulated heavily by the government. Before further regulations are imposed they should be supported by facts and not by assumptions. Such a dangerous precedent ignores the legitimate interest of both producers and consumers of a legal product.

REFERENCES

Central Hudson Gas and Electric corp. vs. Public Service commission 447 U.S. 557 (1980) 561-562.

Crawford, C.T. and Gramm, W.L. (1985). Writhing in the cover memo to *Omnibus Petition for Regulation of Unfair and Deceptive Alcoholic Beverage Advertising and Marketing Practices* (Docket No. 209-46), Federal Trade Commission, p.2 (March 6).

Ogbourne, A.C. and Smart, R.G. (1980). Will restrictions on alcohol advertising reduce alcohol consumption? *The British Journal of Addiction*, **75** 296-298.

Presidential Document (1983). Proclamation 5918 of December 5, 1988, cited in the *Federal Register*, **53** (235) 49287-49288 (December 7).

Seventh Special Report to the U.S. Congress on Alcohol and Health (1990). U.S. Department of Health and Human Services. Public Health Service. Drug Abuse and Mental Health Administration. National Institute of Alcohol Abuse and Alcoholism: Rockville, MD.

Smart, R.G. and Cutler, R.E. (1976). the alcohol advertising ban in British Columbia: Problems and effects on beverage consumption, *The British Journal of Addiction*, **7** 13-21.

Surgeon General C. Everett Koop's Press Conference, May 31, 1989

Waterson, M.J. (1983). *Advertising and Alcohol Abuse*, a report published by the Advertising Association, p.10.

Wilcox, G.B., Franke, G.R., and Vacker, B. (1986). Alcohol beverage advertising and consumption in the United States: 1964-1984. *Department of Advertising Working Paper*, The University of Texas: Austin, p. III (January).

ARE WARNING LABELS EFFECTIVE IN PREVENTING ALCOHOL ABUSE?

CHAPTER 16

The Right to Know

Donna L. Polowchena, M.S.

Introduction

As of November 17, 1989 all alcoholic beverage containers bottled after that date are required to have warning labels attached to them with the following statement:

> Government Warning: (1) According to the surgeon general, women should not drink alcoholic beverages during pregnancy because of the risk of birth defects.
> (2) Consumption of alcoholic beverages impairs your ability to drive a car or operate machinery, and may cause health problems.

Though this requirement has been mandated by Congress, it is still considered to be controversial by some groups and individuals. Part of the controversy appears to revolve around the questions "Are the warning labels a symbolic gesture in support of alcohol abuse prevention and education, or are they an effective public health technique or adjunct to other alcohol education programs? (Engs, 1989). A second part of the issue involves the consumers right to know what is in a product. For this paper I will be taking the point of view that the public health measure of health warning labels on alcoholic beverages was long over due and that as a preventive measure it can be effective in reducing alcohol abuse and alcoholism.

History of Warning Labels for Alcohol Beverage Containers

The history of attempting to require warning labels on alcoholic beverages has been long. Proposals for their enactment were first made in the late 1970s on the national level but were rejected. During the 1980s various consumer and health groups, again, made efforts to have legislation enacted as general public support for health labeling was found. For example, a 1984 Roger survey (Washington Post, 1986) of alcohol problems reported that 64 percent of businesses, government, military, and other leaders endorsed mandatory health warning labels, and 68 percent of the general public agreed.

After much effort on the part of various health and consumer groups, in particular the National Council for Alcoholism and the Center for Science in the Public Interest, legislation was finally passed in the summer of 1989 as part of an omnibus drug bill requiring that all liquor, beer, wine, and wine coolers carry labels warning of risks of drinking during pregnancy and of drinking and driving. Similar to cigarette warning labels, these labels do not create any legal restriction or penalty to those who do not heed the warning. They merely provide cautionary notice that consumption of the product may entail serious consequences in certain situations (Congressional Record, 1988)

For years the alcohol beverage industry has argued that labels would unfairly stigmatize light and moderate drinkers. However, some researchers have felt that any drinking during pregnancy might cause fetal developmental problems. Also, alcoholic beverages when taken in excess can impair the ability to drive while also leading to chronic alcoholism. Because of these potentially life threatening problems, warning information on containers addressing these issues were considered particularly important for potential drinkers falling into these categories.

When the legislation was passed, as part of a compromise with the beverage industry, alcohol advertising was excluded from the labeling requirements. However, individuals involved with groups and organizations making recommendations for public policy (Beauchamp, 1987; New York Times, October 20, 1988) feel that warning labeling on all advertisement including bill boards, point of purchase, radio and television, newspapers and magazines needs to be enacted. This is thought to be important by the fact that the more awareness people have about a substance that can cause harm, the more likely they will make healthy choices concerning its use.

The Consumers Right to Know

The consumer has battled for years for the right to know what is contained in a product. As consumers we all have the right to make well-informed, healthy lifestyle choices. We can only do this if we are given the appropriate information. Warning labels can give health information that can counter the images created by the billions of dollars each year spent by the advertisement industry on a product. Labels for food and consumable products must be more than advertising. They must be educational and provide consumers with information on possible harmful ingredients along with those that are more conducive to good health. Cautionary labeling has often been fought by producers with the claim that it raises the products' cost which would be passed onto the consumer. However, these costs are thought to be minimal and are easily offset by savings in the health care industry and work place productivity.

Up until the passage of recent legislation, alcohol was the only ingestable manufactured consumable good that did not have a warning or ingredient label on it. Tobacco warning labels have been required for over two decades. Producers have often argued that warnings on their products will ultimately lead to warnings on everything from eggs to underwear and that people will ignore warning messages. However, this is not a realistic argument. The reason is that alcohol and tobacco are the only two products which are potentially addictive and sold legally direct to the consumer. This is despite their potential destructive impact on our nation's health. Labels on these products give the consumer the option to choose to use or not use the product. Labels help the consumer become aware of possible consequences with use of the substance and allows the consumer the right to make intelligent informed choices.

Informative labels can help prevent severe illness, congenital conditions and even lives by warning individuals that the product contains ingredients which can cause health problems. There are a number of problems related to alcohol consumption to which the consumer has a right to know. In 1984 the estimated consumption of alcoholic beverages was the equivalent of 2.65 gallons of pure alcohol per persons 14 years of age or older. Heavier drinkers, who constitute 10 percent of the drinking population, account for half the alcohol consumed in the United States (Alcohol and Health, 1987). Alcohol is associated with a wide variety of diseases and disorders.The greatest health hazard from chronic alcohol consumption is liver disease. In 1983 cirrhosis of the liver was the ninth leading cause of death in the U.S.. Nearly half of the accidental deaths, suicides and homicides are alcohol related. Victims are intoxicated in about one third of drownings, homicides and boating and aviation deaths and in about one fourth of suicides. Alcohol creates problems for an estimated 18 million persons 18 years and older (*Alcohol and Health,* 1987).

A very serious consequence of drinking is motor vehicle crashes.They are the most common non-natural cause of death in the United States accounting for more fatal injuries than any other type of accident (NIAAA, 1985).During 1984 more than 44,000 traffic fatalities occurred on the U.S. highways. Forty-three percent of all drivers involved in fatal crashes were intoxicated (*Alcohol and Health,* 1987). The highest group of crash deaths resulted in the 18 year old group. However, they account for only 2.2 percent of the driving population and drive less than 2 percent of the total miles traveled.Moreover, they were involved in 5.5 percent of the alcohol related accidents.

Another serious problem resulting from heavy alcohol consumption during pregnancy is fetal alcohol syndrome (FAS).Over the past two

Table 16.1
Reasons for having health warning labels on alcoholic beverages *

• Warning labels help to reinforce the public education message that alcohol is a dangerous substance.

• Warning labels provide information to people who may not have access to formal medical care, in particular low-income individuals.

• Warning labels encourage physicians and other health professionals to present reinforcing, compatible messages to their patients.

• Warning labels raise the visibility of alcohol abuse and alcoholism problems so that health personnel will be more likely to discuss alcohol related issues with their patients.

• Warning labels on all alcoholic beverage containers increases knowledge among youth that alcohol is a drug with health risks and social consequences associated with its use and misuse.

• Warning labels help counter the glamorous view of alcoholic beverages promulgated through alcohol advertising.

• Warning labels inform the public of the dangers of drinking during pregnancy, the dangers of drinking and driving, the dangers of drinking in combination with other drugs, and the danger of addiction and other health consequences of alcohol abuse.

* Adapted from: *Health Hazards Associated with Alcohol and Methods to Inform the General Public of these Hazards.* U. S. Department of Health and Human Services Report. Rockville, MD, 1980.

---

decades there have been more than 3,000 papers published on this problem alone (*Alcohol and Health,* 1987). It is estimated that the overall FAS prevalence is from 1 to 3 cases per 1,000 live births based upon estimates in various American and European cities. Among women who are alcohol abusers the prevalence ranges from 23 to 29 cases per 1,000 population. Serious cases of FAS appear to be found only in mothers who are chronic alcoholics and drink heavily during pregnancy (*Alcohol and Health,*

1987). However, this is considered to be the severe end of a continuum of fetal damage that can be produced by prenatal alcohol exposure. Lower levels of maternal drinking may also have some measurable effects on the fetus.It is important to note that "data so far do not suggest a threshold level of drinking below which there is no effect on the unborn child" (*Alcohol and Health*, 1987 p. 85). It is not known why some fetuses are more susceptible to FAS compared to others. Because of the many unknowns concerning alcohol consumption during pregnancy, to be on the cautionary side, many health professionals and groups recommended that pregnant women abstain from alcohol (*Alcohol and Health*, 1987).

Alcoholic beverage producers certainly do not want consumers to associate drinking with mental retardation, alcoholism, cirrhosis of the liver and death on the highways. However, they do little to inform drinkers about health and safety risk. According to Neil Postman (New York Times, March 20, 1988), it is estimated that about $2 billion worth of promotional campaigns annually are presented by the alcohol beverage industry. Children see more than 100,000 beer commercials on television before they are old enough to legally drink and drive. Postman feels that the ads do more than sell the assumption that drinking is not just safe, but is essential to a happy, successful life.

According to this same article, some alcohol beverage companies do sponsor occasional advertisements to remind consumers to drink "moderately." However, in many cases the advertisements may be designed to undercut prevention oriented legislative inititives rather than to educate drinkers about health risks. It also has been estimated that the heavy drinkers account for half of all sales. If these drinkers drank less, sales and profits would plummet.

Labels as Public Health Education Vehicle

Warning labels on all alcoholic beverage containers, including cans and bottles of beer, bottles of wine and liquor ensure that the message is consistently before the public eye. If public health education messages are to be optimally effective, in terms of promoting increased awareness and behavior change, information needs to be repeated frequently over time and from a variety of sources. Many of the studies investigating the effect of warning labels appear to suggest that they are effective in conjunction with other types of educational messages and public health programs. There have been some studies concerning the effectiveness of warning labels. Since 1975 packaged processed foods have been required by law to bear a nutrition label if it was fortified with additional nutrients (Richardson,1987). One study indicated that after diet sodas were required to carry a warning that saccharin causes cancer in animals, soft drinks sales slowed (Orwin, Schucker and Stokes, 1984).

In 1982 the FDA asked food manufacturers to voluntary label the sodium content of their products. A study by Heimbach (1986) found that public concern about high sodium intake increased as increases in sodium labeling on products occurred. Simultaneously there were mass media and public health high blood pressure education programs discussing the problems of sodium intake. Another study with shelf labeling of food products containing low or reduced sodium, calories and fat, resulted in increased sales compared to those products without the information (Schucker,1986). During the study period, other related public health and media campaigns occurred. The researchers for both of these investigations concluded that perhaps all the educational and media efforts together, including labeling,caused an increase in concern and in healthier consumer choices as it was not possible to determine the effectiveness of labels in isolation from the other educational efforts.

There have been some studies that indicate that people do read labels in certain circumstances. Studies of prescription inserts to inform consumers of the dangers and proper use of a drug found that most patients read the information provided with the prescription.Patients showed an increased knowledge about the side effects and dangers of the medication (Mazis,Morris,and Gordon, 1987). A study by Morris(1980) found sales of a brand of estrogen dropped sharply after media reports were broadcast linking estrogens to cancer. Declines in sales continued following a mandatory insertion of an information sheet a few years later warning of possible side effects of the drug.

The closest analogous substance to alcohol is tobacco. Comprehensive anti smoking education programs and policies began in 1964 with the publication of the Surgeon General's report concerning the health consequences of smoking (Richardson,1987). Cigarette warning labels were first placed on cigarette packages in 1965 but had little immediate effect in consumption. After public education programs began in 1968, a decrease in smoking occurred. Richardson concluded that it may have been a combination of these efforts and not any one in particular which caused a decreased consumption of cigarettes in 1979. These various reports appear to imply that a combination of warning labels, media publicity, public education, changes in public attitudes, and anti smoking commercials have been the primary factors in changes of health behaviors.

Summary

In summary the consumer has a right to know what ingredients he or she is consuming and what the possible health consequences of the product are so that informed choices can be made. Likewise warning labels on alcoholic beverages, in conjunction with expanded educational programs, mass media campaigns, higher federal alcohol excise taxes and restriction of advertisement in the mass media all need to be part of a public health education program as a preventive measure for alcohol abuse and alcoholism.

REFERENCES

Beauchamp, D. (1987). What can we learn from the tobacco experience ? Paper presented: Alcohol Policy Conference V, Charleston, NC.
Committee on Commerce, Science and Transportation. (August 10, 1988) Congressional Record, U.S. Senate:Washington, D.C.
Engs, R.C. (1989). Do warning labels on alcoholic beverages deter alcohol abuse ? *The Journal of School Health*, **59** (3) 116-118
Heimbach, J.T. (1986) The growing impact of sodium labeling. Read before the 46th Annual meeting of the Institute of Food Technologists, Dallas.
Mazis, M.B., Morris, L.A., and Gordon, E. (1987). Patient recall and attitudes about two forms of oral contraceptive patient information. *Medical Care*, **16** 1045-1054.
Morris, L.A.(1980). Estrogenic drugs-patient package inserts, in Morris, L.A., Mazis, M.B. and Barofsky, E. (Eds). *Product labeling and health Risks—Banbury Report 6*, Cold Springs Harbor Laboratory: Cold Springs Harbor, N.J.
NIAA Alcohol Epidemiologic Data System (1985). *Country Problem Indicators 1975-1980. U.S. Alcohol Data Reference Manual*, Vol. III. Rockville, MD.
New York Times, March 20, 1988.
New York Times, October 26, 1988.
Orwin, R.G., Schucker, R.E., and Stokes, R.C. (1984). Evaluating the life cycle of a product warning: Saccharin and diet soft drinks. *Evaluation Review*, **8** (6) 801-822.
Richardson, P. et al. (1987). *Review of the Research Literature on the Effects of Health Warning Labels: A report to the United States Congress*, Macro System, Inc.:Silver Springs, MD.
Sixth Special Report to the U.S. Congress on Alcohol and Health. (1987). U.S. Department of Health and Human Services. NIAAA: Rockville, MD.
Schucker, R.E. (1986). Merchandising nutrition information. *Cereal Food Worlds*, **31** (7) 461-463.
Washington Post, July 2, 1986.

CHAPTER 17

Health Warning Labels
On Alcoholic Beverages

David J. Pittman, Ph.D

A controversial issue in the field of alcohol policy is the federal government requirement that health warning labels be placed on containers of all alcoholic beverages (distilled spirits, wine, and beer); this policy has seriously divided not only organizations but individuals who have worked together harmoniously over the last quarter of a century to bring greater public awareness to the serious problems of alcoholism and alcohol abuse in American society and to provide increased private and public funding for the prevention and treatment of this disease. The crux of the argument between the opponents and proponents of health warning labels is whether such action would raise the public's awareness of problems associated with alcohol use and would prevent the development of new cases of alcoholism, or whether such action is an exercise in futility since warning labels are simplistic and cosmetic reactions to a complex problem.

Historical Context of Warning Labels

As Mark Keller (1978) has pointed out, the idea of warning labels on containers of alcoholic beverages is far from being a new idea. Keller cites the proposal of cautionary labels by a 1945 Massachusetts Legislative Special Commission to Study the Problems of Drunkenness which was as follows:

> Directions for use: Use moderately and not on successive days. Eat well while drinking, and if necessary, supplement food by vitamin tablets while drinking. Warning: if this beverage is indulged in consistently and immoderately, it may cause intoxications (drunkenness), later neuralgia and paralysis (neuritis) and serious mental derangement such as delirium tremens and other curable and incurable mental diseases, as well as kidney and liver damage (Keller, 1978).

Such a label was rejected in Massachusetts.

Legislation was introduced in the 96*th* Congress (1978–81) by Senator Strom Thurmond of South Carolina to have containers of alcoholic beverages containing more than 24 percent alcohol (distilled spirits) labeled with a conspicuous warning that drinking may be injurious to one's health. Similar legislation has been introduced by Thurmond in previous sessions of the U.S. Congress and hearings were held by the Senate Alcoholism and Drug Abuse Subcommittee on his legislation in the previous session of the 95*th* Congress in 1978, but no legislation resulted from these hearings.

In early 1978, the Bureau of Alcohol, Tobacco, and Firearms (BATF) of the U.S. Department of Treasury asked for public comments on the issue of health warning labels on containers of alcoholic beverages in view of the increased attention being given to the fetal alcohol syndrome. The public comments were reviewed by a panel of three individuals from outside the government who reached no consensus on whether health warning labels would be effective or not. In early 1979, the BATF deferred any action on warning labels; instead they placed major responsibility for a massive educational campaign to alert the general population (especially women in the child-bearing ages and the medical and allied professionals) to the consequences of excessive and/or abusive drinking, on the alcohol beverage industry as well as the National Institute on Alcohol Abuse and Alcoholism (NIAAA). Both private and governmental groups mounted massive educational campaigns in this area.

In a surprising development the U.S. Senate on May 7, 1979, adopted an amendment co-sponsored by Senators Thurmond and Hatch of Utah to the renewal legislation (SB-440) for the NIAAA program authority to require warning labels on containers of beverage alcohol containing more than 24 percent alcohol (distilled spirits) leaving wine and beer, both containing less than 24 percent alcohol content, exempt from this amendment. The Thurmond-Hatch amendment required the display of the statement: "Caution: Consumption of alcoholic beverages may be hazardous to your health" (*Wall Street Journal*, 1979).

In September 1979 the Senate Subcommittee on Alcoholism and Drug Abuse held hearings on the feasibility of health warning labels which supplemented those previously held by the same Subcommittee in January 1978, then under the chairman ship of former Senator Hathaway. Senator Riegle stated on December 19, 1979, in the Senate that "there is an emerging consensus in the medical and alcoholism fields in support of warning labels. The consensus is not unanimous, but it is impressive nevertheless" (*Congressional Record*, 1979).

However, the House of Representatives' Subcommittee on Health and the Environment, under the chairmanship of Representative Henry Waxman, neither held hearings on this question nor was the health label amendment voted on when the House approved its version of SB-440, the renewal legislation for NIAAA authority.

A compromise was reached between the Senate and House on mandated health warning labels which in effect called for another study. The exact wording of the compromise which is embodied in the new Section 334 to the Comprehensive Alcohol Abuse and Alcoholism Prevention Treatment and Rehabilitation Act of 1970 was:

> Sec. 334. (a) Not later than June 1, 1980, the Secretary of Health, Education and Welfare, acting through the Assistant Secretary for Health, and the Secretary of the Treasury, acting through the Assistant Secretary for Enforcement and Operations, shall jointly report to the President and the Congress—
>
> (1) the extent and nature of birth defects associated with alcohol consumption by pregnant women.
>
> (2) the extent and nature of other health hazards associated with alcoholic beverages, and
>
> (3) the actions which should be taken by the Federal Government under the Federal Alcohol Administration Act and the Federal Food, Drug and Cosmetic Act with respect to informing the general public of such health hazards.
>
> (b) Subsection (a) shall not be construed to limit the authority of the Attorney General, the Secretary of the Treasury, or the Secretary of Health, Education, and Welfare under the Federal Alcohol Administration Act or the Federal Food, Drug, or Cosmetic Act (*Congressional Record*, 1979).

Throughout the 1980s demands for health warning labels on containers of alcoholic beverages by consumer, medical, public health, and new temperance advocates continued to escalate. Various cities, led by New York in 1983, and followed by others such as Philadelphia, Los Angeles, Columbus, etc., mandated retail establishments dispensing alcohol to require health warning posters. In 1987, California authorities, acting on the law required by their Proposition 65 initiative, labeled alcohol as a reproductive toxin; in 1988 warning posters noting this action were mandated throughout that state where alcoholic beverages were sold.

The health warning advocates moved to include more than fetal damage in their labels; they pressed that drink warnings should include references to alcohol's being a drug and other health problems that could result from the ingestion of alcoholic beverages. More specifically, in 1988, the proposed Thurmond-Conyers law would have required producers of alcoholic beverages to use five rotating warning labels. These were:

WARNING: The Surgeon General has determined that the consumption of this product, which contains alcohol, during pregnancy can cause mental retardation and other birth defects.
WARNING: Drinking this product, which contains alcohol, impairs your ability to drive a car or operate heavy machinery.
WARNING: This product contains alcohol and is particularly hazardous in combination with some drugs.
WARNING: The consumption of this product, which contains alcohol, can increase the risk of developing hypertension, liver disease, and cancer.
WARNING: Alcohol is a drug which may be addictive.

In the mid-1980s the alcohol beverage began to be a target of product liability suits for their alleged lack of informing consumers about the risks of addiction and health damage. Legal action was brought against Brown-Forman and G. Heileman Brewing Company in Illinois in 1986 for alleged failure to warn that their products were addictive. Further suits involving alleged fetal damage by alcohol use were filed in Seattle, Washington. Probably, given their concern with the potential product liability awards, the alcohol beverage industry acquiesced to health warning labels on their products in 1988. Therefore, the Omnibus Drug Act of 1988 enacted by the U.S. Congress required that all containers of alcoholic beverages produced for domestic consumption carry the following warning labels effective November 19, 1989:

1. According to the Surgeon General, women should not drink alcoholic beverages during pregnancy because of the risk of birth defects.
2. Consumption of alcoholic beverages impairs your ability to drive a car or operate machinery, and may cause health problems.

The controversy over warning labels and the best way to avoid fetal damage from excessive consumption of alcohol can be linked to broader concerns in the nation. In 1986, the U.S. Congress enacted the "Emergency Planning and Community Right to Know Act", which related to reporting requirements involving the emission of certain noxious chemicals into the atmosphere and the stockpiling of these dangerous chemicals (*Insight*, 1988). The "Right to Know" not only the ingredients but the risks of various products is a major aspect of the consumer movement. Moreover, given the fact that the American society is a health-centered one and the inability of medical science to determine a safe level of drinking during pregnancy leads inevitable to the recommendation by some in the new temperance movement of gender prohibition, i.e., women in the child-bearing years with the ability to conceive should abstain from alcoholic

147

beverages since damage may occur to the fetus before the woman is aware she is pregnant.

Scientific Evidence of the Effectiveness of Health Warning Labels

There is not even one scientific study to support the point of view that health warning labels would raise the public's awareness of alcohol problems and alcoholism or that labels would have any effect on the drinking patterns of American citizens, which are deeply ingrained in the sociocultural fabric of the society. Furthermore, an overwhelming majority of Americans either abstain or are light or moderate drinkers. Only approximately six to seven percent of the adult population become alcoholic.

A warning label that excessive consumption of alcoholic beverages may damage your health comes at the end point of personal drinking decision-making—namely after the purchase of the alcoholic beverage. Do we scientifically know whether or not a label will be read by the purchaser? Also, how does a warning label affect the consumption of alcoholic beverages ordered in restaurants, taverns, and cocktail lounges where the health warning or posters are rarely in view? Or would governmental regulations later require that all glasses in which alcoholic beverages are served to customers mandate the printing of labels on them? Or would there have to be specified times when lights would be turned up in the cocktail lounges, taverns, restaurants, etc., in order for the customers to read the labels on their glasses? Or would the server of alcoholic beverages in a commercial establishment have to give a verbal warning to the customer on the potential problems of alcohol use? Further, the economic costs of these new labeling procedures are being passed on to the consumers.

Use of All Products Carry Some Risk

The American Congress and the massive bureaucratic structure which it has created should be cognizant that almost all products may have some deleterious effects upon certain individuals. Salt is counter-indicated in cases of hypertension; thus the question becomes, should it carrying a warning label? Sugar is counter-indicated for diabetics; therefore should it carry a warning label? This list could be expanded *ad nauseam* to the point of absurdity. Unfortunately, in the rush by zealots to protect us from ourselves, there is real danger that there will be so many cautions and warnings about the possible negative consequences of products to certain categories of individuals that serious health hazards, where the danger is real to an overwhelming majority of the population, will be ignored by the customer. In short, health warning labels should be used only when the negative health consequences of the products are based on sound scientific studies such as is the case with cigarette smoking.

Conclusion

Despite these developments, a warning labels on containers of beverage alcohol is no more than a symbolic action without any substance, which would imply that America's alcoholism problem (which is probably less extensive than in the first half of the 19th century (Rorabaugh, 1976)) could be solved by simplistic and superficial devices that have never proved effective with any other major health problem. The further damage is that warning labels may deceive some people into believing that concrete action is being taken by the government to reduce the health hazards of excessive drinking; in fact, health warning labels neither address the question of the multiple etiology of alcohol problems and alcoholism nor develop more effective primary prevention programs in this area.

We need to determine why some people drink to excess or have alcohol problems, and in most cases why humans have been drinking since the beginning of human history without the majority of them developing alcohol problems; these are the primary research questions to which our attention should be addressed, and we should not be deceived by simplistic answers (such as the Neo-Prohibitionist philosophy) to the complexities of alcohol problems.

More positive approaches to alcohol problems, but infinitely more expensive than cosmetic health warning labels on the agent alcohol, are the educational efforts by private voluntary community agency structures, the alcohol beverage industry, the mass media, and governmental agencies at all levels to inform the public about beverage alcohol usage under varying conditions and at various dose levels.

REFERENCES

Congressional Record (1979). Senate, December 19, p. S19121.
Insight (1988). May 23, p. 9.
Keller, M. (1978). "Letter to Senator Hathaway of Subcommittee on Alcoholism and Drug Abuse", January 28.
Rorabaugh, W.J. (1976). "Estimated U.S. Beverage Consumption, 1790–1869", *Journal of Studies on Alcohol*, **37** 357-364.
Wall Street Journal (1979). May 8, p. 14.

SHOULD WOMEN BE ADVISED TO ABSTAIN COMPLETELY FROM ALCOHOL DURING PREGNANCY?

CHAPTER 18

Drinking In Pregnancy: A Recommendation For Complete Abstinence

Sterling K. Clarren, M.D.

A teratogen is an environmental agent capable of producing birth defects. As alcohol (ethanol) became established as a human teratogen in the 1970s, the United States Surgeon General was prompted to advise women who were pregnant or planning to become pregnant that it was best for them to abstain from drinking alcohol containing beverages through-out gestation (US Department of Treasury, 1980). I believe, the Surgeon General's simple statement was correct then and now, although it belies issues of great complexity. In order to properly understand the statement, it is necessary to review two topics: what is known about dose-response or the teratogenic threshold for alcohol- related birth defects, and what changes in popular behavior can be expected from public awareness campaigns concerning alcohol consumption in pregnancy based on a professional statement of danger?

The theory of teratogenic threshold explains that environmental substances rarely cause malformations under all circumstances. Danger to the fetus occurs when exposure is above a critical dose at a critical time in gestation, a "period of vulnerability" (Shepard, 1982). When the exposure is above a critical concentration at a vulnerable time then a sensitive organ, tissue line, or cell type (but generally not the fetus as a whole) may be injured or destroyed. For some teratogens the critical dose is sufficiently high and/or the periods of vulnerability are sufficiently limited that little fetal harm is ever done. Other teratogens are effective at low dose exposures in widespread periods of gestation. The teratogenic impact of ethanol seems to fit more closely into the latter category.

Ethanol flows freely through the placenta and is poorly metabolized by the fetus. Fetal exposure to ethanol is directly reflected in the maternal blood alcohol concentration (BAC). To date, no study has correlated BAC's in pregnant women with fetal outcomes. Such studies would obviously have major methodologic and ethical problems. Consequently, researchers have tried to correlate maternal reported consumption of alcohol as an indirect measure of BAC to fetal outcomes. Correlating reported maternal alcohol consumption to fetal response can only produce broad estimates of teratogenic threshold for several reasons. First, it is difficult to obtain accurate intake information. Few people measure liquor or wine accurately into a glass. Individuals may report "no more than one drink per night", yet if they are questioned further it is found that "the drink" may have anywhere from one half-ounce to four or five ounces of liquor. People may forget or deny liquor consumption that occurred days, weeks or months prior to an interview. Second, even if people were to have consumed identical volumes of alcohol, absorption and peak blood alcohol concentrations would still vary widely based on the individuals' sizes, their fat/lean body mass ratios, their rates of alcohol consumption, and whether they ate while drinking.

Third, after absorption, degradation of alcohol is primarily determined by the activity of two liver enzymes, alcohol dehydrogenase and aldehyde dehydrogenase. The activity of these enzymes may be varied by racial background, individual genetic background and/or liver disease. Finally there may be other factors that determine ethanol metabolism. In our laboratory, for example, alcohol has been given via nasogastric catheter to non- human primates (*M. nemestrina*) who were fasted overnight. The animals' BAC's were sequentially measured over several post consumption hours. Even under these standard conditions peak BAC's varied by 20% to 25% in the same animal given the same dose on different days (Clarren et al., 1987).

Structural malformations are generally regarded as proof of fetal response to teratogenesis. It is probable that there is a specific period of vulnerability for each major or minor malformation during the first trimester, with the exception of the brain which is rapidly developing and changing throughout gestation. The brain must be thought of as a large collection of neuronal systems in which each system has its own periods of teratogenic vulnerability (Alling, 1985). While the brain may be susceptible to alcohol throughout much of gestation, its pattern of alteration may be different in different exposure sequences. Functional as well as structural anomalies of the brain need to be considered as possible teratogenic outcomes. Generalized growth deficiency can also be considered a malformation; length and weight are most severely effected by teratogens in the second half of pregnancy.

Agent concentration and gestational timing can not be the sole determinants of fetal response to alcohol. There are several case reports of fraternal twinning in which one twin was more severely affected than the other (Christoffel and Salasky, 1975). Presumably, fetuses have a genetic resistance to teratogenesis that are not evenly shared. It also remains an open question to what extent other maternal factors like generalized malnutrition (Fischer et al., 1982), specific vitamin or mineral deficiencies (Dreosti, 1986), or exposures to other drugs (King and Fabro, 1983) might potentiate the effects of ethanol exposure at different doses.

Another difficulty in interpreting dose response data in many human studies of alcohol related birth defects is the practice of reporting cohort doses in terms of "averaged consumptions." It is understandable that investigators have used averaged consumption scores which are obtained by dividing daily intake reports by periods of time like weeks or months. After all no two fetuses have ever been exposed to the *exact* same drinking pattern throughout gestation and consumption data will inevitably be imprecise given the explanations above. However, *widely* varying drinking patterns may be merged through the averaging approach. A woman drinking 30 gms of alcohol each day and a woman drinking 210 gms of alcohol once per week would have the same averaged weekly consumption score. It is possible that each of these exposure patterns is teratogenic or that only one is—but surely the impacts of these exposure patterns would be different. When studies report relatively moderate drinking to be associated with a teratogenic impact (Kline et al., 1980; Streissguth et al., 1981), is this true for the cohort over all or are some subgroups in the cohort skewing the results?

At present little is known about the ability of the fetus to repair itself from early gestational teratogenesis. There is evidence that women who stop drinking during pregnancy have larger, healthier babies.(Rosette et al., 1980). But there is also evidence that early gestational alcohol exposure correlates with abnormal behaviors in the offspring independent of later gestational effects by the mother to reduce or eliminate alcohol use (Ernhart et al., 1987; Streissguth et al., 1989; Larsson et al., 1985).

One outcome from alcohol teratogenesis is the fetal alcohol syndrome (FAS). This specific disorder is defined by brain dysfunction, growth deficiency, specific minor malformations of the face and other assorted major and minor anomalies (Clarren and Smith, 1978). FAS usually is found in children of chronic alcoholics (Clarren, 1981). Alcoholics presumably achieve BAC's above alcohol's teratogenic threshold often enough to affect numerous embryo/fetal vulnerable periods. Not all infants born to alcoholics have FAS, however. Is this because of important difference in consumption patterns, maternal metabolism, fetal resistance, cofactors, or combinations of these? No one yet knows.

Although not all infants born to alcoholics have FAS, this does not mean that they are necessarily "normal." Neither does it mean that fetuses exposed to alcohol in non-alcoholic pregnancies are without teratogenic risk. Physicians or psychologists can never prove an individual is fully normal, they can only demonstrate that a person is abnormal or normal on the tests given at a specific time. Prospective studies in humans and in animals clearly demonstrate that alcohol can produce isolated malformations or affect brain structure, and/or function without producing the major and minor malformations and growth deficiencies which help to define FAS (Streissguth et al., 1989; Clarren et al., 1988; Streissguth et al., 1986; West, 1986). Alcohol related brain teratogenesis can be manifest as attention and behavior problems as well as difficulties with memory and learning (Streissguth et al., 1989). Some, but not all, of these problems would be identified by I.Q. testing. Subtle problems might not be detected until an affected child is well into school (Streissguth et al., 1989). Imaging studies of brain structure are not capable of detecting damage at the cellular or neurochemical level. At this time, virtually no information is available on how many periods of vulnerability for brain teratogenesis exist in humans, or what the specific threshold dose for any neurologic structure or system may be.

In summary, alcohol can produce an identifiable birth defect syndrome, fetal alcohol syndrome, which is generally associated with frequent, heavy alcohol exposures. Binge patterns of drinking or moderate consumption of alcohol may be associated with brain dysfunction in isolation. The limits for dose-response producing central nervous system damage in isolation are not known. Certainly some small amount of liquor taken on only rare days in pregnancy should be below threshold in any pregnancy—but it is likely that it will never be possible to guarantee an absolutely safe low dose of alcohol for any period of pregnancy for a specific individual.

An official position representing professional opinion on a matter of public health is only the beginning of a campaign to affect public behavior. The issues involved in mounting a campaign concerning the dangers of gestational alcohol use are complex. Who is to be warned? Everyone? Women? High risk women (who are they)? Who is to do the warning? The government, the media, the scientific community, the liquor manufacturers? Should the campaign be directly aimed at a targeted population of drinkers or should it be aimed at groups like doctors, teachers, or spouses who could then work with the target population. What fetal problems are to be targeted by the campaign, the prevention of FAS or all alcohol related birth defects? Can a reasonable reduction in fetal morbidity be easily measured? Will the campaign have negative as well as positive consequences? Can the campaign be assessed, sustained and improved over time? Who should take on the responsibility of answering these questions?

The Surgeon General's advice represents, in my opinion, the only responsible professional advice that can be offered for alcohol use in pregnancy. The only absolutely safe gestational alcohol exposure is no exposure. I believe it is the position from which a public health campaign must be mounted even though it is a most problematic beginning. Alcoholics and intermittent alcohol abusers are the highest risk target populations. Yet the alcoholic woman's denial of her alcohol use and dependence is a primary component of her condition. Public awareness campaigns of simple, direct information are not likely to influence her. However, methods for identifying and confronting pregnant alcoholics and directing them towards treatment are being developed and need to be encouraged (Minor and Van Dort, 1982; Rydberg, 1985; Rosett et al, 1978; May and Hymbaugh, 1989). The non-alcoholic who is concerned about having a healthier baby can learn from health recommendations and can alter her behavior. Unfortunately, variations in media and professional advice may confuse her (Little et al., 1981; 1983). Even if all non-alcoholic women understood and accepted the Surgeon General's advice, the situation would be difficult. Often women do not know they are pregnant in the first crucial weeks of gestation. In order to fully avoid alcohol's teratogenic impact, women would need to avoid alcohol use in all periods of unprotected sexual intercourse from menarche to menopause.

The medical profession and the scientific community can not alter the facts to make life less complicated. Alcohol related birth defects will not be prevented by academic wrangling over subtle differences in the relative safety of different low dose alcohol exposures. The prevention of FAS and related conditions will only occur when effective methods for identifying and treating alcoholics prior to pregnancy are coupled with convincing advise that helps non-alcoholic women reduce or eliminate their alcohol consumption at times of risk.

REFERENCES

Alling, C. (1985). Biochemical maturation of the brain and the concept of vulnerable periods. In *Alcohol and the Developing Brain*. Rydberg U., (Ed.). Raven Press: New York, pp. 5-10.

Christoffel, K.K and Salasky, I., (1975). Fetal alcohol syndrome in dizygotic twins. *Journal of Pediatrics,* **87** 963-967.

Clarren, S.K. (1981). Recognition of the fetal alcohol syndrome. *Journal of the American Medical Association,* **245** 2436-2439.

Clarren, S.K., Astley, S.J., and Bowden, D.M. (1988). Physical anomalies and developmental delays in non-human primate infants exposed to weekly doses of ethanol during gestation. *Teratology,* **37** 561-570.

Clarren, S.K., Bowden, D.M., and Astley, S.J. (1987). Pregnancy outcomes after weekly oral administration of ethanol during gestation in pigtailed macaques (Macaca nemestrina). *Teratology,* **35** 245-254.

Clarren, S.K. and Smith, D.W. (1978). The fetal alcohol syndrome. *New England Journal of Medicine,* **298** 1063-1067.

Dreosti, I.E. (1978). Zinc-alcohol interactions in brain development. In *Alcohol and Brain Development.* West, J.R. (Ed.). Oxford University Press: New York, pp. 373-405.

Ernhart, C.B., Sokol, R.J., Martier, S., Moron, P., Nadler, D., Ager, J.W., and Wolf, A. (1987). Alcohol teratogenesis in the human. 2. A detailed assessment of specificity critical period and threshold. *American Journal of Obstetrics and Gynecology,* **156** 33-39.

Fischer, S.E., Atkinson, M., Brunap, J.K., Jacobson, S., Sehgal, P.K., Scott, W., and Van Thiel, D.H. (1982). Ethanol-associated selective fetal malnutrition: A contributing factor in the fetal alcohol syndrome. *Alcoholism: Clinical and Experimental research,* **6** 197-201.

Kink, J.C. and Fabro, S. (1983). Alcohol consumption and cigarette smoking: effect on pregnancy. *Clinical Obstetrics and Gynecology,* **26** 437-448.

Kline, J., Stein, Z., Shrout, P., Susser, M., and Warburton, D. (1980). Drinking during pregnancy and spontaneous abortion. *Lancet,* **2** 176-180.

Larsson, G., Bohlin, A.V., and Tunell, R. (1985). Prospective study of children exposed to variable amounts of alcohol in utero. *Archives of Disease in Childhood,* **60** 316-321.

Little, R.E., Grathwohl, H.L., Streissguth, S.P., and McIntyre, C.E. (1981). Public awareness and knowledge about the risks of drinking during pregnancy in Multnomah County Oregon. *American Journal of Public Health,* **71** 312-314.

Little, R.E., Streissguth, A.P., Guzinski, G.M., Frathwohl, H.L., Blumhagen, J.M., and McIntyre, C.E. (1983). Change in obstetrician advise following a two year community educational program on alcohol use and pregnancy. *American Journal of Obstetrics and Gynecology,* **146** 23-28.

May, P.A. and Hymbaugh, K.J. (1989). A macro-level fetal alcohol syndrome prevention program for Native Americans and Alaska Natives: Description and evaluation. *Journal of Studies on Alcohol,* **50** 508-518.

Minor, M.J. and Van Dort, B. (1982). Prevention research on the teratogenic effects of alcohol. *Preventative Medicine,* **11** 346-359.

Rosett, H.L., Ouellette, E.M., Weiner, L. and Owens, E. (1978). Therapy of heavy drinking during pregnancy. *Obstetrics and Gynecology,* **51** 41-46.

Rosett, H.L., Weiner, L., Zuckerman, B., McKinlay, S., and Edelin, K.C. (1980). Reduction of alcohol consumption during pregnancy with benefits to the newborn. *Alcoholism: Clinical and Experimental Research*, **4** 178-184.

Rydberg, U. (1985). Inpatient treatment of pregnant women with abuse of alcohol and drugs-prognosis for mother and child. *The Second Malmo Symposium on Alcohol*. Ferrosan, A.B., (Ed.). Department of Alcohol Diseases: Malmo, pp. 69-73.

Shepard, T.H. (1982). Detection of human teratogenic agents. *Journal of Pediatrics*, **101** 810-815.

Streissguth, A.P., Barr, H.M., Sampson, P.D, Bookstein, F.A., and Darby, B.L. (1989). Neurobehavioral effects of prenatal alcohol: Part I. Research Strategy. *Neurotoxicology and Teratology*, **11** 461-476.

Streissguth, A.P., Barr, H.M., Sampson, P.D, Parrish-Johnson, J.C., Kirchner, G.L., and Martin, D.C. (1986). Attention, distraction and reaction time at age 7 years and prenatal alcohol exposure. *Neurobehavioral Toxicology and Teratology*, **8** 717-725.

Streissguth, A.P., Martin, D.C., Martin, J.C, and Barr, H.M. (1981). The Seattle longitudinal prospective study on alcohol and pregnancy. *Neurobehavioral, Toxicology and Teratology*, **3** 223-233.

U.S. Department of the Treasury and the U.S. Department of Health and Human Services. (November, 1980). Report to the President and Congress of health hazards associated with alcohol and methods to inform the general public of these hazards.

West, J.R. (1986). *Alcohol and Brain Development*. Oxford University Press: New York.

157

CHAPTER 19

Is Occasional Light Drinking During Pregnancy Harmful?

Ernest L. Abel, Ph.D.
Robert J. Sokol, M.D.

Introduction and Background

In the last two decades more than 5,000 articles have been published on the effects of alcohol during pregnancy (Abel, 1984b; 1989). One might assume we'd now have some consensus about the dangers of occasional light drinking during pregnancy. Unfortunately, this isn't so. Our own sober (no pun intended) conclusion, based on a *critical* evaluation of the literature, is that there are no known clinically important risks to the fetus from an occasional drink during pregnancy (see below for our definition of "occasional" and "light"). Here are our reasons:

1. Personal Experience

About two-thirds of all Americans drink to some extent (Malin et al., 1982). Our mothers and your mothers are probably among these 66%. One of us is a Dean of a Medical School (R.J.S.); the other is a Professor in Obstetrics and Gynecology (E.L.A.). While we are both very hairless on top and somewhat funny-looking, we are both of normal size and stature, are both slightly pudgy, do not suffer from any visible birth defects, and though you may disagree with us, (for what we are arguing), we think we are of normal intelligence.

In other words, we don't look or act as if we have suffered as a result of our mothers' having had a drink or two during their pregnancies. We have also peered carefully at the minds and bodies of our children. While it's too soon to know for sure, none of them seems to be any more funny looking than we are, none of them seems to have suffered any loss of IQ points from the occasional drinks our spouses may have taken, and our food bills reflect their overwhelming commitment to eating.

Now it's your turn reader—do you or any of your children seem to have suffered as a result of an occasional motherly drink? Do you personally know of anyone that has?

2. Historical Evidence

When this country was on its way to nationhood, drinking was the norm. Our founding fathers and mothers drank far more than we do today. George Washington was a whiskey distiller, John Adams drank a tankard of hard cider every morning, Thomas Jefferson invented the presidential cocktail party (Rorabaugh, 1979). Historical information about drinking by women is hard to come by, but in the early 1800s there were an estimated "100,000 female drinkers" and many more "who consumed from one-eighth to one-quarter of the nation's spirituous liquor" (Rorabaugh, 1979). We may be mistaken (because of the adverse effects of our own in-utero alcohol exposure), but we don't believe that the people who wrote our Constitution, Declaration of Independence, our Bill of Rights and the other laws by which we live, lost any IQ points by being exposed to more alcohol in-utero than we ourselves were. (In raising this argument, we are more than aware of Dr. Johnson's precept concerning patriotism being the last refuge of the scoundrel).

3. Lies, Damn Lies, and Statistics

A) Lies. There is no practical objective way of knowing how much anyone drinks. We as researchers are therefore forced to rely on what people admit to when they are asked how many drinks they have a day, a week, a month, or something like this. But, how much is in a "drink?" We assume one drink is the same as another and each contains about 1/2 oz of alcohol. This just shows how naive we are. A bartender may use a "shot" glass but who else does? The amount of beverage actually consumed in a drink can vary from one to twelve ounces (Weiner et al., 1983). If you pour most of your pint into a tall glass and I just pour a finger into mine, we'll both say we've had only one drink. If you were asking questions about income you wouldn't ask "how many times do you get paid a month?", would you? You'd want to know not only how often but how much someone gets paid. This would tell you a lot provided a dollar has the same value for everyone. But suppose you had Canadians and Americans in your study. Both might say they make $250 a week, but these dollars have different values in terms of what they will buy. Or suppose you asked Israelis and Britons how much they make. If both say they make 250 "pounds", do they make the same? 'Nuff said. You get the point.

B) Damned Lies. Simply asking someone who drinks a lot about how much he/she drinks is naive. People who drink a lot don't like to admit it. They deny. Technically speaking, they lie. Sometimes they lie a lot. Trust a used car salesman before you trust what an alcoholic tells you about his or her drinking.

Self-reports of drinking during pregnancy are always suspect. Relating the dangers of a given number of "drinks" per day to a particular risk to the fetus based on this information is sophomoric. Because of denial, actual alcohol intake is underreported by the abusive drinker — the individual most likely to be at risk for giving birth to a child with alcohol-related birth defects (Ernhardt et al., 1988; Jacobson et al., 1989; Martier et al., 1989). The risk to the fetus of what might appear to be "2 drinks a day" is undoubtedly the result of much higher intake.

   C) Statistics. Alcohol is but one of many possible risk factors, such as social class, maternal illness, genetic susceptibility, smoking, diet, past health history, pregnancy complications, use of drugs and exposure to environmental pollutants. In epidemiology, statistical techniques are used to try to "even out" as many of these cofactors as possible. The goal is to match people as closely as possible except for their alcohol use. If you are going to do this carefully, you especially need to control for heredity. Charles Dickens made this point cogently in *Pickwick Papers* when he wrote about a meeting of "The Brick Lane Branch of the United Grand Junction Temperance Association." One of the new members was "Betsy Martin, widow, one child and one eye. Goes out charring and washing by day; never had more than one eye, but knows her mother drank bottled stout, and shouldn't wonder if that caused it."

   Consider IQ scores. If you are studying the causes of subnormal IQ, isn't it reasonable to start with parental IQ? Claire Ernhardt and her coworkers (1981) did this when they examined the effects of lead in children. They found lead was associated with decreased scores on cognitive and verbal tests but when parental IQ was incorporated into the analysis, the relationship was no longer significant. No studies in fetal alcohol research have bothered to include parental IQ as a factor. In a recent study, Ann Streissguth and her coworkers (1989) used parental education as a surrogate for IQ, the assumption being the more years in school, the higher the IQ. She then matched subjects on parental school years. Black children were included in the test but race could not be considered in the regression analysis because of the "relatively small number" of black children. If these were so few, why were they included at all? This point would be totally academic except for the fact that the only 2 children with fetal alcohol syndrome in the original Seattle study were both born to the same woman who was black! (Hanson et al., 1978). Black race has also been found to be a major factor in susceptibility to prenatal alcohol effects (Sokol et al., 1986), and Streissguth et al. (1989) state in their conclusions that "the important covariates have been taken into account before claiming a teratogenic effect" when in fact, the covariate for race was not.

   For subjects who are mentally retarded using parental school education might be reasonable. But the Streissguth et al. study dealt with trivial differences in IQ scores of 4- year-old children — less than 5 points. If you or I stay up too late at night, our I.Q.s would probably slip by more than 5 points? If you want to control for parental IQ—measure parental IQ.

What's In A Name?

Not only do we as researchers have to worry about obtaining reliable drinking histories, we need to agree on definitions or criteria for "moderate", "social", "light" and "occasional" drinking. But we still have no consensus in terminology. "Moderate" or "social" drinking in one study can include women who are "heavy" drinkers in another. Even the same research group may use these terms inconsistently. For example, Streissguth and her coworkers defined 4 drinks per day as "social" drinking in one study (Streissguth et al., 1980), 2 drinks a day as "heavy" drinking in another (Martin et al., 1977) and "never more than 3–4", as "social" in yet another (Landesman-Dwyer et al., 1978).

Unrealistic labels have also been used by researchers describing observations in animals. For example, Clarren and Bowden (1982) described the amount of alcohol producing a blood alcohol level of 200–300 mg% in non-human primates as "moderate." Similarly, in their study of alcohol's impact on craniofacial development in mice, Sulik et al. (1981) administered dosages of alcohol producing peak BALs of 193–215 mg% and discussed these levels in terms of "social" drinking. If these levels represent "moderate" or "social" drinking, the people drinking this much probably do most of their socializing in a stupor.

What then is an "occasional" or "social" drink? We realize any specific amount is arbitrary. We are prepared to be arbitrary. We suggest that a BAL of less than 0.04g% is compatible with "social" drinking. This is equivalent to 2 drinks (containing 1 oz. absolute alcohol) consumed over a 2 hour period for someone weighing 140 lb. (University of Michigan Alcohol Research Center). We know of no evidence to suggest that this amount consumed occasionally, e.g., once or twice a week, will cause bad things to happen to unborn babies.

What about studies that say spontaneous abortion rates are increased about twofold for women drinking 1–2 drinks per day or less during pregnancy, you say? (Harlap et al., 1980; Kline et al., 1980). We say the increased risk in these studies is almost certainly due to the heaviest drinkers who only represent a small proportion of the study population— in other words, these studies suffer from the "lies, damn lies and statistics" quandary. In the Harlap et al. (1980) study the number of "heavy" drinkers (more than 2 drinks/day) was reported as only 0.5% of the study population. This is a lot less than the national median and modal consumption for pregnant American women (Abel, 1984a). Either the people in this study are an unusual group (which raises other issues of representativeness) or we're dealing with an instance of the "used car salesman" syndrome—women in this study considerably underreported their alcohol consumption. A reasonable interpretation is that the risk for spontaneous abortion was present only among the 2–4% heaviest exposed pregnancies (Sokol, 1980).

Kline et al. (1980) retrospectively compared women who aborted spontaneously with a control group and concluded that as little as two drinks a week were a risk factor for spontaneous abortion. While this study controlled for smoking, use of other drugs and diet, it didn't control for social class since all women in this study were on public assistance. When Kline repeated her study with private patients the relation between drinking and spontaneous abortion was no longer there (Kolata, 1981).

Studies of abortion following alcohol exposure in nonhuman primates are very, very consistent in finding that the blood alcohol threshold level for spontaneous abortion is around 205 mg% (Clarren et al., 1987; Scott and Fradkin, 1984; Altshuler and Shippenberg, 1981). In dogs, the BAL threshold is almost identical (Ellis and Pick, 1980). These studies in non-human primates and dogs are impressive in their consistency and in their support for suspicion of underreporting in human studies.

How about lowered birth weight, one of the more reliably observed effects associated with *in utero* alcohol exposure in humans and animals? (Abel, 1984a).

In an often cited report, Little (1977) found that consumption of 2 drinks per day produced a decrease in birth weight of 160 g. However, drinking ranged from 0 to 5 drinks a day, and 3 of the mothers in this study could have been classified as alcohol abusers. Only seven of the 801 children in the study weighed under 2500 g. Little (1977) did not indicate the birth weights of the children born to the alcohol abusers or the drinking behavior of the mothers of the low birth weight infants. It's more than likely that the alcohol abusers accounted for most of the relationship.

In another study alleging to show significant effects of "occasional" drinking, Streissguth and her co-workers (1980) reported that eight-month-old children had significantly poorer performances on the Bayley tests after statistical adjustment for a number of confounding variables. However, infants born to women drinking more than 8 drinks per day were lumped in with those whose mothers drank 2 or more drinks per day. When Hank Rosett reanalyzed these data by specific dose and each infant was included only once, only the mental scores of the infants exposed to the higher amounts were significant — and their average score was still a normal 98! (Rosett and Weiner, 1984).

Sutton's Law

There is good reason to believe thresholds exist for various adverse alcohol-related birth defects and it's reasonable for clinicians to recommend abstinence to patients contemplating pregnancy or already pregnant. Unfortunately, the patient who places her unborn offspring at greatest risk, i.e., the abusive drinker or alcohol-dependent woman, is the individual least willing or able to identify herself as a risk drinker or to become abstinent.

When someone asked Willie Sutton why he robbed banks, he answered, "That's where the money is..." The occasional or light drinker is like the nickel in the cookie jar. The real loot, in terms of preventing alcohol-related brain damage, isn't in the cookie jar — it's in the vault, in among the risk drinkers. These are the women we must identify and help to become abstinent. Willie had the right idea? Go where the money is.

REFERENCES

Abel, E.L. (1984a). *Fetal Alcohol Syndrome and Fetal Alcohol Effects.* Plenum Press: New York.

Abel, E.L. (1984b). *Fetal Alcohol Syndrome and Effects.* Greenwood Press: Westport, Connecticut.

Abel, E.L. (1989). *Alcohol-related Birth Defects.* Greenwood Press:Westport, Connecticut.

Altshuler, H.L. and Shippenberg, T.S. (1981). A subhuman primate model for fetal alcohol syndrome research. *Neurobehavioral Toxicology and Teratology* , **3** 121–126.

Clarren, S.K. and Bowden, D.M. (1982). Fetal alcohol syndrome: A new primate model for binge drinking and its relevance to human ethanol teratogenesis. *Journal of Pediatrics,* **101** 819–824.

Clarren, S.K., Bowden, D.M., and Astley, S.J. (1987). Pregnancy outcomes after weekly oral administration of ethanol during gestation in the pig-tailed macaque (Macaca menstrina). *Teratology,* **35** 345–354.

Ellis, F.W. and Pick, J.R. (1980). An animal model of the fetal alcohol syndrome in beagles. *Alcoholism: Clinical and Experimental Research,* **4** 123–134.

Ernhart, C.B., Landa, B., and Schnell, N.B. (1981). Subclinical levels of lead and developmental deficit—a multivoriate follow-up reassessment. *Pediatrics,* **67** 911.

Ernhart, C.B., Morrow-Tlucak, M., Sokol, R.J., and Martier, S. (1988). Underreporting of alcohol use in pregnancy. *Alcoholism: Clinical and*

Experimental Research, **12** 506–511.

Hanson, J.W., Streissguth, A.P., and Smith, D.W. (1978). The effects of moderate alcohol consumption during pregnancy on fetal growth and morphogenesis. *Journal of Pediatrics*, **92** 457–460.

Harlap, S. and Shiono, P.H. (1980). Alcohol, smoking and incidence of spontaneous abortions in the first and second trimester. *Lancet*, **2** 173–176.

Jacobson, S.W., Sokol, R.J., Jacobson, J.L., Martier, S., Kaplan, M., Ager, J., Billings, R., and Bihun, J. (1989). How much underreporting of pregnancy drinking can be detected by one year postpartum? *Alcoholism: Clinical and Experimental Research*, **13** 344.

Kline, J., Shrout, P., Stein, A., Susser, M., and Warburton, D. (1980). Drinking during pregnancy and spontaneous abortion. *Lancet*, **2** 176–180.

Kolata, G.B. (1981). Fetal alcohol advisory debated. *Science*, **214** 642–645.

Landesman-Dwyer, S., Keller, S., and Streissguth, A.P. (1978). Naturalistic observation of newborns: Effects of maternal alcohol intake. *Alcoholism: Clinical and Experimental Research*, **2** 171–177.

Little, R.E. (1977). Moderate alcohol use during pregnancy and decreased infant birth weight. *American Journal of Public Health*, **67** 1154–1156.

Malin, H., Coakley, J., Kaelber, C., Mussch, N., and Holland, W. (1982). An epidemiological perspective on alcohol use and abuse in the United States. In National Institute on Alcohol Abuse and Alcoholism. Alcohol Consumption and Related Problems. NIAAA: Rockville, MD, 99–153.

Martier, S.S., Ager, J.W., Sokol, R.J., Jacobson, J., Jacobson, S., and Bottoms, S.F. (1989). Identification of pregnancy risk-drinking: Two viruses of tolerance. *Alcoholism: Clinical and Experimental Research*, **13** 344.

Martin, J., Martin, D.C., Lund, C.A. and Streissguth, A.P. (1977). Maternal alcohol ingestion and cigarette smoking and their effects on newborn conditioning. *Alcoholism: Clinical and Experimental Research*, **1** 243–247.

Rosett, H.L. and Weiner, L. (1984). *Alcohol and the Fetus*. Oxford University Press: New York.

Rorabaugh, W.J. (1979). *The Alcoholic Republic*. Oxford University Press: New York.

Scott, W.J., Jr. and Fradkin, R. (1984). The effects of prenatal ethanol in cynomolgus monkeys *Macaca fascicularis. Teratology*, **29** 49–56.

Sokol, R.J. (1980). Alcohol and spontaneous abortion. *Lancet*, **1** 1079.

Sokol, R.J., Ager, J., Martier, S., Debanne, S., Ernhart, C., Kuzma, J., and Miller, S.I. (1986). Significant determinants of susceptibility to alcohol teratogenicity. *Annals of New York Academy of Sciences*, **477** 87–102.

Streissguth, A.P., Barr, H.M., Martin, D.C., and Herman, C.S. (1980). Effects of maternal alcohol, nicotine and caffeine use during pregnancy on infant mental and motor development at 8 months. *Alcoholism: Clinical and Experimental Research*, **4** 152–164.

Streissguth, A.P., Barr, H.M., Sampson, P.D., Darby, B.L., and Martin, D.C. (1989). IQ at age 4 in relation to maternal alcohol use and smoking during pregnancy. *Developmental Psychology*, **25** 3–11.

Sulik, K.K., Johnston, M.C., and Webb, M.A. (1981). Fetal alcohol syndrome: Embryogenesis on a mouse model. *Science*, **214** 936–938.

Weiner, L., Rosett, H.L., Edelin, K.C., Alpert, J.J., and Zuckerman, B. (1983). Alcohol consumption by pregnant women. *Obstetrics and Gynecology*, **61** 6–12.

ARE SCHOOL BASED ALCOHOL/DRUG EDUCATION PROGRAMS EFFECTIVE?

CHAPTER 20

School-based alcohol and drug education programs can be effective

Stuart Fors, Ph.D.

Introduction

The availability of all kinds of drugs (Johnston, O'Malley, and Bachman, 1987) makes it a virtual certainty that young people will be put in a position of deciding whether or not to use them. For the purpose of this paper, drugs include psychoactive substances that are available either legally or illegally. For the most part, drugs that are generally considered to be medicines are excluded. For example, within this framework we find legal drugs such as alcohol and nicotine that are illegal for some age groups, as well as marijuana, the simple possession of which has been decriminalized (de factor or de jure) in most states, and cocaine/crack and heroin which are not legal under any circumstances.

The issue to be discussed in this chapter is the extent to which schools can be justifiably promoted as a *primary* site for drug education efforts. Do schools have a clear role (beyond the "3 R's") in education about health/ social issues? If schools have a role, how should it be described or defined? What are the limits of involvement and the expectations?

More specifically, this paper will:

1) Clarify the role, goals, and scope of school-based drug education;
2) Argue that school-based drug education can, and does, work; and
3) Present suggestions for strengthening programs.

Many of the thoughts in this paper reflect empirical and anecdotal evidence from the drug education literature as well as my personal views that have developed in my 25 years as a teacher of health/drug education at the middle, secondary, and university levels.

The Schools and Drug Education

Schools have a mandate from society to contribute to the physical, social, emotional, moral, and intellectual development of young people.

How moral issues are to be approached has not been resolved. Some say schools should be more involved, with specific moral directives; others say moral education should be left to the family and church. Nonetheless, schools are faced with major challenges, and education about drugs is just one of many that requires a commitment of time, money, and expertise. The federal government views the school as a major site where the "war" on drugs can be waged. Hundreds of millions of dollars are being pumped into the educational pipeline through direct grants and allocations to each state. Someone, somewhere, believes that drug education works.

The role of the school has been clarified and expanded in the last 5–10 years (see, for example: Lohrmann and Fors, 1986; U.S. Department of Education [USDOE] — 1986, 1988; Goodstadt, 1989). While there is no consensus on the specifics, the general areas of involvement include the following:

1. School drug policies—issues such as smoke-free schools, penalties for use, possession, sale, or under the influence of drugs, first aid for drug emergencies;

2. Primary intervention—drug education that may be offered in a myriad of ways; and

3. Secondary intervention—programs for high risk students (those exhibiting problem behavior directly related to drugs or predictive of drug abuse).

Evidence That School-Based Drug Education Works
Interpretation of Evidence/Effectiveness

One of the major roadblocks to evaluating drug education programs is the inability of program planners to agree on the basic goals and objectives of drug education. For example, if a goal is "drug free youth" (USDOE, 1988), our standard for effectiveness will be a decrease toward zero in the consumption of all drugs. On the other hand, if "responsible use" (Engs and Fors, 1988) is a goal, success occurs if moderate drinking prevails and/or if there is a significant decrease in driving after drinking (or an increase in the use of designated drivers).

Over the past 25 years we have witnessed a decrease of 25–30 percent in the prevalence of smoking in adults (Surgeon General, 1989). This has resulted in over 750,000 smoking-related deaths that were either avoided or postponed. Additionally, the percentage of high school seniors who smoke daily has been reduced by 35–40 percent (28.8–18.7) (Johnston et al., 1987). Drug taking by middle and high school students, with the exception of alcohol, has *decreased* in the past ten years. Lloyd Johnston, of the Institute for Social Research at the University of Michigan, who

168

coordinates the annual drug use survey of high school seniors was quoted as saying, "The continued decline in drug use suggests that anti-drug campaigns educating the young about drug use are being heard." (Staff, 1989). Another newspaper article said this: "Prevention programs are generally credited for a marked drop nationwide in casual drug use..." (Straus, 1989). The following section will provide what I believe is specific evidence that some programs, in some places, are working for some people.

Research Reports

That school-based drug education has a positive effect on knowledge is well recognized. For some, this would be satisfactory evidence of success and we need go no further. But not for most! Bangert-Drowns (1988) concluded on the basis of his meta-analysis of 33 programs that were evaluated between 1968 and 1986 that, "alcohol and drug education successfully increased drug-related knowledge, but was less successful in changing attitudes, and least successful in changing the drug-related behaviors of students" (p. 254). He continues, "... the public record shows that substance abuse education has, for the most part, failed to achieve its primary goal, the prevention of drug and alcohol abuse." (p. 260). Something else is needed! This is not new. Health behavior scholar, Godfrey Hochbaum admonished us in 1969 that "...we must pay much more attention to how a child can apply his health knowledge and overcome the difficulties he may encounter" (Hochbaum, 1969, p. 18).

Botvin (1986) summarized his view of the "state of the art" by saying, "The progress made in the past few years provides considerable cause for optimism" (p. 369). "More than 20 research studies testing programs based on these two prevention models (social influences, personal and social skills) have demonstrated significant reductions in substance use (typically cigarette smoking)" (p. 373). He recognized some methodological limitations, and he stressed the potential of these strategies for use with programs that focus on multiple drug behaviors.

An expert Advisory Panel convened by the National Cancer Institute in December, 1987, concluded that, "... school-based smoking prevention programs in the U.S. have had consistently positive effects, though these effects have been modest and limited in scope" (cited in Glynn, 1989, p. 183).

Connell, Turner, and Mason (1985) reported the results of the School Health Education Evaluation project. This project looked at the effects four health curriculums (these were not limited to substance abuse prevention) had on approximately 30,000 students in more than 20 states over a period of three years. The authors concluded that knowledge, attitudes, health-related skills (i.e., decision-making skills) and selected behaviors were significantly different in the experimental groups. Self-report behavioral data included cigarette smoking. Three times as many comparison group students began smoking during the first half of the 7th grade as experimental group students. A strong argument is made for the establishment of coordinated health education programs that continue "through several grades" (p. 317).

Pentz, et al. (1989) reported on a large scale substance abuse prevention project in the Kansas City, Kansas/Missouri metropolitan area. Over 22,000 6th and 7th grade students received a school-based educational program that is being introduced sequentially into different schools over a six-year period. One-year follow-up data indicate significantly lower use prevalence rates for alcohol, cigarettes, and marijuana in the intervention schools when compared with delayed intervention schools. The net increase in prevalence in the intervention schools was half that of the comparison schools. This project also included parental involvement and media coverage.

Walter, Vaughan, and Wynder (1989) reported on their evaluation of a six year sequential health curriculum titled, "Know Your Body" that focused on cigarette smoking and diet as cancer risk factors. They followed a cohort beginning in the 4th grade in 1979 and continuing through the 9th grade. Of the 911 original subjects, 593 had data collected at both baseline and termination points. Of interest for this review was the significantly lower prevlance of current smokers (3.5%) in the intervention schools compared with the non-intervention schools (13.1%). The study results are limited in their external validity by the nature of the study subjects. The location was in Westchester County, New York, which is one of the most affluent areas of the United States.

Anecdotal Evidence/Reports
Hard-core researchers, raise your warning flags! Reports that write of good feelings, lots of smiles, intuition, and other miscellaneous subjective "data" provide good reason to pause, but there are other good reasons to read further. Just because the project was not the idea of a funded researcher and therefore it does not include a sophisticated evaluation is no reason to discard it out-of-hand. The challenge is to sort through the numerous glowing reports and determine whether or not to accept the "results" at face value. Given the usual limitations, I am herewith submitting examples of "testimonials" that have appeared in two publications (National Institute on Alcohol Abuse and Alcoholism [NIAAA] and National Institute on Drug Abuse [NIDA], 1986; Southeast Regional Center for Drug-Free Schools and Communities [SERC], 1988).

"The results of the analyses of the first post-test data for this project indicate early treatment effects on the awareness of curriculum content and the frequency of alcohol use." (NIAAA and NIDA, 1986, p. 22).

"A study conducted in 1984 to determine differences in the frequency and early onset of drug use in communities with Project Charlie compared to those not using a prevention program, showed significant differences." (NIAAA and NIDA, 1986, p. 26).

". . .the overall conclusion has been that when high team activity schools are compared to low or no team activity schools at each of the three grade levels (elementary, junior, and senior high), the high team activity schools average considerably more positive impact on substance use, attitudes, and knowledge." (NIAAA and NIDA, 1986, p. 29).

"Self-report survey data, an increase in the number of students participating in organizations actively promoting the no-use message, official arrest data, and a decline in the number of students suspended or expelled from school all point to success." (SERC, 1988, p. 12).

"Statistics show that there were no alcohol or other drug use-related offenses in the two years, 1985–86 and 1986–87." (SERC, 1988, p. 14).

"A repeat of PRIDE Survey in 1986 showed that student use of alcohol and other drugs had decreased in every category." (SERC, 1988, p. 16).

All of the programs from which a quote was taken regarding effectiveness included a school-based drug use/abuse prevention curriculum as part of a comprehensive community/school program. Should these results be taken "with a grain of salt?" My opinion is no. While many, if not most of the programs may not have incorporated all of the basic theoretical, educational, and behavior change principles such as those advocated by Botvin (1986) and Goodstadt (1986), they are still worthy of our inclusion on the side of programs that "work." That is, by some pre-established standard, whether it is knowledge gain, attitude change, drug use reduction, arrest reduction, lower DUI behaviors, or emergency room visits, program directors/evaluators have concluded that to varying degrees school-based drug education works for them.

Summary

It would be a serious mistake to make a blanket statement that drug education works, without some caveats. To me that would be akin to saying that 500 mg of penicillin in capsules four times a day will work for all people for all health problems in all circumstances. We understand that is nonsense and certainly for some people, downright dangerous. Goodstadt

(1989) wrote of inconsistencies in effects:

> 1. Program effects vary among sub-groups of students;
>
> 2. Program impact is inconsistent across outcome measures; and
>
> 3. Individual program have produced both positive and negative outcomes. (p. 247).

Assuming Goodstadt's conclusions are accurate, we should avoid "throwing the baby out with the bathwater." That is, discarding potentially strong programs out-of-hand because in one evaluation they do not measure up to a pre-selected standard.

Evidence has been presented that school-based drug education has worked as measured by knowledge, attitude, skill and/or behavioral effects. This is particularly true for cigarettes where a clear and consistent message from all parts of our society supports the educational effort. There is plenty of evidence that some programs have not worked, but rather than dwell on what did not work, I suggest we carefully scrutinize those programs that have been successful.

When we analyze drug education programs, we need to look not just at the results, but at three possible factors that can determine success or failure (Green and Lewis, 1986):

> 1. Theoretical basis—for scope and sequence, for educational strategies, for specific content;
>
> 2. Implementation process — the theoretical basis may be adequate, but if teachers do not teach the program the way it was designed, how can the program have a chance to succeed? This argues strongly for well designed teacher in-service and committed teachers; and
>
> 3. Evaluation strategy—if instrumentation and design are weak or faulty, then we must be concerned with a Type I or Type II statistical error. In either case, the "true" results are not uncovered.

While school-based drug education seems to be working in some situations (and we should celebrate those successes), programs still seem to be missing the youth at higher risk. Ten percent of those people who drink, consume 50 percent of the alcohol (Secretary of Health and Human Services, 1987), and this seems to be the trend with other drugs. There is relatively widespread experimentation (primarily with marijuana) that results in a small percentage of hard core users experiencing the majority of the problems that accompany abuse.

Unfortunately, school-based drug education may only be a "band aid" for high risk youth. Peele (1987) expressed the dilemma this way, "Our

172

inability to engage many youngsters in meaningful achievement activity or to provide a large number with a minimal degree of social integration vitiates our drug education programs for the groups we are most concerned to reach." (p. 425). And finally, Representative Charles Rangel (D-NY) was quoted as saying, "Until we solve the problems of joblessness, homelessness, family instability, lack of education, and poverty, we will never end the despair that is the root cause. . .for many in the first place" (Thomas, 1989).

REFERENCES

Bangert-Drowns, R. (1988). The effects of school-based substance abuse education—a meta-analysis. *Journal of Drug Education*, **18** 243–264.

Botvin, G. (1986). Substance abuse prevention research: Recent developments and future directions. *Journal of School Health*, **56** 369–374.

Connell, D., Turner, R., and Mason, E. (1985). Summary of findings of School Health Education Evaluation: Health promotion effectiveness, implementation, and costs. *Journal of School Health*, **55** 316–321.

Engs, R. and Fors, S. (1988). Drug abuse hysteria: The challenge of keeping perspective. *Journal of School Health*, **55** 26–28.

Glynn, T. (1989). Essential elements of school-based smoking prevention programs. *Journal of School Health*, **59** 181–188.

Goodstadt, M. (1986). Alcohol education research and practice: a logical analysis of the two realities. *Journal of Drug Education*, **16** 349–365.

Goodstadt, M. (1989). Substance abuse curricula vs. school drug policies. *Journal of School Health*, **59** 246–250.

Green, L. and Lewis, F. (1986). *Measurement and evaluation in health education and health promotion.* Mayfield: Palo Alto.

Hochbaum, G. (1969). Changing health behavior in youth. *School Health Review*, 1 (September) 15–19.

Johnston, L., O'Malley, P., and Bachman, J. (1987). *National trends in drug use and related factors among American high school students and young adults, 1975–1986.* NIDA: Rockville, MD.

Lohrmann, D. and Fors, S. (1986). Can school-based educational programs really be expected to solve the adolescent drug abuse problem? *Journal of Drug Education*, **16** 327–339.

National Institute on Alcohol Abuse and Alcoholism and National Institute on Drug Abuse (1986). *Proceedings of the 1st National Conference on Alcohol and Drug Abuse Prevention.* NIAAA and NIDA: Rockville, MD.

Peele, S. (1987). Running scared: We're too frightened to deal with the real issues in adolescent substance abuse. *Health Education Research*, **2** 423–432.

Pentz, M., Dwyer, J., MacKinnon, D., Flay, D., Hansen, W., Wang, E., and Johnson, C.A. (1989). A multi-community trial for primary prevention of adolescent drug abuse—Effects on drug use prevalence. *Journal of the American Medical Association*, **261** 3259–3266.

Secretary of Health and Human Services (1987). *Sixth special report to the U.S. Congress on alcohol and health.* DHHS: Washington, D.C.

Southeast Regional Center for Drug-Free Schools and Communities (1988). *Noteworthy programs and practices: Summaries of programs and strategies in support of drug-free youth in the southeast.* Atlanta. Southeast Regional Center for Drug-Free Schools and Communities.

Staff (1989, March 1). Teen drug use down sharply in class of '89. *Atlanta Constitution.*

Straus, H. (1989, September 5). "No" is easier said than done. *Atlanta Constitution.*

Surgeon General (1989). *Reducing the health consequences of smoking: 25 years of progress.* Executive summary. Rockville, MD: Thomas, K.,U.S. Dept. of H&H.S. , (1989, June 22). Anti-drug campaigns' effectiveness debated. *Atlanta Journal and Constitution.* p. D–4.

U.S. Department of Education (1986). *What works: Schools without drugs.* USDOE: Washington, D.C.

U.S. Department of Education (1988). *Drug prevention curricula: A guide to selection and implementation.* USDOE: Washington, D.C.

Walter, H., Vaughan, R., and Wynder, E. (1989). Primary prevention of Cancer among children: Changes in cigarette smoking and diet after six years of intervention. *Journal of the National Cancer Institute*, **81** 995–999.

CHAPTER 21

A Review of School-Based Drug Education Programs: Do We Expect Too Much?[1]

Louis Gliksman, Ph.D.
Cynthia Smythe, M.Ed.

Concerns about alcohol and drug abuse have existed in our society for decades. In addition to trying to deal with the issue of treatment—how do we help those who are in trouble—we have also been concerned with the issue of prevention—how do we stop these problems from occurring in the first place. Most of the prevention efforts that have been developed over the years have focused on children in the school system—for the most part children who are in grades 6 and above. The reasons cited for the emphasis on this particular group are numerous. For example, we have heard that our children are our future and we must do whatever is necessary to ensure that they don't fall under the spell of drugs; and if we get to these kids before they use any drugs we increase the likelihood of success. In point of fact, one of the primary reasons for this emphasis is decidedly practical. It is easier to develop programs and implement them for this particular group because they are a captive audience. We know where to find them and how to convey information because that is what the school system has been doing for years. We have been following this approach blindly in spite of the questions and issues with which we have been confronted over the decades, the most fundamental of which is whether this programming approach is having the desired effect. While we have taken cursory looks at individual approaches and have changed approaches over the years, we have not really addressed the issues fundamental to this type of approach to prevention.

Drug prevention programs for school-aged children should generate a number of specific questions. For example, how effective is any one school program in preventing drug (i.e., alcohol, illicit drugs, and tobacco) abuse? Are programs methodologically sound enough for consumers to

[1]The views expressed in this document are those of the authors and do not necessarily reflect those of the Addiction Research Foundation.

trust the results and act on them? Are there principles for effective programming that can be gleaned from the hundreds of programs developed and implemented thus far? Can programs alone or policies alone be effective in preventing use/abuse? These and other similar issues will be addressed by reviewing some of the more current literature on school-based programming. In order to put our discussion into perspective, we will begin with a brief review of the history of school-based prevention programming. It should be remembered that many of the changes in the underlying philosophies of these approaches reflect the values of our society at that time, probably more than they reflect the current state of knowledge about attitude and behavior change. We will focus primarily on alcohol and tobacco use among school-aged children and adolescents, and will conclude our discussion by trying to make recommendations for future programming based on our interpretation of what went before.

An Historical Perspective of School-Based Programming

The following history of school-based alcohol programming is based partially on a 1976 review paper by Gail Milgram. Alcohol education in the U.S. has its roots in the history of the Temperance Movement which emerged in the 1840s. The movement urged all states to require teaching the "evils of alcohol" in school and by 1880 this was accomplished. It wasn't until the 1930s and the repeal of prohibition that alcohol education began to change. The objectives of alcohol education at that time were to stress abstinence during the growing period and then responsibility for substance use after growth had finished.

The decade of the 40s can be characterized by two opposing forces: evils of alcohol versus objective information. The first approach emphasized the extensive and serious damage done to health by alcohol. The latter approach stated that students were not to be scared into abstinence but were instead to be given simple facts based on scientific truths.

A change in the philosophy of alcohol education can be noted in the 50s. There are few references left to the evils of alcohol and many more to the teaching of scientific facts. There is also a move at this time toward alcohol education becoming part of a total health education curriculum. However, analyses of curricula found that alcohol education was dealt with on a hit-or-miss basis and material was often inaccurate.

Alcohol education in the 60s favored the objective scientific approach. It was felt that specific information and systematic instruction about alcohol was necessary to help students form a personal decision when older. It was in this decade that people became interested in the effect of teacher variables on students, (i.e. how comfortable was the teacher when discussing these issues).

The 70s brought a potpourri of approaches: the ever present evils of alcohol; the concept of responsible drinking; a call for objective honest information; and a new movement for "alcohol is a drug approach." Analyses of alcohol education literature from this decade show that most education material was produced for teachers and college and high school students with little for elementary students. A review of curriculum guides shows little stress on alcohol and highway safety or teenage drinking.

This brings us to the 80s. In this decade the predominant approach, based on the work of Fishbein and Ajzen (1975), incorporates the notion that attitudes are determinants of behavior, and involves creating programs that will reduce abusive behavior by increasing knowledge and improving attitudes. A second approach that is quickly gaining popularity is the Social Influence model based on McGuire's (1964) social inoculation theory and Bandura's (1977) social learning theory. This model emphasises the external influences that push adolescents toward drug use, particularly the media and key people in the adolescent's life. The approach acknowledges the vulnerability of adolescents by promoting such programs as "Just Say No" and Life Skills Training.

The drug education literature is rife with articles denouncing the effectiveness of the knowledge-attitude-behavior paradigm. However, it is difficult to know whether the programs themselves are ineffective or the evaluations are so poor that any effects are masked. A few examples follow. Staulcup, Kenward, and Frigo (1979) reviewed 21 primary alcohol prevention projects and found no link between knowledge or attitude change and behavior change. The authors plead for better evaluations, standardized measuring instruments and longitudinal studies.

Kinder, Pape and Walfish (1980) reviewed 25 studies and found knowledge gains but no attitude or behavior changes. They again plead for better methodology in the evaluations and for valid measures. Some tentative changes in attitudes and behavior in adult populations make the authors wonder if education should be directed toward specific populations using specific variables.

During this same period, a review of 127 program evaluations was done by Schaps, DiBartolo, Moskowitz, Palley, and Churgin (1981) who found the programs generally ineffective. However, when looking at the 10 best researched, high-intensity programs, they found some positive effects. The authors suggest that the evaluations be more methodologically rigorous with program outcomes better linked to the actual program elements.

It appears that in the absence of positive effects, the alternative has been to blame the methodology and not the program itself. This may be true, but there is a real paucity of evidence to back this up.

177

However, these somewhat discouraging reviews also did lead to some philosophical papers about the nature of the knowledge-attitude-behavior paradigm itself; the value of these programs generally; and the reasons for the limited success of most programs. In 1983 Weisheit published a paper about why programs fail. He believed abstinence-oriented programs of necessity failed since the large majority of teenagers drink. Because of this failure, the responsible use paradigm emerged. Theoretically, responsible use makes sense, but Weisheit claims it is hard to define and difficult to implement and evaluate clearly. Therefore, success is unlikely. Since most primary prevention fails with teenagers in any case, he suggests we use different markers of success than the conventional ones. A program may be deemed successful if it makes parents and taxpayers happy and the school feels it is doing its job.

Goodstadt (1986) cites five previous reviews that are consistent in their findings of little evidence of effectiveness. Because the evaluation methodology in these studies is inadequate and the results too inconsistent or negative, the findings are not helpful for future programming. He suggests several reasons for these results: programs may be thought to fail because the evaluations fail to assess differential effects on subgroups of the target audience; although knowledge is relatively easy to influence by many types of programs, attitudes and behaviors are extremely difficult to modify; drug education programs fail to provide links with other areas of school curriculum; too little emphasis is placed on implementation of the program and too little time spent delivering the program; and there is a failure to distinguish between process and outcome evaluation.

In 1984, Polich, Ellicksen, Reuter, and Kahan in a Rand report on adolescent drug use make a strong argument for the Social Influence model. They say approaches up to now have failed because they make incorrect assumptions about why adolescents use drugs. They feel giving information or trying to change values is a waste of time. Adolescents use drugs because of peer influence and they must learn counter arguments or be inoculated against further use/abuse.

Specific sure-fire variables began to emerge in the literature around this time. Connell, Turner, and Mason (1985) evaluated the School Health Education program in the U.S., a total health curriculum that involved 30,000 children in 20 states. As usual, they found knowledge gains, but also some increases in attitudes and self-reported skills and practices. These latter increases correlated with the number of classroom hours committed to the program. The authors recommend 40–50 classroom hours necessary for effective changes.

Pickens (1985), in his review, suggested other variables that may contribute to program effectiveness: prior drug experience of the target group;

178

teacher variables; and the developmental stage of the target group vis-a-vis drug use.

Tobler (1986) in her meta-analysis of 143 adolescent drug prevention programs found Peer programs most effective for the average adolescent and Alternative programs best for the "at risk" group. However, Bangert-Drowns (1988), in his meta-analysis criticized Tobler's methodology and found most programs ineffective.

The SWRL Report (1988) on Prevention Goals, Methods and Outcomes found the Social Influence approach, particularly the "Just Say No" program, has limited effectiveness by itself, particularly with alcohol. The authors recommend prevention should start earlier than junior high and programs should aim to reduce underlying problems in drug users.

In 1989 Moskowitz published a large critical review of the research literature. He classifies most programs into one of three models: knowledge/attitude; values/decision making; and social competency and finds none very effective. Moskowitz says that with alcohol education it is difficult to articulate goals—is it abstinence or responsible use? Confusion also arises because there are minimum drinking age laws but most teenagers drink. With smoking education there is a clear message—abstinence. The present social climate is also ensuring the success of anti-smoking programs.

Reviews of smoking prevention studies reveal more successes than those in the area of alcohol education—probably for the reasons stated by Moskowitz. Flay (1985) reviewed 27 studies using psycho-social approaches to prevention and found serious methodological flaws in the research to date. He also found problems with assigning whole schools to experimental or control conditions since some schools have greater numbers of smokers than others. However, in spite of these limitations, he feels that programs based on the Social Influence approach can be successful some of the time, and that these programs have prevented further increases in smoking by up to 50% for up to three years. In 1985, Flay et al. also published the results of the Waterloo Smoking study. This program involved students from 22 matched schools in experimental and control conditions. The core program given in the first three months of grade 6 had three components: information elicited Socratically from the students; development of skills to resist the social influence of family, peers and media to smoke; and decision-making skills and commitment not to smoke. Flay et al. (1985) found the curriculum affected the smoking onset process—particularly for those students already at risk.

Biglan et al. (1987) looked at a program teaching refusal skills from the point of view of subject attrition and found that smokers dropped out of the treatment condition at higher rates than non-smokers. Therefore,

179

they concluded, it is hard to generalize the results of programs to those adolescents who are likely to become habitual smokers.

Two papers, one by Cleary, Hitchcock, Semmer, Flinchbaugh, and Pinney (1988) and one by Kozlowski, Coambs, Ferrence, and Adlaf (in press, 1989) criticize the effectiveness of the Social Influence model. Cleary et al. conclude that such programs have small effects of uncertain duration on smoking behavior. Kozlowski et al. argue for an integrated substance abuse program since smokers are also other non-medical drug abusers. They feel it is alright to impart information but don't try to change attitudes. Policy is probably more effective and less expensive in preventing smoking than much of the existing programming.

Conclusions

The history of successes of school-based drug education programs has not been a positive one. The general consensus appears to be that although there are individual successes, school-based drug education prevention programs, regardless of their underlying principles, have generally not proven themselves to be effective or are inconsistent in their effectiveness at best. Any positive effects from these programs, have been with respect to changes in knowledge. Changes in attitudes are not consistently found and positive changes in behavior are rarely found to be associated with these programs. We are left with the hope that this knowledge gain will ultimately be instrumental in changing attitudes and behavior, an assumption that we cannot make with any degree of certainty (Goodstadt, 1989).

However, before we dismiss the benefits of school-based programming out of hand, we should re-examine two possibilities for the negative view espoused above—that problems of methodology and/or a lack of integration of approaches may account for a lack of positive findings. Previously, we suggested that poorly designed studies that ask the wrong questions have been the reason for a lack of positive findings, and suggested that this may indeed be a poor excuse. However, the possibility exists that this is indeed an accurate statement. In fact, Milgram (1987), in the course of articulating a variety of potential reasons for the lack of positive findings, suggests that this may in fact happen with regularity. The potential reasons include the following: (i) the goals of the program may be non-specific making outcome assessment difficult; (ii) the program content may not meet student needs; (iii) teachers delivering the program may be untrained and/or uncomfortable with the material; (iv) programs may not be lengthy enough to be effective; and (v) evaluations of these programs may not be conceived properly so that the right questions are not asked. Some of these are problems associated with the program and others are problems of evaluation design. While all are possible, it seems unlikely that methodological issues are high on the list of possibilities. Increased attention to evaluation issues in the literature recently should have reduced the possibility of this being proposed of poor evaluations accounting for failure. The fact that it is still being proposed suggests that the problem lies with the products and not the method of evaluation.

Goodstadt (1988), rather than focusing on the negative findings, takes a constructive approach and proposes that the problem is that these programs which focus on the individual student may be insufficient in themselves. There is a need for both drug education and drug policies to prevent use/abuse. The implication is that education by itself may not be sufficient, but that it requires a policy component to complement it which acknowledges and reinforces the messages in the drug education component and at the same time recognizes the large number of students who do not use or abuse drugs.

The most recent educational thrusts have taken such an integrated approach and built the two components into school system interventions. The concept of integration is the cornerstone of the Addiction Research Foundation's program thrust in the school system. It acknowledges that the issue of alcohol and drugs must be dealt with in a comprehensive manner.

It suggests a coordinated curriculum component ideally running from kindergarten to grade 12, and one which involves a number of courses. It incorporates strategies for early identification which will help those beginning to be at risk, and proposes a policy component which specifies the rules for students and teachers and their obligations with respect to alcohol and drugs.

Implicit in the program is the acknowledgment that community support is integral to the program's success and other interventions, such as parenting programs, community campaigns are being designed to reinforce the messages in the schools and ensure that there is consistency. The success of this approach will be monitored and the years to come will determine its utility.

This document has intentionally taken a decidedly research oriented approach in the discussion of these school-based initiatives. We recognize and acknowledge at the outset that the subjective experiences of program developers and implementors may be different, but the objective criteria are the sole basis on which we are able to gauge program effectiveness. We also recognize that these findings generally represent short term interventions, and it is possible that the true value of these interventions may not be apparent for several years when their information and strategies may be more relevant.

181

REFERENCES

Bandura, A. (1977). *Social learning theory*. Prentice-Hall: Englewood Cliffs, NJ.

Bangert-Drowns, R. (1988). The effects of school-based substance abuse education—a meta-analysis. *Journal of Drug Education*, **18**(3) 243–264.

Biglan, A., Glasgow, R., Ary, D., Faller, C., Gallison, C., Thompson, R., Glasgow, R., and Lichtenstein, E. (1987). Do smoking prevention programs really work? Attrition and internal and external validity of an evaluation of a refusal training program. *Journal of Behavioral Medicine*, **10**(2) 159–171.

Cleary, P., Hitchcock, J., Semmer, N., Flinchbaugh, L., and Pinney, J. (1988). Adolescent smoking: Research and health policy. *The Millbank Quarterly*, **66**(1) 137–171.

Connell, D., Turner, R., and Mason, E. (1985). Summary of finding of the School Health Education evaluation: Health promotion effectiveness, implementation, and costs. *Journal of School Health*, **55**(8) 316–321.

Fishbein, M. and Ajzen, I. (1975). *Belief, attitude, intention and behavior: An introduction to theory and research*. Addison-Wesley Publishing Co: Reading, MA.

Flay, B. (1985). Psychosocial approaches to smoking prevention: A review of findings. *Health Psychology*, **4**(5) 449–488.

Flay, B., Ryan, K., Best, J., Brown, K., Kersell, M., d'Avernas, J., and Zanna, M. (1985). Are social-psychological smoking prevention programs effective? The Waterloo Study. *Journal of Behavioral Medicine*, **8**(1) 37–59.

Goodstadt, M. (1986). School-based drug education in North America: What is wrong? What can be done? *Journal of School Health*, **56**(7) 278–281.

Goodstadt, M. (1988). *Education and baseball bats: Drug education versus school drug policies*. Paper presented at the Alcohol Policy VI Conference, Ann Arbor, Michigan, December 1, 1988.

Goodstadt, M. (1989). Drug education: The prevention issues. *Journal of Drug Education*, **19** 197–208.

Kinder, B., Pape. N., and Walfish, S. (1980). Drug and alcohol education programs: A review of outcome studies. *International Journal of Addiction*, **15**(7) 1035–1054.

Kozlowski, L., Coambs, R., Ferrence, R., and Adlaf, E. (1989). Preventing smoking and other drug use: Let the buyers beware and the interventions be apt. *Canadian Journal of Public Health*, in press.

McGuire, W. (1964). Inducing resistance to persuasion: Some contemporary approaches. *Advances in Experimental and Social Psychology,* **1** 191–229.

Milgram, G. (1976). A historical review of alcohol education research and comments. *Journal of Alcohol & Drug Education,* **21**(2) 1–16.

Milgram, G. (1987). Alcohol and drug education programs. *Journal of Drug Education,* **17** 43–57.

Moskowitz, J. (1989). The primary prevention of alcohol problems: A critical review of the research literature. *Journal of Studies in Alcohol,* **50**(1) 54–88.

Pickens, K. (1985). Drug education: The effects of giving information. *Journal of Alcohol & Drug Education,* **30**(3) 32–44.

Polich, J., Ellickson, P., Reuter, P., and Kahan, J. (1984). Strategies for controlling adolescent drug use. *The Rand Publication Series.*

Schaps, E., DiBartolo, R., Moskowitz, J., Palley, C., and Churgin, S. (1981). A review of 127 drug abuse prevention evaluations. *Journal of Drug Issues,* **11** 17–43.

Staulcup, H., Kenward, K., and Frigo, D. (1979) A review of federal primary alcoholism prevention projects. *Journal of Studies in Alcohol,* **40**(11) 943-968.

The Southwest Regional Educational Laboratory. (1988). *Prevention goals, methods and outcomes.* The Southwest Regional Educational Laboratory: Los Alalmitos, CA., 1–13.

Tobler, N. (1986) Meta-analysis of 143 adolescent drug prevention programs: Quantitative outcome results of program participants compared to a control or a comparison group. *Journal of Drug Issues,* **16**(4) 537-567.

Weisheit, R. (1983). The social context of alcohol and drug education: Implications for program evaluations. *Journal of Alcohol & Drug Education,* **29**(1) 72-81.

183

CHAPTER 22

Alcohol/Drug Education: School and Community Factors

Gail Gleason Milgram, Ed.D.

Introduction

America's belief in the ability of its educational systems to solve social problems has fueled dramatic growth in school-based programs. The renewed interest in alcohol and drug prevention and education programs is but one example of the problems schools are expected to tackle. There are many essential elements for alcohol/drug education to be comprehensive and integrated in the school's curriculum: a clear and articulated philosophy, realistic goals and obtainable objectives, content and methods that support the program, trained educators, and strategies that meet the needs of the students. A key factor in any educational program is the community's support, as the philosophical base and policy structure for the school's program evolves from the community. Building a bridge between the community and the school to create programs that are reinforced by both elements is an important task for prevention in the 1990s.

The School

Fors notes the school's mandate to contribute to the development of young people and the major challenges faced by the institution (1990). Weishert et al. studied whether the schools are appropriate settings for prevention programs and they found that although students might not be receptive to all the information and activities provided in this setting, they do not "tune-out" school-based prevention programs (1984). Alcohol and drug education programs in schools date back to the 1800s, yet they have often lacked comprehensiveness. Gliksman and Smythe stress the importance of integration within the school's curriculum as the cornerstone of the school's alcohol/drug program (1990).

Many programs have not defined prevention or clarified goals. Since selecting obtainable goals is directly related to the positive impact of the program and the ability to measure its results, prevention of what and for whom needs to be presented in a realistic fashion. The following list of questions is designed to clarify goals and philosophical issues (Milgram, 1987):

> Will the educational program attempt to prevent alcohol/drug use for life or until a certain age, to minimize risks related to use, to prevent alcohol/drug related problems, to prevent societal ills related to alcohol and drugs or to prevent alcohol/drug dependency?
>
> Philosophical issues related to alcohol/drugs also need to be clarified: Is alcohol accepted as part of American society? Are any drugs accepted for use by society? Is there a distinction between low-risk and high-risk drinking/drug taking? It is possible for individuals to make responsible decisions regarding the use of alcohol/drugs? Can responsible decisions regarding alcohol/drugs be made by adolescents?
>
> Programmatic issues also need to be addressed: At what age and with what content will alcohol/drug education be included in the school's curriculum? Will alcohol and other drugs be combined or handled separately? Will relevant evaluation measures be built into the program?
>
> Belief statements on alcoholism/drug dependency must also be accepted. Is alcoholism/drug dependency a disease? Do people recover from alcoholism/drug dependency with appropriate treatment? What impact does the alcoholism/drug dependency have on the significant others in the person's life?

A clear and articulated philosophy provides the support for policy development and educational program implementation. Other critical components for an alcohol/drug education program are alcohol/drug content materials and methods that support the goals and objectives and trained educators who understand and support the program. Identifying the needs of the students and incorporating the reality of the adolescent world into the program are also essential aspects. An open and non-threatening classroom atmosphere facilitates the educational process. Since the classroom is a peer group, it is essential that the students interact with each other and discuss positive alternatives in high-risk situations. Perry's review of adolescent prevention programs suggests that peer-led strategies can be an effective method for drug abuse and health-promotion programs (1987).

Student Assistance Programs (SAPs), which are designed to help young people who are experiencing problems, are relatively recent addition to the school-based prevention area. The SAP assesses problems, promotes early intervention, and refers the young person to treatment when necessary. The issue of alcohol/drug problem educators must also be considered by the school system: If an impaired educator is not receiving help, it will negatively impact on the programs designed for students. The alcohol/drug-dependent teacher or administrator needs to receive treatment. If treatment options are not part of the school system's personnel policy and procedures, the person's problem may become more severe.

Unfortunately, many systems emphasizes some aspects of alcohol/drug education and neglect others. For example, a school may purchase an excellent curriculum guide but neglect to train their educators in its use. Another example is a school system that limits the alcohol/drug education to one educational level (e.g., high school) or to one period of time (e.g., prom/graduation). When evaluation of alcohol/drug education programs occurs, and this is relatively infrequently, measurement of success is usually based only on the existing pieces. The role of possible missing elements is not considered. That is, it would be difficult to assess program impact on students' behavior if the program has not been developed and implemented in a comprehensive fashion.

The evaluation is often conducted immediately at the end of the program, and may not measure the program's full impact. Milgram's review of alcohol and drug education programs notes that too often programs are expected to produce dramatic effects in relatively short periods of time; when this doesn't occur, support is often withdrawn (1987). Bry suggests that evaluation studies should have a follow-up time of more than two years to allow for changes in behavior to appear (1978). Staulcup et al. recommends that the evaluation project be supported for longer than three years (1979), and Gliksman and Smythe point out that the value of school-based initiatives may not be apparent for several years (1990). Not only is there a need to build in longer follow up evaluations of school-based programs but measures of the program's impact on behavior need to be incorporated into the program's design.

Another issue which needs to be addressed is that too often program success is defined by political, rather than behavioral, measures. If individuals (e.g., school/community) are pleased with the program and feel that the program is successful, which it may or may not be, then program success is assumed, not studied (Gliksman and Smythe, 1990). This may create a difficult situation later when the school/community discovers that alcohol/drug problems still exist. The education program is then blamed for the failure when, in point of fact, the program may not have been well constructed or properly evaluated in the first place.

A problem, identified in reviewing the reviews of the literature, is that combined are many studies of varying levels of sophistication, grade levels, subject groups (e.g., age, socioeconomic level, geographic region), curricula, etc. Therefore the results resemble a hodgepodge and provide little in the way of future direction (Goodstadt, 1986; Gliksman and Smythe, 1990; Milgram, 1987). The lack of comprehensive and replicated evaluation research makes it difficult to provide information on what works for whom at what point in time.

The Community

The community is composed of many significant groups: businesses, churches, civic groups, courts, government, health care providers, helping professionals, police, school systems, etc. The philosophical position on alcohol/drugs and dependency, which is necessary for school-based prevention programs, must evolve from and with the community, as community support is essential for the educational programs. Also, if a community denies that a problem exists, this must be addressed. Realization that the problem can be dealt with can motivate the community to mobilize; the community can provide information on the range and diversity of patterns of alcohol and drug use. Community members can assess the needs of the community, coordinate the efforts of the many diverse groups, and support implementation of effective programs.

Community awareness of significant alcohol/drug issues has been targeted by the federal government (e.g., minimum age of purchase of alcohol), national groups (e.g., NCA, MADD, SADD), and campaigns by local organizations (e.g., Rotary Clubs, Jaycees) on significant topics, such as drinking and driving. Community governments also have a strong interest in prevention programs and can help develop community coalition groups and support organizations working on alcohol/drug problems. Corporate America is also supporting a range of programs for schools (e.g., curriculum development, teaching aids, educational kits), providing alcohol/drug messages through media resources (e.g., billboards, TV/radio public service announcements, videos) and funding community based projects (Adams and West, 1988). Work site prevention strategies (e.g., personnel policies, health promotion programs, and community projects) have also been implemented by many corporations.

The input and interaction of the parents in a community is a critical component in school-based alcohol/drug education. It is essential that parents be informed of the school system's policies on alcohol/drug use and problems and be given information regarding the alcohol/drug education program that is being conducted in the schools. Parents should know what type of program is in effect, in which grade levels the alcohol/drug education program is being conducted, and who is responsible for teaching the material (e.g., classroom teacher, health educator, school nurse). How the school is dealing with students who have an alcohol/drug problem should also be shared with the parent population. In addition, the manner

187

in which the assistance program interfaces with parents and the community needs to be delineated. Parents should know how to access the program, what help is available in the school, and what outside referral resources are used. Support groups for parents have developed in many communities to help parents deal with issues of raising their children, facing alcohol/drug problems, and developing strategies to handle problem situations. Parent groups have also written letters of concern regarding alcohol/drugs in their community, offered support to school-based programs, raised money for necessary elements of school programs and designed strategies to help young people and their parents (Allen, 1986).

The bridge between the school and community enables the flow of alcohol/drug information and motivates discussion on specific topics. Community support also reinforces the school's messages and ensures consistency (Gliksman and Smythe, 1990). Communities and schools have developed strategies to work together to solve a common problem. The Seattle Social Development Project in the Seattle school system focuses on training teachers and parents in identifying risk factors in alcohol/drug abuse and in developing skills to deal with these issues; the relationship between children and the significant adults in their lives is considered more important than the given curriculum. The Family Interaction Program, developed by the staff of the Summer Tobacco and Alcohol Risk Reduction (STARR) Project in Sumner, Washington, is based on the premise that family participation in alcohol/drug education will enhance the classroom prevention program. Training sessions for participating parents include alcohol/drug information, decision making, coping skills, self-concept and the activities in the Family Activity Book; the program complements the *Here's Looking at You, Two* curriculum and provide strategies and methods for families and schools to work together (Mecca, 1984).

The growth in community-based prevention emanates from the belief that the community is well suited to a multi-faceted program (Saltz, 1988). Though little research exists on the success of community based alcohol/drug programs, the positive results from other community health promotion programs (e.g., cardiac health, anti-smoking, fitness) support the development of community alcohol/drug education programs. Research on what is successful will help show communities how to define and expand their role in this area. Program replication in other communities will be stimulated by the success achieved by the program in one community.

Acknowledgement

The author gratefully acknowledges the help and assistance provided by Marilyn Z. Carpenter during the preparation of this manuscript.

REFERENCES

Adams, T. and West, B (1988). The private sector: Taking a role in the prevention of drug and alcohol abuse for young people. *Journal of Drug Education*, **18** (3).

Allen, T. (1986). Adolescent substance abuse and the role of families, schools, and communities. In: Ackerman, R.J., ed. *Growing in the Shadow: Children of Alcoholics*. Health Communications: Pompano Beach, FL.

Bry, B.H. (1978). Research design in drug abuse prevention: Review and recommendations. *The International Journal of Addictions*, **13** (7).

Fors, S. (1990). School based alcohol and drug education programs can be effective. In: Engs, R., ed. *Controversies in the Addiction Fields*: Vol I. Kendall-Hunt Publishing Co: Dubuque, IA.

Goodstadt, M.A. (1986). Alcohol education, research and practice: A logical analysis of the two realities. *Journal of Drug Education*, **16**.

Gliksman, L. and Smythe, C. (1990). A review of school-based drug education programs: Do we expect too much? In: Engs, R., ed. *Controversies in the Addictions Field*: Vol I. Kendall-Hunt Publishing Co: Dubuque, IA.

Mecca, A.M. (1984). Parent education. In: Mecca, A.M., ed., *Comprehensive Alcohol and Drug Prevention Strategies*. California Health Research Foundation: Sacramento, CA.

Milgram, G.G. and Nathan, P.E. (1986). Efforts to prevent alcohol abuse. In: Michelson, L. and Edelstein, B., eds. *Handbook of Prevention*. Plenum Publishing Corporation: New York.

Milgram, G.G. (1987). Alcohol and drug education programs. *Journal of Drug Education*, **17** (1).

Perry, C.L. (1987). Results of prevention programs with adolescents. *Drug and Alcohol Dependency*. **20**.

Saltz, R.F. (1988). Research in environmental and community strategies for the prevention of alcohol problems. *Contemporary Drug Problems*, **15**.

Staulcup, H., Kenward, K. and Frigo, D. (1979). A review of federal primary alcoholism prevention projects. *Journal of Studies on Alcohol*, **40** (11).

Swadi, H. and Zeitlin, H. (1987). Drug education to school children. Does it really work? *British Journal of Addiction*, **82**.

Tether, P. (1987). Preventing alcohol-related problems: the local dimension. In: Stockwell, T. and Clement, S., eds. *Helping the Problem Drinker: New Initiatives in Community Care*. Croom Helm: New York.

Weishert, R.A., Hopkins, R.H., Kearney, K.A., and Mauss, A.L. (1984). The school as a setting for primary prevention. *Journal of Alcohol and Drug Education*, **30** (1).

SHOULD ABSTINENCE BE THE ONLY TREATMENT MODEL FOR ALCOHOLISM AND PROBLEM DRINKING?

CHAPTER 23

Abstinence and Non-abstinence Goals in Treatment: A Case Study in the Sociology of Knowledge

John Wallace, Ph.D.

Introduction

It is unfortunate that the issues involved in treatment goals for alcoholics often seem to have been argued in terms of simplistic assertions. The dogmatic assertion that no alcoholic can control his or her drinking precludes the possibility that spontaneous remissions may occur in alcoholism as they do in other diseases. Moreover, the assertion ignores the many formal and informal observations of periods of moderate alcohol consumption that occur routinely in the lives of persons considered to be alcoholic. An equally simplistic assertion is the statement that some (number of) alcoholics can control their drinking. Since it requires documentation of only a single successful case to provide such an assertion to be true, the assertion is trivial. Instead of attempting to debate the merits of either dogmatic or trivial statements, it would probably prove more profitable to consider several critical questions. These are as follows:

1. How many persons diagnosed as alcoholics are likely to be able to drink in a controlled, moderate, attenuated, normal, or nonproblem manner?;
2. Over what temporal intervals can such drinking behavior be sustained?;
3. Do reliable treatment technologies exist for achieving non-abstinence goals for diagnosed alcoholics?;
4. What risks are inherent in various definitions of "controlled", "moderate", or "nonproblem" drinking and for whom are such risks apparent?
5. Is it possible to differentiate those persons who are likely to succeed at nonabstinent treatment goals from those persons not likely to succeed at such goals?
6. Is the scientific data base on nonabstinent drinking goals reliable?
7. Do documented spontaneous remissions of alcoholism justify chang-

192

ing treatment goals and procedures from abstinence to nonabstinence goals and methods?

These questions from the basis for the following discussion.

The Roots of Controversy

Numerous early studies provided observations concerning non-abstinent but apparently nonproblem drinking behavior among alcoholics. Pattison, Sobell, and Sobell (1977) and Sobell and Sobell (1978) compiled a bibliography of approximately 80 articles that, in part, and in some manner, addressed the issue of controlled or moderate drinking among alcoholics. The majority of these articles did mention or report some degree of controlled, moderate, nonproblem, or "improved" drinking of varying durations among problem drinkers or alcoholics. Wallace (1983) examined this collection of articles and concluded that, "while there are studies in this collection which require serious attention, it would be misleading for anyone to advertise the entire collection as constituting 'strong scientific evidence' in favor of controlled drinking as a viable treatment goal" (p. 481). Nathan (1985) apparently reached a similar conclusion: "when you look carefully at the series of studies on which the presumed efficacy of controlled drinking treatment was based, you quickly come to realize that only one study, the very well-known study of Mark and Linda Sobell (1973, 1976) yielded positive data. While there were other studies which, when viewed through the microscope of the statistician, yielded data encouraging to advocates of controlled drinking treatment, basically only the Sobell study yielded data that strongly encouraged the view that controlled drinking treatment could work" (p. 172).

Perhaps the most important of the early studies concerning the feasibility of nonabstinent goals for alcoholics was the classic paper by D.L. Davies (1962). In this paper, Davies described his followup of seven men discharged from London's Maudsley Hosptial before 1955. The seven men had been picked out of a large group of ninety-three men with diagnoses of "alcohol addiction" who were involved in a routine follow up system. What attracted D.L. Davies to these seven men was their apparent ability to drink normally over periods of time ranging from seven to eleven years.

One investigator, Griffith Edwards, did not ignore the important empirical questions raised by Davies' research and conducted a further followup of the seven patients Davies had originally followed (Edwards, 1985). Edwards' results directly contradicted the observations of Davies. Following re-investigation, Edwards reported that five of the seven putative normal drinkers "experienced significant drinking problems"

193

both during Davies' original follow-up period and subsequently, that three of these five at some time also used psychotropic drugs heavily, and that the two remaining subjects (one of whom was never severely dependent on alcohol) engaged in trouble-free drinking over the total period (Edwards, 1985, p. 181).

In effect, only one man out of ninety-two subjects with what might today be called diagnoses of "alcohol dependence" was able to sustain a pattern of moderate drinking. Working with a group of hospitalized, *gamma* alcoholics at Patton State Hospital in California, Sobell and Sobell (1973) reported impressive findings in favor of controlled drinking behavior therapy over abstinence treatment at followup. A three year independent followup of the Sobell patients by Caddy and colleagues (Caddy et al., 1976) continued to report superior outcomes for patients treated with controlled drinking behavioral therapy versus patients given abstinence-oriented treatment.

Despite optimistic reports by the Sobells and subsequently by Caddy et al. (1978), Pendery, Maltzman, and West (1982) on further independent re-followup of these patients could not confirm the substantial amounts of successful controlled drinking that had been reported earlier. For example, Caddy et al. reported that 50 percent of the patients treated with controlled drinking therapy functioned well on 100 percent of the days during year 3 of the followup. Pendery, Maltzman, and West, however, described the six *highest* functioning patients differently (See Table 23.1).

These patients, described in Table 23.1, according to Caddy et al. had functioned well for 100 percent of the days the *3rd* year after controlled drinking treatment! Large discrepancies such as these between the earlier characterization of these patients as "functioning well" and the subsequent characterizations in the refollowup report by Pendery, Maltzman, and West have raised serious doubts about the validity of the claims for sustained successful controlled drinking by the Sobell experiment's patients.

A third major study, the Rand Report, by Armor, Polich, and Stambul (1976) and Polich, Armor, and Braiker (1981) resulted in the following: media enthusiasm over the initial claims of large numbers of moderate drinking alcoholics; skeptical reaction from the alcoholism field; criticism of the field for reacting in an emotional, subjective, dogmatic, and ideological manner; subsequent extensive revision downward of the estimates of the numbers of persons capable of sustained moderate or nonproblem drinking.

Since numerous prior reports had pointed to the possibility that some small number of alcoholics might undergo spontaneous remissions, the Rand Report's findings of moderate drinking for *brief* periods by patients treated at eight National Institute on Alcohol Abuse and Alcoholism (NIAAA) funded treatment centers might otherwise be considered trivial. What made the findings appear significant were 1) the *large number* of alcoholics who were reported to be drinking normally, and 2) the apparent misunderstandings by the press, lay community, and some members of the academic behavioral science community (e.g., Marlatt, 1983; Peele, 1988) that the report documented sustained *long-term* moderate or nonproblem drinking.

Numerous persons, lay and professional, confused the followup points used in the Rand reports with the lengths of the windows on actual drinking behavior. While the studies were described as the 6-month, 18-month, and 4-year studies, the 6-month and 18-month studies involved asking the subjects about their drinking behavior for the 30 days immediately preceding the followup interview. The 4-year study attempted to measure the patient's quantity and frequency of drinking in terms of the 30 days before the subject's last drink. Hence, none of these reports by the Rand authors provided direct observations on *sustained* moderate or nonproblem drinking among alcoholics. In effect, the Rand study results on brief periods of nonproblem drinking among alcoholics were trivial since they essentially confirmed what clinicians and recovering alcoholics themselves have known for some time: brief periods of moderate or nonproblem drinking are common among alcoholics and not exceptional (Wallace, 1985). The second issue raised by the Rand reports concerned the large number of alcoholics that were reported to be drinking normally. This issue, however, must be viewed in terms of three considerations: 1) the length of the followup period; 2) sampling bias due to loss of subjects; and 3) reliability and validity of measurement of quantity and frequency of consumption in the Rand studies.

The Rand 18-month study reported that 22% of the subjects in these eight NIAAA funded treatment centers were normal drinkers, a rate of normal drinking that was most unexpected by prior observations. Actually, when the data are examined by individual treatment centers, they are even more deviant in terms of previous research and clinical observations. For example, of the patients in "Treatment Center B" who were drinking at all, 70 percent were described by the Rand authors as normal drinkers! While small numbers of persons admitted to an alcoholism treatment center can be expected to show subsequent nonproblem drinking, these rates were simply too deviant to be considered reliable. Is it possible that they were spuriously high due to a combination of bias on outcome, invalid measurement of normal drinking, and an extremely brief followup window?

With regard to bias on outcome, the loss of large numbers of subjects from the data base pointed directly to this possibility. While the Rand

Table 23.1

Description of Caddy et al.'s highest functioning controlled drinkers according to Pendery, Maltzman, and West*

CD-E1 Subject and multiple collaterals state he drank heavily throughout year 3, during which he resided in three states. He used an assumed name on his driver's licence because of an outstanding alcohol-related felony bench warrant issued in year 2. In February, year 3, police were called by neighbors of subject's mother, when he threatened violence and caused a disturbance while drunk, and in April, he was too drunk to attend his brother's funeral. (This trend continued and in year 4 he was arrested for drunk drinking and rehospitalized.)

CD-E5 Subject states that "the third year included some of my worst drinking experiences. In August 1972, after drinking more than a fifth of liquor per day, I went to the San Bernadino Alcoholism Services for help. I was having shakes and other withdrawal symptoms and was very sick physically. By then, a physician had told me I had alcohol cirrhosis of the liver." A record of the subject's application for treatment there, his wife's statement, documentation of subsequent hospitalization for alcoholism treatment, and continued deterioration of his health are consistent with his self-report.

CD-E11 Subject and collateral state that year 3 was his worst year. His records show he spent time in jail, in a state hospital, and in a Veterans Administration hospital because of actions he committed while intoxicated. Toward the end of year 3, he had additional arrests, including one for drunk driving.

CD-E13 Subject and multiple collaterals state that he was abstinent throughout year 3. He states, however, that this was in spite of the controlled drinking treatment. He became abstinent only after additional alcohol-related incarcerations in hospitals, jail, and road camp. He then spent 5 months of year 2 at Twelve Step House, an AA-oriented alcoholism recovery home, to which he attributed his abstinence.

CD-E15 Subject and multiple collaterals state he was drinking excessively (sometimes as much as a fifth per day and some beer) when he was not going to be at work. (His blood alcohol of 0.34 percent on a recent admission to a hospital confirms his high reported tolerance.) He had not yet experienced serious alcohol withdrawal symptoms during year 3 and did not require hospitalization. According to his family, however, his health was already beginning to deteriorate, leading to repeated alcohol-related medical problems and hospitalizations from 1976 to the present.

CD-E18 Subject and collateral state that he successfully controlled his drinking throughout year 3, although, "it would not be entirely accurate to say I never drank excessively." We found no evidence of alcohol-related problems in any major life area. In our view, this subject, who apparently had not experienced physical withdrawal symptoms, might have been appropriately designated an alpha (psychologically dependent) alcoholic.

* Pendery, Maltzman, and West 1982, p. 173.

196

authors argued that their samples were not biased on outcome, further analyses by Wallace (1979; 1989a) disputed these arguments. Wallace noted that the Rand authors relied upon their *composite remission* rates to demonstrate that their samples were not biased on outcome due to loss of large numbers of subjects. The composite remission rate was made up of the combined abstinence and normal drinking rates for the various centers and was reported to be uncorrelated with subject drop out rates. Wallace ran separate analyses for abstinence and normal drinking. When abstinence rates for the eight treatment centers were correlated with their subject loss rates, Wallace obtained a significant correlation of +.79. This correlation of +.79 between abstinence rates and subject loss rates contrasted sharply with the Rand author's correction of -.07 (nonsignificant) for composite remission rates and subject loss rates. Moreover, Wallace's analysis of the correlation between normal drinking rates and subject loss rates was -.14 (nonsignificant). In effect, a measure of acceptable reliability and validity, abstinence rates, showed substantial bias on outcome while a measure of questionable reliability and validity, normal drinking, showed no bias on outcome. How can this internal contradiction in the Rand data be explained? The most parsimonious and likely explanation for this contradiction is simply that the Rand data were not only contaminated by substantial bias on outcome due to loss of subjects but were further contaminated by *invalid* measurement of normal drinking. As a result of sample bias, the Rand outcome rates for both normal drinking and abstinence in the 18-month study were spuriously high. Furthermore, the invalid measurement of normal drinking, indicates an even lower true rate for normal drinking. Moreover, the extremely short followup window of only 30 days worth of drinking behavior used in the Rand study, contributed further to the spuriously high reported normal drinking rates. In short, the total sample normal drinking rate of 22 percent that the Rand authors reported that aroused so much controversy was a product of improper data analysis, bias due to large dropout rates, invalid measurement of normal drinking, and a brief followup window.

Methodological improvements characterized the 4-year Rand report, particularly with regard to sampling and subject followup (Polich, Armor, and Braiker, 1981) However, problems with invalid measurement of "nonproblem" drinking (labeled normal drinking in the earlier studies) and also with the brief follow window remained. The Rand authors reported that one-quarter of the sample underreported their actual consumption of alcohol. Also, quantity and frequency of consumption were still measured over too brief a period (30 days before the subject's last drink). Under these circumstances, the Rand authors' *brief* nonproblem drinking rate in the 4-year study was 14 percent (corrected for invalid measurement of quantity and frequency of consumption). The authors did provide an estimated rate of long-term nonproblem drinking of 7 percent. Correcting this estimated sustained rate for invalid measurement as well as other factors suggests a long term nonproblem drinking rate of approximately 3 to 4 percent. This corrected long term nonproblem drinking rate from the 4-year study is clearly markedly lower than the 22% entire sample brief normal drinking rate of the 18-month study that attracted such media attention and provoked intense controversy.

In the final analysis, the Rand reports (as well as the D.L. Davies study and the Sobell experiment on controlled drinking) are more appropriately construed as episodes in the sociology of knowledge rather than exemplars of rigorous scientific research. These studies, in my opinion, told us considerably more about the beliefs, attitudes, values, behaviors, prejudices, biases, and knowledge processes of some persons in the social and behavioral science communities than they did about the behavior of alcoholics.

Recent Negative Findings

Important studies on nonabstinence treatment outcomes for alcoholics have been provided by Foy et al. (1984), Rychtarik et al. (1987), Pettinati et al. (1982), and Helzer et al. (1985). The experiment by Foy et al. and Rychtarik et al. was significant since it provided perhaps the closest attempt to date at replication of the controversial Sobell and Sobell (1973) experiment discussed earlier. Because of numerous differences between the Foy et al. experiment and the Sobell experiment, it cannot be taken as an exact replication. The ingredients, however, were quite similar. Both studies used hospitalized, chronic alcoholics, provided patients with training in behavioral drinking management techniques, and followed patients for a long time.

Foy et al. randomly assigned patients to broad-spectrum behavioral treatment including controlled drinking skills training or to the same broad-spectrum behavioral treatment package without the controlled drinking skills component. Hence, all patients received the same treatment program with the exception that some got drinking management training as well and others did not.

The results showed that adding a controlled drinking component to a package of behavioral therapy components resulted in abusive drinking in the short run (6-month followup) but had no further effect, negative or positive, after six-month followup. Long-term followup of these patients revealed virtually no sustained controlled drinking (Rychtarik et al., 1987). Of those patients who appeared to be engaging in brief controlled drinking at the point of the 7- to 12-month followup, *none* were able to sustain such behavior over time. For the entire sample, only 2 patients appeared to have achieved stable moderate drinking. While controlled drinkers did poorly in this research, so did abstainers, only 2 of whom were able to achieve stable abstinence through the behavioral methods employed. Hence, in this research as in the Sobell research, behavioral training methods were largely ineffective in producing either stable controlled drinkers or stable abstainers.

Pettinati and colleagues (1982) followed patients for four years after treatment. These investigators reported a 3 percent long term controlled drinking rate.

In discussing this study (Peele, 1988 p. 378) claimed that "in populations such as these, abstinence through a lengthy followup period is exceedingly rate." Wallace (1989b, p. 264), however, pointed out that, in fact, in the Pettinati study, *"abstinence throughout the four-year followup was not exceedingly rare, as claimed by Peele, but substantial."* As Pettinati et al. (1982), p. 213) commented: "A substantial percentage of patients (29%) were able to maintain abstinence and show overall good life-adjustment throughout the four years." They added the statement that "abstinence with good adjustment in the first year is the only status that seems to have any stability over the four-year period."

It would appear then that part of the strategy for advancing acceptance of nonabstinent treatment goals for alcoholics is to denigrate the achievements of abstinence-oriented treatment programs even when the actual data do not justify such denigration. Hence, positive outcomes of abstinence-oriented programs are often dismissed, ignored, or distorted while studies purporting to show the case that studies of abstinence-oriented treatment effectiveness have been carried out on very poor prognosis patients who were unlikely to recover without major social rehabilitative efforts far in excess of what one normally expects of alcoholism treatment as such. Wallace et al. (1988), Patton (1979), and Hoffman and Harrison (1986) have all shown that abstinence-oriented programs can be effective with treatment populations whose social circumstances do not preclude an adequate response to brief alcoholism treatment.

An important study by Helzer et al. (1985) found very little evidence for stable moderate drinking among 1,289 alcoholics discharged from medical and psychiatric treatment facilities. Only 1.6 percent of the subjects met Helzer et al. very liberal definition of stable moderate drinking for the three year period preceding the followup interview. Nonmoderate drinking in this research was defined as 7 or more drinks a day on four or more days in any one month. As Wallace pointed out (1989b, p. 265), "In effect, provided that medical, legal, or social problems were denied and not detected, an alcoholic could drink as much as six drinks a day for twenty-seven days on each and every month and be categorized as a moderate drinker. Moreover, this same alcoholic could also get drunk three times each month, or thirty-six times per year for a total of 108 episodes of intoxication over the 3-year followup period and still be considered a moderate drinker." Despite such very liberal criteria, Peele (1988, p. 378) was distressed that Helzer and colleagues would "disqualify from remission" any alcoholic who "got drunk four times in any one month in a three year period."

In general, then, consideration of the major studies that have claimed successful nonabstinent outcomes of treatment of alcoholism and of studies that have failed to support such claims indicates the following: 1) nonabstinent outcomes such as reduced drinking and nonproblem drinking appear possible for only very small numbers of persons who have been diagnosed as alcoholics; 2) such outcomes are far more likely to occur over brief temporal spans than over lengthy periods; 3) such outcomes are more likely to be reported from methodologically inadequate studies than as a result of scientifically rigorous investigations; 4) a reliable treatment technology for producing normal drinkers out of alcoholics does not exist; 5) while some observations suggest that level of alcohol dependence may be related to brief remission of alcoholism (e.g., Foy et al., 1984; Orford et al., 1976) it is not possible to predict with an acceptable degree of accuracy, the small numbers of alcoholics who may succeed at nonabstinent treatment goals from the vast majority of alcoholics who cannot; 6) nonabstinent treatment goals may be appropriate for some persons with drinking problems other than alcoholism (e.g., Sanchez-Craig and Wilkinson, 1987); 7) while certain types of problem drinkers may be able to moderate their intake of alcohol, alcoholics are at considerable risk for grave physical, psychological, and social consequences if they continue to drink alcohol and they should be so informed. In the face of such severe consequences, small numbers of spontaneous remissions do not justify routine attempts to train alcoholics to drink in a controlled or nonproblem manner; 8) claims in support of nonabstinent goals for alcoholics will continue to be made and will probably be extended to include drug addicts as well. Such claims must not be accepted uncritically by the behavioral science community but must be subjected to rigorous evaluation and criticism.

Summary

As we have seen, a close examination of the details of the major pieces of empirical research upon which prior enthusiastic claims have been based suggests that such claims have been greatly exaggerated. Nonabstinence goals for alcoholics, for the most part, have been achieved in very small numbers of alcoholics for only very brief periods of time. This fact should be borne in mind as new claims in favor of nonabstinence goals are made and revisions in the traditional goal of abstinence for alcoholics are recommended.

REFERENCES

Armor, D.J., Polich, J.M., and Stambul, H.B. (1976). *Alcoholism and treatment.* Rand Corporation: Santa Monica, CA.

Caddy, G.R., Addington, H.J., and Perkins, D. (1978) Individualized behavior therapy for alcoholics: a third year independent double-blind follow-up. *Behavior Research and Therapy,* **16** 345–62.

Davies, D. (1962). Normal drinking in recovered addicts. *Quarterly Journal of Studies on Alcohol,* **23** 94–104.

Edwards, G. (1985). A later follow-up of a classic case series: D.L. Davies's 1962 report and its significance for the present. *Journal of Studies on Alcohol,* **46** (3) 181–190.

Foy, D.W., Nunn, L.B., and Rychtarik, F.G. (1984) Broad-spectrum behavioral treatment for chronic alcoholics: Effects of training controlled drinking skills. *Journal of Consulting and Clinical Psychology,* **52** (2) 218–230.

Helzer, J.E., Robins, L.N., Taylor, J.R., Carey, K., Miller, R.H., Combs-Orme, T., and Farmer, A. (1985). The extent of long-term moderate drinking among alcoholics discharged from medical and psychiatric treatment facilities. *New England Journal of Medicine,* **312** (26) 1678–1682.

Hoffman, N.G. and Harrison, P.A. (1986). *The CATOR 1986 Report.* Ramsey Clinic Publications: St. Paul.

Marlatt, G.A. (1983). The controlled drinking controversy: A commentary. *The American Psychologist,* **38** 1097–1110.

Nathan, P.E. (1985). Alcoholism: A cognitive social learning approach. *Journal of Substance Abuse Treatment,* 169–173.

Orford, J., Openheimer, E., and Edwards, G. (1976). Abstinence or control: The outcome for excessive drinkers two years after consultation. *Behavior Research and Therapy,* **14** 409–418.

Pattison, E.M., Sobell, M.B., and Sobell, L.C. (1977). *Emerging Concepts of Alcohol Dependence.* Springer: New York.

Patton, M. (1979). *Validity and Reliability of Hazelden Treatment Followup Data.* Hazelden Education Services: Center City, MN.

Peele, S. (1988). Can alcoholism and other drug addiction problems be treated away or is the current treatment binge doing more harm than good? *Journal of Psychoactive Drugs*, **20** (4) 375–383.

Pendery, M.L., Maltzman, I.M., and West, L.J. (1982). Controlled drinking by alcoholics? New findings and a reevaluation of a major affirmative study. *Science*, **217** 169–175.

Petinatti, H.M., Sugerman, A.A., DiDonato, N., and Maurer, H.S. (1982). The natural history of alcoholism over four years after treatment. *Journal of Studies on Alcohol*, **43** (3) 201–215.

Polich, J.M., Armor, D.J., and Braiker, H.B. (1981). *The Course of Alcoholism: Four Years After Treatment*. Report prepared for the National Institute on Alcohol Abuse and Alcoholism, U.S. Department of Health, Education, and Welfare. Rand Corporation: Santa Monta, CA.

Rychtarik, R.G., Foy, D.W., Scott, T., Lokey, L., and Prue, D.M. (1987). Five to six-year follow-up of broad-spectrum behavioral treatment for alcoholism: Effects of training controlled drinking skills. *Journal of Consulting and Clinical Psychology*, **55** (1) 106–108.

Sanchez-Craig, M. and Wilkinson, D.A. (1987) Treating problem drinkers who are not severely dependent on alcohol. In M.B. Sobell and L.C. Sobell (eds.) *Moderation as a Goal of Treatment for Alcohol Problems: A Dialogue*. Haworth Press: New York.

Sobell, M.B. and Sobell, L.C. (1978). *Behavioral Treatment of Alcohol Problems*. Plenum: New York.

Sobell, M.B. and Sobell, L.C. (1976). Second-year treatment outcome of alcoholics treated by individualized behavior therapy: Results. *Behavior Research and Therapy*, **14** 195–215.

Sobell, M.B. and Sobell, L.C. (1973). Individualized behavior therapy for alcoholics. *Behavior Therapy*, **4** 49–72.

Wallace, J. (1979) Alcoholism Treatment Revisited. Originally appeared in *World Alcohol Project*, **2** (1) 1979. Reprinted in Wallace, J. (1989a) *Writings*. Edgehill Publications: Newport, RI.

Wallace, J. (1985). Predicting the onset of compulsive drinking in alcoholics: A biopsychosocial model. *Alcohol*, **2** 589–595.

Wallace J. (1989a). Alcoholism treatment revisited. In Wallace, J. *Writing*. Edgehill Publications: Newport, RI.

Wallace, J., McNeill, D., Gilfillian, D., MacLean, K., and Fanella, F., (1988). I. Six-month treatment outcomes in socially stable alcoholics: Abstinence rates. *Journal of Substance Abuse Treatment*, **5** 247–252.

Wallace, J. (1983). Alcoholism: Is a shift in paradigm necessary? *Journal of Psychiatric Treatment and Evaluation*, **5** (6) 479–485.

Wallace, J. (1989b). Can Stanton Peele's opinions be taken seriously? *Journal of Psychoactive Drugs*, **21** (2) 259–271.

CHAPTER 24

Toward Client Choice In Treatment For Alcohol-Related Problems*

Martha Sanchez-Craig, Ph.D.

Current Principles in Treatment

"With alcoholics, choice is no longer possible, whether to drink or not to drink, or of the amount consumed, or the effects of that amount upon them, or the occasions upon which drunkenness occurs." This quotation is taken from The New Primer on Alcoholism by Marty Mann (1968, p. 9), a respected authority in the alcohol field; it synthesizes the beliefs of most alcoholism treatment personnel today. Mann's assertion is extremely questionable in light of available evidence. It is argued in this presentation that the widespread acceptance of the belief that "choice is no longer possible" in the matter of drinking can act as a deterrent to seeking treatment. Furthermore, I propose that if clients have choices thrust upon them, treatment can be made more acceptable and effective.

The first choice that prospective clients must make is whether for them it is true that "choice is no longer possible." In traditional alcoholism programs, asserting that "choice is possible" is unacceptable and labelled as "denial"—a symptom of the disease. In flexible treatment programs, clients beliefs are accepted whether they indicate that choice is possible or not possible, and treatment decisions are profoundly influenced by these perceptions. Within a flexible framework, the issue for clinicians is to learn about the sort of advice that clients should receive in order to be able to make informed choices.

We have found that many clients, particularly those who are new to treatment, consider conventional programs incompatible with their self-concept and unsuited to their needs (Sanchez-Craig, Wilkinson, and Walker, 1987). Often they report having postponed treatment because of restrictions of personal choice which they expected from treatment profes-

•This article is a summary of a paper presented at the 40th Anniversary Conference of the Addiction Research Foundation, held in Toronto, Canada, October, 1989. It is published in the proceedings of the Conference. Permission for re-printing by Kendall-Hunt Publishing Company, Dubuque, Iowa, was granted by the organizers of the Conference.

sionals. Specifically they fear that: they will have to accept the label "alcoholic"; they will be given no option but life-long abstention as the goal; and the schedule of treatment will be incompatible with meeting personal and professional obligations, i.e., there will be no choice about the scheduling of treatment. All these fears are usually justified, and they can make the prospect of accepting treatment seem more undesirable than the problems from drinking. Thus, the consequences of drinking have to be dire before treatment becomes the lesser of two evils.

For the past 12 years our objective has been to develop and test treatment methods that meet the perceived needs of problem drinkers, by providing them with greater choice in treatment. Our methods derive from the assumption that clients have the capacity for self-control, are good judges of their own capabilities, but have *learned* a harmful habit. We try to ensure that the philosophy of the program and the self-concept of the clients are compatible. The methods, which are described in a manual for therapists (Sanchez-Craig, 1984), have been refined on the basis of evaluations of the procedures, their outcomes, and the expressed needs of the clientele (Sanchez-Craig et al., 1987; Sanchez-Craig and Wilkinson, 1986–87; Sanchez-Craig and Wilkinson, in press; Sanchez-Craig, in press).

Choices we ask clients to make relate to: *the nature of treatment*— upon completion of the initial assessment, the nature and philosophy of our program are described to the client, treatment alternatives are discussed, and the client chooses; *the goal of treatment*—this may be abstinence or some considered and specified level of consumption, and can be modified in light of experience; *the scheduling of sessions*—clients negotiate with their therapist times that are of mutual convenience; *the involvement of others*—it is never a condition of participation that clients must involve others in their treatment (e.g., spouse, family, employer, Alcoholics Anonymous); and *the termination of treatment*—in consultation with the therapist clients decide when treatment should terminate, either because of successful completion, or failure to achieve the goals, or incompatibility with the treatment method.

Constraints of Choice in Treatment Programs
The view of alcoholism as a progressive and irreversible disease dictates essential elements of effective intervention: clients must learn and accept that they have "the disease" (i.e., a permanent physiological abnormality) and, based on the construct of "loss-of-control" or "impaired control", they must accept that life-long abstinence is the only realistic goal. Rejection of these conditions is seen as symptomactic of the disease, namely, "denial." In addition, many program insist that important persons

204

in the client's life become involved in the treatment process in order to undermine the client's denial and avoid inadvertent "enabling" of the condition. Many programs insist upon participation in Alcoholics Anonymous to help maintain sobriety and adherence to the disease ideology. The idea that there are a number of essential educational and therapeutic components of effective intervention justifies programs of predetermined duration (typically lasting from three to twelve weeks, with follow-up periods of one to two years).

Evidence Favouring Choice in Treatment

Generally speaking, behavioral scientists would agree that treatments tend to be more effective if they are consistent with the clients' self-concepts and beliefs about the condition being treated. This indicates that, where alternative effective treatments are available, choice should be permitted so as to match clients' perceptions with the dispensed treatment. In the treatment of alcohol problems this general proposition is most relevant to: the model of alcohol dependence, the goal of treatment, and the clients' concerns about the privacy of the treatment. The most contentious and extensively evaluated of these issues is that of goal.

The consistent finding of controlled-drinking outcomes among some treated alcoholics, even after their participation in abstinence-directed programs (e.g., Armor, Polich, and Stambul, 1976; Nordstrom and Berglund, 1987) is the impetus to offering moderation of drinking as the goal. In a study with 70 "early-stage" problem drinkers (Sanchez-Craig, Annis, Bornet, and MacDonald, 1984) we found that when abstinence was imposed upon them, most did not achieve it; they disregarded the assigned goal and approximately 70% developed patterns of moderate drinking on their own. In the study, clients were randomly assigned to one of two conditions of a treatment program: in one condition abstinence was the only available goal ("no choice group"); in the second condition clients could choose between abstinence and controlled drinking ("choice group"). The two groups did not differ significantly on relevant pretreatment characteristics, or levels of drinking reported over a two-year follow-up period.

First, we found that abstinence was considerably less acceptable to the clients than controlled drinking: only 34% of those who had abstinence assigned to them accepted it as their longer-term goal; of those who were offered a choice, 85% opted for controlled-drinking. The drinking outcomes for the two groups were very similar, with most clients reporting moderate drinking at six months follow-up; such outcomes remained stable to the end of the follow-up period (Sanchez-Craig et al., 1984). It should be noted, however, that clients in the abstinence condition had more

205

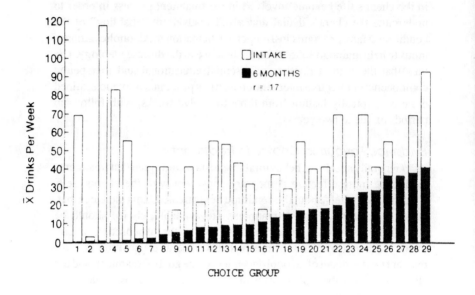

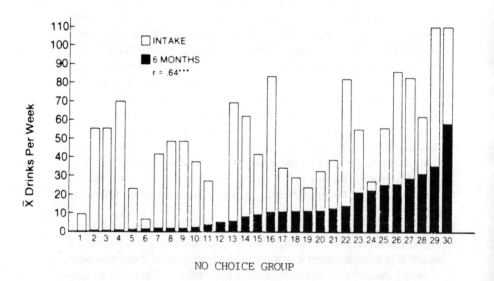

Figure 24.1 Mean weekly alcohol consumption at intake and six months follow-up for the Choice Group and the No Choice Group.

206

difficulty in developing moderate drinking than clients who were specifically trained in the procedures. Furthermore, the abstinence group requested significantly more aftercare sessions than the group who chose their own goals. In short, we found that restriction of choice interfered with treatment gains (Sanchez-Craig and Lei, 1986).

Figure 24.1 illustrates the average weekly consumption for each client in the "choice" (top panel) and "no choice" (lower panel) groups at assessment and six month follow-up. In each graph the clients are placed in ascending order of scores on mean number of drinks per week at follow-up. Note that in the "no choice" group the finding is typical—heavier consumption at intake to the program was predictive of heavier consumption after. However, this relationship was not seen in the "choice" group because of the very marked reduction in drinking by some of the heaviest drinkers coming to the program. Thus, we concluded that, for the types of clients we recruited to the program, heavier drinking before treatment should not preclude giving choice of goal.

In our subsequent treatment studies with "early-stage" problem drinkers (Sanchez-Craig, Leigh, Spivak, and Lei, 1989; Sanchez-Craig, Spivak, Davila, and Bianca, in preparation) we found that, when given choice, most select moderate drinking as their longer-term goal. Thus, if programs of secondary prevention are to be successful in attracting clients, we believe that it must be generally known that moderation is considered a feasible objective of treatment. As part of the same strategy for early intervention, it is important to offer clients the opportunity to participate in programs where it is clear they will not be labelled as "alcoholic", except if they choose the term.

Strategies for Increasing Opportunities for Client Choice

There is an entrenched and committed alcoholism treatment establishment and industry, whose members are very unlikely to modify their views of what constitutes appropriate intervention. The best strategy for increasing clients' choice will be to introduce notions of flexible treatments into the training of health-care professionals, and encourage those professionals to identify and target problem drinkers who are currently avoiding the treatment system. This is a grandiose plan because professional education largely ignores alcohol and drug dependence as an important area of concern. Also, since the recommended strategy focuses upon secondary prevention, it will confront the problems inherent in attempting to develop prevention programs generally. For example, in the area of heart disease, transplantation is a more glamorous activity than prevention education. Similarly, it is inevitable that heroic recoveries from alcoholism involving public confessions are more newsworthy than private resolutions before the problem becomes severe.

Probably the best hope for achieving the objective of developing strong programs of secondary prevention will be to persuade governments to give greater priority to funding this activity, and the training of necessary staff. Today such programs are rare.

Future Choices

As our prevention program has developed, we have gradually increased the amount of responsibility that is placed upon clients during treatment. The amount of therapist contact has been reduced with the aid of "self-help" materials which we tested in a controlled study (Sanchez-Craig et al., 1989). We found that females were generally more successful than males in moderating drinking over the one-year follow-up. Females were particularly successful in the conditions of the study where the treatment was aided by "self-help" materials. We are now replicating this study to determine whether, in fact, women do best when they are guided to resolve the problem largely on their own.

It seems that many persons overcome their alcohol problem through their own efforts (e.g., Clark and Cahalan, 1976; Fillmore, 1974), and probably many do with some simple advice (e.g., from their physician). Today little is known about the extent to which these resolutions occur, and about the characteristics of those who benefit from simple advice. Thus, it seems essential to study how people respond to direct advice, and to purely motivational advice. With support from NIAAA, my colleague Dr. Karen Spivak is now conducting a community study which may provide some clues on this matter.

She placed three one-day advertisements in local newspapers offering *educational materials* to those who were concerned about their drinking, but wished to quit or reduce their consumption without professional help. The response to such advertisements was encouraging: approximately 180 persons expressed interest in receiving the materials and in becoming subjects of the study. It involves an initial one-hour interview to conduct a brief assessment and to give out the educational materials, plus two follow-up assessments (at 3 and 12 months). At random, subjects received one of the following: a 2-page pamphlet outlining guidelines and steps for achieving sensible drinking; a 30-page manual explaining the steps outlined in the pamphlet; and a package with information on alcohol effects. Many subjects said that they decided to participate in the study because they thought that having the assessment and the educational materials could help them to establish whether they had a problem, and if they needed professional help. At the time of preparing this paper, Dr. Spivak had conducted 3-month follow-up assessments for half of the participants; 10% indicated that they would prefer to work with a professional, rather than to continue on their own. It remains to be seen how many subjects choose either of these routes by the end of the study.

Conclusion

In conclusion, the arguments laid out suggest the desirability of offering clients choice in treatment, particularly before their alcohol problem is very severe. The ultimate choice that a potential client must make it whether to take treatment or not. For those who are seeking treatment for the first time, a good initial strategy could be to motivate them to solve the problem on their own with the aid of self-help materials and opportunities to check their progress. This strategy may prove fruitful in two important respects: it could make treatment delivery more efficient, and it would satisfy the clients' need for self-control.

REFERENCES

Armor, D.J., Polich, M., and Stambul, M.B. (1976). *Alcoholism and Treatment*. The Rand Corporation: Santa Monica, CA.

Clark, W.B. and Cahalan, D. (1976). Changes in problem drinking over a four-year span. *Addictive Behaviors*, 1 251–259.

Fillmore, K. (1974). Drinking and problem drinking in early adulthood and middle age. *Quarterly Journal of Studies on Alcohol*, 35 819–840.

Mann, M. (1968). *New Primer on Alcoholism*. Holt Rinehart and Winston: New York.

Nordstrom, G. and Berglund, M. (1987). Aging and recovery from alcoholism. *British Journal of Psychiatry*, 151 382–388.

Sanchez-Craig, M. (1984). *A Therapist Manual for Secondary Prevention of Alcohol Problems. Procedures for Teaching Moderate Drinking and Abstinence*. Addiction Research Foundation: Toronto.

Sanchez-Craig, M. Brief didactic treatment for alcohol and drug-related problems: An approach based on client choice. *British Journal of Addiction*, in press.

Sanchez-Craig, M., Annis, H.M., Bornet, A., and MacDonald, K.R. (1984). Random assignment to abstinence and controlled drinking: Evaluation of a cognitive-behavioral program for problem drinkers. *Journal of Consulting and Clinical Psychology*, 52 390–403.

Sanchez-Craig, M. and Lei, H. (1986). Disadvantages to imposing the goal of abstinence on problem drinkers: An empirical study. *British Journal of Addiction*, 81 502–512.

Sanchez-Craig, M. and Wilkinson, D.A. (1986–87). Treating problem drinkers who are not severely dependent on alcohol. In M.B. Sobell, and L.C. Sobell (Eds.), *Drugs & Society*, **1** The Haworth Press, Inc.: New York.

Sanchez-Craig, M., Wilkinson, D.A., and Walker, K. (1987). Theory and methods for secondary prevention of alcohol problems: A cognitively-based approach. In W.M. Cox (Ed.), *Treatment and Prevention of Alcohol Problems: A Resource Manual.* Academic Press: New York.

Sanchez-Craig, M., Leigh, G., Spivak, K., and Lei, H. (1989). Superior outcome of males over females after brief treatment for the reduction of heavy drinking. *British Journal of Addiction*, **84** 395-404.

Sanchez-Craig, M., Spivak, K., Davila, R., and Bianca, A. Superior outcome of females over males after brief treatment for the reduction of heavy drinking: Independent replication and report of therapist effects. Ongoing research supported by Grant No. ALCP-1 5 R01AA06750–03, in preparation.